Contents

D1332704

Foreword to the third edition

Kathleen Hickey was a much admired teacher whose work with dyslexic children and adults has been deeply influential. She always acknowledged her debt to others, particularly in the United States, but her own contribution was unique. Her understanding of the principles of multisensory learning was not merely theoretical: it led her to create the detailed, structured and practical material that is set out in this book. She understood that methods which fail a substantial number of learners must be regarded as generally inadequate, prompting new thought for all, not just remedy for some. She instinctively knew how important was the experience of success, and she made sure that no student remained unaware of what had been achieved. She herself knew what it was to bear a disability, and she would correct, sometimes fiercely, those who paid more regard to the problem than the person.

The outcome of her knowledge, skill and experience was the Kathleen Hickey language kit, which she published herself, with the help of Elizabeth Adams in 1977. It was a pioneering work. Others have built on it, and many use its ideas and methods without knowing their origin. It has not been superseded. The context in which it is used, however, is always changing, as are the expectations of learner and teachers. The legal framework of teaching has been transformed since 1988, there has been more research, and the demands of parents and the public have become more insistent. A second edition, in book rather than kit form, was issued by the present publishers in 1992, edited by Jean Auger and Suzanne Briggs. Now, the continuing need for the book has prompted a third edition, edited by Margaret Combley, and illustrated by Richard Gent. The new edition preserves Kathleen Hickey's original word, which has helped and influenced so many, but it also bears the impress of all of those who have secured its continuance. Many learners and teachers will be grateful for a book that so effectively shows what can be done, and how, while respecting the professionalism of teachers and the autonomy of learners.

Professor Tyrrell Burgess
Edinburgh
August 2000

Foreword to the second edition

Kathleen Hickey's Language Training is built on principles of education derived from study and reflection on experience. In presupposing that teacher and learner will relate to each other as expert and client, it represents the epitome of professionalism. In her position as head of the first remedial centre in Surrey in the early 1960s, Miss Hickey was called upon to rescue boys and girls from from the ignominy of failure in learning to read, write and spell English. In carrying out her duties, she became critical of a system of education that accepted a substantial incidence of failure for which 'remedial' measures were required. The principle that she developed–the Hickey Principle–was that all children should achieve mastery of basic education and nobody should suffer the burden of illiteracy. Where there is evidence of widespread failure, it is encumbent on teachers to reconsider the whole of what is offered and to evolve methods that are universally apt. This is quite different from seeking to remedy defeat. Miss Hickey's solution was to provide a comprehensive multisensory approach for all. To this end she wrote *Dyslexia: A Language Training Course for Teachers and Learners*.

Recognising the outstanding quality of Miss Hickey's work, the Earl of Radnor expressed the hope, in his foreword to the first edition in 1977, that it would be widely used. His confidence has been fully vindicated: professionals and parents continue to demand the Hickey Kit. It is in the hope of making her ideas more readily available to all that the editors offer this second edition: *The Hickey Multisensory Language Course*

When she was preparing the original kit, and for some years after its publication, Kathleen used to demonstrate its use with pupils, teachers and parents in her own home. In schools and at teachers' meetings all over Britain, she trained a number of colleagues who are continuing her work both in training other teachers and in teaching children.

The editors of this second edition were at the time both teachers influenced by Miss Hickey and they adopted the Hickey philosophy in their teaching. Working on this new edition, has been for each of them a labour of love and dedication: love for Miss Hickey who taught them so much and dedication to the welfare of underachieving children in the English-speaking world.

Jean Augur wrote up the story of her family's struggle to get effective help for her three sons: in *This book doesn't make sens cens sns scens sense: living and learning with dyslexia.* Mrs Augur says that the breakthrough came when she attended a lecture by Miss Hickey. 'That lecture was a revelation', she says–and forthwith began to focus on dyslexia. Suzanne Briggs also has a dyslexic son and despite her wide experience and good contacts, could find no help with his problems until she met Miss Hickey.

My own observation over the years was that, once Miss Hickey had established the Multisensory pattern, no boy or girl brought to her notice for help left after even a single hour's session without a modicum of success and clear awareness of exactly what had been learnt. Young people, and some not so young, who had been variously diagnosed, criticised, rubbished or turned into rebels or passive resisters, began to believe in themselves and in their ability to learn.

The editors and I trust that this new presentation of the Hickey Kit will ensure that anyone finding problems with reading, writing and spelling will receive the systematic support it offers.

Elizabeth Adams
1992

Foreword to the first edition

Perhaps it might safely be said that dyslexia is far more readily recognised as a disability now than previously. It might also be said that in this more general recognition there lies an appreciation that those disabled in this way represent a human problem and, in all probability, an economic disaster.

Nevertheless, recognition is not enough. Teachers must be trained to deal with this disability and children themselves, once diagnosed, must be taught. Miss Hickey's book, incorporating as it does a course for teachers and children, must mark an important advance towards this end.

It is, in all probability, the first book of this kind to be published in this country, and it should go a long way to alleviate the anxieties felt by pupils, parents and, indeed, teachers themselves, who rightly are often worried at not having the knowledge to teach the dyslexic child.

To a large extent this book was created at the request of teachers themselves, who recognised the need for such a book through their own teaching experience. Kathleen Hickey, an early pioneer of remedial education, with her wide experience of dyslexia derived both from this country and the United States of America, is ideally suited to respond to this request and to produce this book. This is no experiment in teaching, but the product of practical experience.

I can only hope Dyslexia: A Language Training Course for Teachers and Learners is used as widely as possible. If it is, I know it will be of inestimable value to very many people. It should provided a very strong strand in the lifeline so desperately needed by those disabled by dyslexia, and it should help to end the appalling situation in our society whereby young people of intelligence are allowed to finish their period of statutory education as illiterates.

Earl of Radnor
1977

Preface to the third edition

Kathleen Hickey was an instinctive, talented teacher. She became one of the pioneers of dyslexic teaching in Britain. Her language programme fused together traditional 'remedial' teaching methods with the multisensory structured programmes developed for dyslexic children in the USA. Long before we had a well-developed concept of dyslexia as a language processing difficulty, Hickey stressed the importance of kinaesthetic response, involving verbal patterns, as part of multisensory learning. These principles were in vogue in the 1970s, and are still current.

However, in the past 30 years the context of education has changed quite radically. The Education Reform Act (1988) resulted in the National Curriculum, to which all children have an entitlement. The Education Act (1993) required the DfEE to issue a Code of Practice (1994) on the identification and assessment of Special Educational Needs. The Code clearly states that schools and teachers have statutory duties to identify and assess special needs. Any child who has 'significantly greater difficulty in learning than the majority of children of his age' must be identified by the class teacher, and given an Individual Educational Plan, which sets targets for learning and provides differentiated work so that these targets can be achieved. Parents must be given opportunities to be involved, both in setting the targets and implementing the teaching programmes. There is a Special Educational Needs Co-ordinator (SENCo) in each school who can support with advice and materials, and can call on outside agencies (educational psychologists, support teachers, speech and language therapists). The intention is that children with mild specific difficulties/dyslexia should have their needs met within the classroom. If their literacy difficulties hamper access to the full range of National Curriculum subjects, alternative methods of recording and learning must be explored. Developments in computers and word processors are making these alternative methods more and more accessible and attractive. Children with more severe dyslexic problems will go forward to statutory assessment, and extra resources will be put into the school to support the special need. 'Dyslexia friendly schools' are becoming a reality in most LEAs.

The National Literacy Strategy

In the 1970s, Hickey warned eager young teachers that it takes 30 years for new ideas to reach the classroom, and as we enter the twenty-first century, we are witnessing her influence in the spirit and the details of the Literacy Hour. All primary schools were compelled by law to introduce a structured literacy hour for all pupils by December 1998, using the National Literacy Strategy Framework For Teaching (DfEE 1998) as a structure for delivery of the National Curriculum. Schools can be exempted only if they can convince the DfEE that their alternative plans are as good as those proposed by the Framework. It has been developed in an interactive and dynamic way. Pilot studies have issued, trialled and adapted earlier versions of the Framework and have thus benefited from best practice in classrooms and in other settings.

The Literacy Hour provides a structured, sequential programme, which will satisfy many of the special needs of the dyslexic child: reading skills are explicitly taught; it is based on a wide range of current research; it allows for uneven abilities within the individual; and it includes simple, searching assessments. Echoes of Hickey are seen in the involvement of kinaesthetic feedback, emphasis on structured phonic tuition, teaching of spelling choices, teaching of spelling rules covering morphemes, and the use of games and activities to ensure automaticity. Dyslexic children need an Individual Education Plan giving opportunities for the 'over-learning' and guidance in selecting learning methods appropriate to topic and individual, but at least the mainstream classroom can now provide a basic programme, which is more accessible and relevant. Key Stage 3 teachers in secondary schools have a clearly defined, well-formed structure to build on when reinforcing weak literacy skills. The extra help necessary to ensure that the dyslexic child reaches full potential will continue to depend on definitions within individual negotiations, but the Code of Practice (DfE 1994) ensures that the parent has a key role in such discussions.

Literacy as a language process

Hickey stressed the point that her book provided a 'Language Training Course', not a manual for teaching literacy skills. Subsequent research has confirmed her instinct that reading and writing are language processes (see Snowling and Stackhouse (1996) for an accessible overview). There is a wealth of evidence pointing to the importance of phonological awareness to the acquisition of reading and spelling skills. Babies link the action surrounding them with the speech they hear, then with the sounds they make. As their awareness of sound develops, their links or 'mappings' become more refined. By the time children meet formal reading tuition, most of them have well-developed sound awareness. Poorly developed phonological awareness, with weak and 'fuzzy' internal representations of sound, has become a defining attribute of the dyslexic child. Performance on tasks that demonstrate awareness of rhyme, ability to manipulate sounds within words, speech perception and speech production, is highly correlated with reading ability. This body of research has increased our awareness of the need for specific training in this area. To this end, Chapter 3 has been added, and the Hickey Lesson Plan modified.

Other evidence points to the importance of integrated approaches to reading and writing. Observation studies carried out by Marie Clay (1993) and her Reading Recovery trained teachers, and academic studies of educationalists (Adams 1990) stress the integrated, interactive nature of literacy learning. Key features of successful literacy learning are knowledge of a range of strategies, combined with the ability to call on the appropriate strategy with flexibility and speed. In the same sentence a reader may need to use knowledge of context, word recognition and graphic knowledge, grammatical knowledge, and phonics – and need the ability to orchestrate this range of strategies. For this reason, the 'Stories for Fun', which were added to the second edition, have been omitted. They do give satisfaction and pleasure to some children who have been blocked, but can lead to over-reliance on phonic decoding. Worst of all, they let teachers off the hook of providing relevant and appropriate texts as part of each lesson. This edition prefers to confine decoding practice to words and sentences, and uses a range of normal texts for reading experience. Use of whole texts has been incorporated into the Hickey lesson plan, and the techniques are described in Chapter 3.

Organisation of the Language Training Programme

I have used both editions of the Hickey on teacher training courses. My students found Hickey's Summary of Teaching Points (*aficionados* will remember them as the 'pink pages') unnecessary. These points are already in the programme, and are easier to follow as they are illuminated by activities for the learners. The second edition divided the summary of the structure into three parts, which made it difficult to find one's way about the book. This edition has dispensed with the Summary altogether. The list of reading cards provides a clear, simple structure, and that has been placed at the beginning of the structured programme. The teaching points have been listed alphabetically in the index at the back of the book, so that anything the learner is finding difficult can be accessed easily. The reference numbers have been omitted. The index allows flexibility; any points that the teacher wants to leave until later in the structure can be quickly accessed and 'back-tracked'.

Linguistic information

This is not a linguistics manual, and generalisations are intended to elucidate and simplify concepts and knowledge for dyslexic learners with literacy difficulties. Experts will have to be tolerant where they see over-simplifications. Hickey's Part I explains the linguistic background. Rather than repeat information in the teaching pages, a series of worksheets for the learner illustrate rather than explain the teaching points. They are called 'example' worksheets and are for teachers to copy and adapt. This approach means that the work can be more easily fitted into a flexible classroom structure, and teachers can make the sheets available to helpers.

Diacritical marks continue to be simplified. Letters or letter names are given in inverted commas: 'a'. Following the convention adopted by speech and language therapists, sounds are indicated by slanted brackets: /b/, /sh/. The short vowels are marked with a breve: /ă/. The long vowel is marked with a macron: /ā/. The indeterminate vowel sound (the 'schwa') has the phonic sign /ə/.

Word lists

Augur and Briggs moved the lists of vocabulary from an appendix into the text of the programme. This was a big improvement and saved a lot of flipping through the pages. I have simplified the word lists. Nonsense syllables are no longer listed, as many of the games using onset and rime give experience in reading nonsense syllables. Further experience comes from reading syllables within longer words.

It has been assumed that the teacher can use the lists, adding suffixes and prefixes to base words, either as they need them to illustrate a teaching point, as they appear in print, or as they are required for writing. Some of the really bizarre words have been omitted from the lists, but many have been included – some learners who still need help with the simplest phonics will be intelligent, mature, and have wide vocabularies. Even without these advantages, the words can be useful for vocabulary extension, and can be approached as nonsense syllables. The bottom line is, however, that this is not a targeted workbook but a resource for teachers and learners – they have to use their judgement to select and adapt the materials.

Spelling patterns

Vowel patterns are covered in example worksheets. I have omitted Hickey's short vowel frame. It is far too elaborate for the simple teaching point that it makes, and the spelling choices for /ŏŏ/ and /ĭ/ are already covered by the spelling pack routine. The long vowel frame has been simplified. If a spelling pattern is very rare, the words have been listed as irregular. Sometimes the card has been omitted (e.g. break, /ā/). Sometimes it has been suggested that the teacher might like to omit it (e.g. toe, /ō/).

Margaret Combley

Preface to the second edition

We worked closely with Kathleen on the original language course, or 'kit' as she somewhat derogatively preferred to call it. She described one of us (JA) as the sounding-board for her ideas as she formulated her thoughts. It was obvious from the beginning that, far from producing just another teacher's aid in kit form, she was creating a work of major importance, the influence of which is to be recognised in very many papers and teaching materials subsequently produced by others.

Kathleen's original idea was to produce a step-by-step training course that anyone could pick up and use with any failing pupil in any situation. However, because of the intensity of the format and the amount of information she included, it quickly became evident that the programme had become too complicated to be followed by anyone other than those fully trained in its use. As a result, training courses were set up under her guidance and then, as now, they were always over-subscribed.

These courses have been held originally at the Dyslexia Institute in Staines, and later at the Institute's branches all over the country. Finally they became the basis of the British Dyslexia Association's Teaching Diploma. The programme is very structured and yet leaves wide scope for the teacher's own initiative and imagination. For us personally, as teachers, we see this as one of its greatest assets.

Kathleen always has felt it was every child's right to understand the basic facts about his or her own language–that the more he or she understood of the structure, the more sense he or she would be able to make of it. The English language is very complicated, too complicated to expect children to learn it properly simply by chance. This is particularly so for dyslexic children who can quickly become confused.

Nevertheless, although the original course was written and compiled with the dyslexic pupil in mind, the philosophy underlying it and the information it contains are available and appropriate for all learners. Indeed, with recent concerns about falling standards in reading and spelling, and in the light of the requirements of the National Curriculum, Kathleen's philosophy is more relevant than ever.

In this second edition, we have tried to keep faith with those concepts which Kathleen was trying to promote in this work and have retained most of her original material. We hope that this edition will provide a source of enlightenment and inspiration to a new generation of teachers.

Preface and acknowledgements to the first edition

My interest in teaching reading and writing to children with difficulties began 25 years ago when I found a way to teach a group of young cerebral-palsied pupils who, though educable, were thought to be incapable of learning to read and write. I kept detailed records of their progress. Later, I was able to experiment with different approaches with pupils from 5 years old to adult in a variety of educational establishments and eventually, as the head of Clayhill Centre for Remedial Education, Epsom. Among the children I taught there, who had failed at school for different reasons, one group stood out from the rest. In this group, failure in spelling and fluency of written expression continued, even after they had achieved a high level in reading. Recognising that their problems required special treatment, I developed a systematic approach, the basis of which was to teach reading through writing.

My particular thanks are due to all the children I have taught who have shown me their needs and responded to my efforts to help them; to their parents who have encouraged me with their approval; and to my employers for freedom to experiment, to research and to tutor teachers' courses in language training.

When Samuel T. Orton's work began to interest me, I attended a course in 1969 conducted by Sally Childs; she persuaded me of the value of the Gillingham–Stillman method.

I owe a debt of gratitude to her and the Bath Association for the Study of Dyslexia, for arranging my attendance at a course of language training in the USA and to the Texas Scottish Rite

Hospital, Dallas, for a scholarship to complete this course in 1970 in the Language Unit of the Neurology Department.

My appreciation and thanks are due to Dr Lucius Waites, Paediatric Neurologist and Course Director, for my first real understanding of dyslexia as a constitutional problem; to Aylett Cox, Co-director, and author of *Remedial Techniques in Language Training*; and to the staff of the Language Unit for all I learned from them. I wish particularly to thank Bernice Ruines and Marietta Riddle for their encouragement and the opportunities to observe their work.

My view is that for learning to be effective, it must be self-directed. Whilst appreciating the therapeutic value of the treatment in Dallas in a clinical situation under ideal conditions, I saw the possibilities for its use as a self-learning aid to recovery from early failure in our own schools and as a beginning approach for young dyslexic children to prevent failure.

On my return from the States, I considered ways in which a systematic cumulative course in English, acceptable to British teachers, could be incorporated into the teaching here. Well-proven, successful, self-learning practices already being used would be retained. An essential ingredient must be learning by seeing, hearing, speaking and writing simultaneously (multisensory learning). American terms would need substitutions and the differences in spelling, pronunciation and diacritical marking anglicised. *The Concise Oxford Dictionary* (1956), 4th edition 1951, has been consulted for these changes.

The organisation of the English in the Language Training Course presented here is mainly an adapted version of the Structured Programme developed by Aylett Cox and staff of the Scottish Rite Hospital, which in turn was inspired by the Gillingham–Stillman–Orton team. However, the multisensory techniques described here for learning the regular part of the language are different from those of Gillingham and Stillman (1956) in that they are child-directed rather than teacher-directed. For learning irregular words Fernald techniques are incorporated.

I am grateful to those who have supported my efforts to convert my ideas into practice since my American experience: to Professor Asher Tropp through whose efforts a useful film was made; to The North Surrey Dyslexic Society and, later, the Dyslexia Institute who invited me to be their first Director of Studies; to Wendy Fisher, for enabling the Dyslexia Institute to become a reality and for her personal help and encouragement in getting this book off the ground; to the teaching staff of the Dyslexia Institute for their constructive criticism and individual contributions in finalising the order of the phonograms in the Language Training Course; and in particular to Jean Augur for generously giving time to work on word lists and materials and for her willingness to be a sounding board for my ideas; to Kathleen Jannawa, for the inclusion of her games; to Elizabeth Adams, ex-Surrey Inspector of Education for her continuous encouragement, support and advice throughout the years of endeavour; and to my niece Sarah Kitching for her patience and skilfulness in typing this book.

Finally, I wish to thank Lord Radnor, Chairman of the British Dyslexia Association, for generously sparing the time and energy to write the foreword to this book.

Throughout the text, the term 'he' has been used, but this refers equally to both genders.

Kathleen Hickey

Acknowledgements to the second edition

Suzanne Briggs worked with Kathleen after she had retired from the Dyslexia Institute at Staines. She was a remarkable person as she never allowed her own disabilities to impede her. She had rheumatoid arthritis severely from the age of thirteen and was at the Royal Pinner Hospital until she was twenty three. She sadly died of cancer in March 1984 and she continued to help and advise people to the end.

Suzanne has continued to teach pupils and has enjoyed seeing the progress they have made using the 'Hickey' approach over these last fourteen years. She has really appreciated the support and interest from the teachers who have attended the courses and taken part in the practical workshops.

During her last 4 years Kathleen had already started to revise the second edition of the manual. Jean Augur and I hope that teachers will find the second edition of the manual more user-friendly.

I would like to thank Miss Carolyn Burroughs, Mrs Sheila Berg and others who have helped with the practical pages; these have taken much more time and effort than was anticipated. I would like to thank my family as this work has involved them all: Michael, Harry and Philippa as well as Christopher through whom I met Kathleen.

Finally, thanks to Jane Sugarman and Stephen Cary to whom a whole new aspect of the structure of our language has been revealed in working on this manual!

Suzanne Briggs
1992

Acknowledgements to the third edition

Thanks are due to my Sheffield colleagues at the Rowan School, and to STEPS Learning Support Teachers at the Bannerdale Teachers Centre. Their open-handed sharing of knowledge and expertise have helped me gain insight into ways that the Hickey programme can be integrated with individual programmes in the modern classroom.

Richard Gent's pictures add gentle humour, and they have been much appreciated by the youngsters working at the difficult, sometimes dreary task of consolidating skills where there is little natural aptitude. His artistic skills are self-evident, but I have also appreciated his gift for finding witty and vivid graphic representations of some of the clue words.

Above all I thank my husband, Fred Combley, whose unshakeable confidence in my ability encourages me to attempt impossible tasks, and whose unstinting support ensures their completion.

Margaret Combley
2001

Introduction to the first edition (1977)

In 1968, a group of very distinguished neurologists under the auspices of the World Federation of Neurology drew up and unanimously agreed the following definition of dyslexia:

> A disorder manifested by difficulty in learning to read despite conventional instruction, adequate intelligence and socio-cultural opportunities. It is dependent upon fundamental cognitive disabilities which are frequently of constitutional origin.

Crosby, in the same year (Crosby with Liston 1968), described dyslexia as a symptom resulting from neurological impairments and not a disease or ailment in itself. In *Reading and the Dyslexic Child*, he says that he hopes his book will encourage teachers to search for ways of teaching neurologically impaired children because, although a neurologist can diagnose the symptom, responsibility for its treatment is educational. This educational treatment is being offered here. It has been designed to meet the needs not only of dyslexic pupils, but also of teachers of any pupil with other types of language disorder.

Alongside other more traditional methods, it was developed over several years, both at Surrey County Council's Clayhill Centre, Epsom, and later at the Dyslexia Institute, Staines. The ideas included have been tried and tested and only those that have proved of value have been included. The Language Training Course for teachers and learners is comprehensive, systematic and cumulative. It can be adapted to the needs and abilities of learners of all ages and it is capable of self-direction under the guidance of a teacher. Because the materials are self-corrective the pupil can take responsibility for his or her own progress from the beginning.

Pupils who may not be dyslexic

It is recognised that not all children will need this approach, but many will benefit from its use, particularly in the early stages. Among such pupils will be those who missed the opportunities available at infant level through general immaturity, changes of teachers and methods, prolonged absences from school, undiscovered sensory disabilities, such as eye and ear defects, and the slow learners who need all their school subjects geared to their general rate of learning. Some of these late readers may make progress with extra practice with the usual school approach of 'look and say' reading books and some supporting use of phonics; they may take longer than the average pupil to learn but their difficulties can be overcome by systematic teaching.

Slow learning pupils may also be dyslexic and consideration should be given to this possibility although identification is more difficult in this group.

Children who fail because of inner conflicts arising from environmental conditions are not so easily helped because they cannot give their attention to the process of learning. Their problem is sometimes described as 'primary emotional disturbance'. It may be difficult to tell whether they have the additional problem of dyslexia because confusion enters into most of their activities. When consideration is given to their individual problems and their tensions are relieved, they may make progress, but if this relief is not found they will seldom reach their potential whatever teaching approach is used.

The dyslexic pupil

The adverse effect of failure on the dyslexic pupil's personal development is serious. Usually he does not show signs of anxiety until he starts school and is required to use his faulty sensorimotor systems for learning to read and write. His reaction to failure is one of frustration and these frustrations may lead to emotional problems, which are an added stumbling block to successful learning. In general, children who fail to read and write early may develop all kinds of associated problems. They tend to be nervous and shy, or to become nuisances. They seldom find status in school either with their teachers or, more importantly, with their peers. They may become friendless and solitary, their lack of confidence inhibiting their ability to make friends. Their teachers may try to help them but, defeated and discouraged by lack of progress, may give up and hope the problem will solve itself. Sympathetic and discerning teachers, however, will seek further advice.

Children experiencing difficulties may have had so many negative and frustrating experiences, which reveal their inadequacies, that they may need to be convinced of their ability to learn. Experienced teachers are usually aware, very soon, of which pupil is primarily emotionally disturbed and which is suffering from the effects of failure. A dyslexic pupil when he begins to learn and feel success is distinguished by a certain attitude of objectivity, which is usually lacking in the primarily disturbed child. An a priori approach to additional teaching on the grounds that failure, in all cases, has its roots in emotional causes is not only time wasting but often damaging to the self-concept of the normally intelligent pupil. There is a risk that the child whose classroom failure has been reinforced by inappropriate teaching may become so resistant that he will emerge at the end of school life unequipped to find his true role in society.

Many parents become alarmed when their child does not achieve success in school and their anxieties can be communicated to him As failure persists, parents' anxieties increase. It then appears that the child's failure to make progress is the result and not the cause of anxiety in the home. The efforts of the family to help may only exacerbate the problem because sympathetic encouragement is not enough. The child needs competent teaching.

It sometimes happens that, as a result of failure in school, a child will shut himself off from the teacher in the classroom until he seems unable to listen to instructions or to carry them through in practical tasks. This may lead to a lack of initiative even outside the classroom and a loss of power of concentration. The child may become an inward-looking person with difficulty in making any sort of effort and wasting energy in avoidance tactics. Such a child will not often be trusted by his parents to act responsibly and they will perform tasks for him that other children take normally in their stride. These parents are then open to the charge of being over-protective.

Early identification of a pupil's learning style is vital if the right teaching approach is to be used. This lies in the hands of the teacher and the Language Training Course is an approach which is designed to prevent failure.

Learning by simultaneous use of the required senses

In discussing the nature of the problem, Waites and Cox (1969) described language perception and cognition as the ability to process correctly, pattern and retain (recognise, interpret, assimilate and store) for memory recall the information provided by the sensory systems, and that the primary sensory systems concerned with language perception and development are the auditory, visual and tactile–kinaesthetic. A difficulty in these sensory systems results in language disability.

The pupil with a faulty sensorimotor system loses out on all counts; not only can he not recognise or recall whole words easily, but he also has a problem in learning and blending sounds and phonic units in sequential order, so that neither a 'look and say' nor a 'phonic' approach would be appropriate either by itself or in combination. A dyslexic pupil may fail even with additional help if his special needs are not being met appropriately. Success can only be expected when the language training achieves harmonious interaction of all the senses, i.e. when the learner sees, hears, speaks and writes simultaneously. This is multisensory learning. The learner is using visual, auditory, kinaesthetic and oral abilities in an integrated process, thus encouraging the various parts of his sensorimotor system to support each other in making permanent sound–symbol associations.

The teachers

Most teachers are aware of the importance of encouraging their pupil's fluent spoken language to promote good comprehension and pleasure in reading, coupled with a facility in writing for enjoyment and communication. If these attributes are to be within the scope of a dyslexic pupil, in addition to training in oral and written sentence construction for organising and expressing his thoughts in speech and writing, he needs to acquire the necessary mechanical skills for recognising and producing the printed word. Unless teachers can be helped to recognise the problem and be willing to undertake some training, many dyslexic children will continue to represent the 'hardcore' of the teachers' problems.

It is often said that a slower reader needs only the encouragement of a sympathetic teacher. This may be true of a pupil who has failed for reasons that are primarily emotional. Many sympathetic teachers who have taken up support teaching because they want to help children have been defeated by their own lack of knowledge when they attempt to teach a dyslexic child who cannot make sense of known methods of learning. The teachers need to study how to teach the skills in a way that the dyslexic pupil will understand. Because such a pupil may have experienced many beginnings and failures, he will need to have complete faith and confidence in his teacher; this situation will only come about if the teacher is an expert in his field. Good relationship between teacher and learner will not last without progress.

The Language Training Course allows the key for success to be possible from the beginning and for progress to continue, step by step. Using multisensory techniques, teachers will be able to help a pupil to learn, one at a time, each small unit of language in a definite order, each step building on the previous one. He blends, in sequential order, phonograms into whole words, phrases and sentences, whilst incorporating rules and choices for spelling the sounds. In this way he can build his skill in using the English language gradually and securely.

The Language Training Course is not just one more method of teaching reading. It is a serious attempt to show teachers how to give language training by means of an entirely different concept; to give them a sense of direction; and to challenge them to think in terms of a comprehensive plan of language learning for individuals. The course encourages the teachers' ingenuity and inventiveness in devising materials for practice and consolidation as each new step is learned. The use of games is encouraged to enable the pupil to become self-reliant with programmes relevant to the stage reached by him and devised so that he cannot practise mistakes. Each stage must therefore be planned ahead with self-corrective materials. While being available for guidance and advice, the teacher should organise the work so that the pupil is increasingly able to sustain his own efforts and get to grips with the task of conducting his own self-study, so that eventually, he will no longer need the teacher. As Wiseman said in his Preface to Cane and Smithers (1971):

What distinguishes the successful from the unsuccessful schools seems quite simple – the existence among their teachers of clearly defined objectives, of a workmanlike approach to their task, of a systematic and planned series of exercises and activities, and of an eclecticism in amalgamating various methods and choosing – at appropriate times – the essential from each. 'Good' teachers and 'good' schools are those which know what they want to do, plan how they intend to do it, and structure the activities of the day and the week accordingly, and monitor the progress of their teaching.

The learner

In learning, there must be interaction between the learner and the material to be studied. From the beginning a good teacher will bear in mind that he is a third factor in this process, and will try to withdraw the distraction of his presence. Because this Language Training Course is essentially a pupil-directed approach, it is capable of giving the learner confidence in his own ability to learn. However, the teacher must be vigilant and aware of what is happening all the time.

Dyslexic pupils need each other's support; the Language Training Course can be used as a basis for classroom work or with groups of pupils, each following his own individual programme of work. When their need to practise a certain skill overlaps, they can work in pairs or groups. This kind of organisation takes the pressure off both the learner and the teacher. In one-to-one teaching, the teacher is tempted to point out all the pupil's mistakes, but ways can be found to encourage the pupil to develop a self-critical attitude and to learn to anticipate his dyslexic tendencies so that he will be on guard against making errors. When he does, he can be helped to discover them for himself. When a teacher is continually talking, the learner often stops listening. Some teachers become anxious for the pupil if he does not respond to a question immediately and will supply the answer before the pupil has had time to think, thus increasing his insecurity. Silence will allow him to give his full attention to the task.

Kathleen Hickey

Part I

Chapter 1
Some basic problems that may affect school performance

This chapter describes dyslexia as a developmental difficulty. Signs during the early years are delayed or unusual language development, and poor co-ordination. Within the classroom, the dyslexic child displays distinct and characteristic difficulties in reading approaches, spoken language, writing and spelling. Concentration may be poor and sequencing difficulties may affect organisation. Yet the dyslexic child may be able to excel in activites not involving reading and writing, and belongs in the mainstream classroom, with a teacher who can deal with any problems during the normal course of a lesson.

The dyslexic pupil in school

Any pupil, in any school, at any level of society may exhibit signs of dyslexia, which can occur throughout the ability range among bright, average and dull pupils. It affects mainly the language skills but sometimes other skills reliant on written symbols, such as mathematics and music. The basic constitutional problem may cause a dyslexic pupil to experience different difficulties at various stages in his development.

Characteristics sometimes found in the pre-school child

A teacher discouraged by a pupil's lack of progress and wishing to help the child may consult the parents. In discussion, the parents may reveal that their child had been a late talker, that when he began to speak he was difficult to understand, that he reversed words such as tap and pat, and would say god for dog. He may have failed to show a preference for either hand, eating with his right hand but using his left for playing games requiring manipulation of objects; kicking a ball was equally good or equally poor with either foot. He may have appeared to be somewhat unco-ordinated generally and did not hold tools comfortably, such as a spoon, knife and fork, pencils and crayons.

Apart from these apparently trivial difficulties, he seemed a bright, normal, happy child with no signs of abnormal emotional behaviour. The parents had no reason to expect any special difficulty in school. Signs of anxiety in the child appeared only after he began to go to school and started to bring home his reading book. He began to behave awkwardly and have temper tantrums. He would look at the pictures in the book and would like to have the book read to him, but he would make no attempt to look at the words. The teacher might also be told that other members of the family had similar difficulties and that they were poor readers and bad spellers.

The dyslexic pupil

Seldom, if ever, will a dyslexic pupil exhibit all the characteristics of dyslexia described below. The quality and degree of severity of any particular difficulty varies with each pupil. In learning to read, write and spell, he may have difficulties in:

- Distinguishing between written symbols and distinguishing between sounds.

- Associating sounds with their symbols, i.e. remembering which symbol to write for a particular sound in a given situation or remembering which sound to apply to a written symbol in a given situation, or both.
- Ordering the written symbols correctly to make the visual pattern of words and/or blending the sounds correctly to make the auditory pattern of words.
- Writing from left to right, writing the correct form of a letter or word so that it is not reversed, beginning and finishing in the correct place when writing a letter.
- Dealing with sequential order in time and space: yesterday-tomorrow, or right-left.
- Maintaining concentration.

If he is old enough to read but does not, he is almost certain to have a poor self-esteem because of repeated failure.

A young, non-dyslexic, but generally immature, pupil may have similar difficulties at an early age but lose them as he grows older. Such a pupil should be closely observed in school until it is certain that he is not in need of further help.

The dyslexic pupil's place in the school system

In most cases a dyslexic pupil will be able to take part normally and will quite often excel in classroom activities not involving reading and writing. His place is rightfully in the classroom, growing up with his peers. He needs a teacher who can deal with his requirements there, helping him during the normal course of a lesson either individually or within a small group of children of similar age and ability. In order to do this teachers should be able to recognise dyslexia in a pupil by his approach to, and performance in, certain activities.

Reading

He is unlikely to make progress on a whole word 'look and say' approach to reading because he cannot retain the total appearance of a word and recognise it again in a different or even the same context. In his efforts to make sense he does not hold the symbol sequence and gets a flash impression only. He might also be unable to make progress on a purely phonic approach because of poor auditory discrimination, inability to do sound blending and to hold the sound sequence of the complete word. If he has not become too discouraged to persevere, learning to read may be possible for him eventually, with a mixture of both approaches, but he may in the end reach only a low level of reading skill. In many cases it is the more verbally fluent pupil who 'gets by' in reading because he is able to make intelligent use of the context and guess at, or substitute, suitable words, but due to anxiety to make sense of the context, he reads inaccurately. This tendency to substitute words for others of the same meaning gives an indication of the pupil's lack of training in the mechanics of reading.

Spoken language

Sometimes the dyslexic pupil will speak only in monosyllables and have difficulty in the grammatical structure of something he wishes to say. He may not be able to get his tongue round longer words, leaving out syllables and reversing some of them. For example, <u>preliminary</u> might become <u>preminilary</u> or <u>prelinery</u>. In conversation, he may often be lost for a word and will substitute one with the wrong meaning, but many a bright dyslexic pupil has plenty to say. He can discourse intelligently and interestingly on a variety of subjects. He might be the one who is ready with the answers in oral lessons and contributes most to a group discussion, but if he is not given opportunities to speak up with confidence in oral lessons, he may conceal his good ability with words because he is included to limit his written vocabulary to words he thinks he can spell.

Written work

It is in this area that a teacher will recognise the special difficulties of a dyslexic pupil who will seldom be able to hand in acceptable work requiring satisfactory sentence construction and correct spelling. Even verbally fluent pupils may have difficulty in constructing suitable sentences when attempting to transfer their ideas to writing. Correctly spelt words are difficult to recall and reconstruct. Producing correctly constructed sentences with correctly sequenced, correctly spelt words, represents a mammoth task comprising mental gymnastics and manual dexterity working simultaneously.

In addition to the anxiety associated with written work, the act of writing in itself may require a great deal of effort from a dyslexic pupil, particularly one of primary school age. He may sit in a contorted position and hold his pencil awkwardly when writing, so that bodily tensions interfere with his concentration. Even an older pupil may not be fully oriented towards keeping his writing from left to right, or on a horizontal line. The line may climb up or down the paper. It is quite usual for the left-hand margin to begin in the correct place but gradually slope to the right as each line of writing is indented slightly from the last. It will go diagonally across the paper from top left to bottom right. There may be no spaces at all between words but when a pupil has learned to separate them he may overreact and leave very wide spaces. The general appearance of his written work is often of scattered and unconnected words. If, in addition, his handwriting is badly formed, sometimes almost illegible, it makes for very poor presentation.

Learning lists of random words for spelling is a totally unsuitable activity for a dyslexic pupil. The task can cause a great deal of unnecessary misery. On being given such a list to memorise, he will usually be at the bottom of the class. Even after working on the task faithfully, although he may have remembered all the letters in a word, he is likely to get them in a different order each time he is tested. Many pupils repeat the letter order correctly when working out the spelling of a word, and then write it down incorrectly because they have not been able to sustain the sequence long enough to get it onto the writing surface. Such pupils will often omit letters, syllables, words and even whole sentences for the same reason.

In addition to this, a dyslexic pupil has a tendency to reverse and/or invert certain letters that are similar in shape, 'b' and 'd', 'p' and 'b', 'n' and 'u', 'w' and 'm'. He might reverse words such as 'was' and 'saw', 'top' and 'pot'. If he is left without suitable teaching, whole sentences might be reversed or written mirror-wise. Young non-dyslexic children also reverse the shapes of letters but as they mature they tend to correct this tendency. A dyslexic person may have to contend with this all his life.

Concentration

Because he can excel in subjects not requiring reading and writing, the dyslexic pupil is often recognised for the intelligent person he is. When he produces poor written work therefore, if his teachers do not understand his problems, they may lose patience with him and regard him as lazy and careless, inattentive and lacking in concentration.

In fact a dyslexic pupil may work very hard to overcome his problems without much help from his teachers. Because of all these difficulties, concentration is difficult for him. He has to make a much greater effort than the other children to achieve even poor standards. This extra effort may sap other energies to a large extent and can cause fatigue. Multisensory training can help him overcome this difficulty and improve his concentration.

General behaviour and confusions

A dyslexic pupil may be noticed in the classroom because his behaviour does not conform to that of the rest of the class. A normally intelligent pupil, who cannot understand what he is being taught, may have become so confused and frustrated by continued failures that he puts up a front of apathy and boredom, and seems not to be paying attention. He may find more interesting outlets for his energies in antisocial activities and become a nuisance. He may be fidgety and find it difficult to sit still for long. Should he have the added problem of poor general body co-ordination, he may not move about a crowded classroom easily, frequently dropping his books and pencils and knocking things off desks.

His inability to put things into sequential order may affect other day-to-day activities. He may need help in organising himself and his possessions, and in carrying out instructions which contain more than one phrase or sentence. For instance, if asked to get the red book, third from the left on the top shelf, he may become utterly confused and say 'I don't know what you mean'. This is not because he is incapable of understanding and carrying out the task, but because he cannot organise and sustain the sequence of phrases used by the teacher.

The inability to relate things in space may result in poor differentiation between in and out, left and right, over and under, forwards and backwards.

It may be that he cannot find his way about. This often becomes most evident at secondary school transfer and is rarely understood. The use of maps may confuse him because he is unable to transfer from two- to three-dimensional relationships.

Learning to sequence the alphabet for practical purposes, such as using a dictionary, a telephone directory, or other alphabetical lists, may take up to two years of training.

Only after a period of intense concentrated help might he learn to order things sequentially relating to time, such as the days of the week, the months of the year, past and to on the clock, yesterday and tomorrow.

Further information

The Education Act (1993) and the Code of Practice (DfE 1994) give the dyslexic child the right to be in an inclusive classroom, being supported with recognition, assessment of special educational needs, and differentiated work aimed at addressing those needs. The DfEE have encouraged recognition, sending to every school a laminated card to hang up in the staff-room, with 'Handy Hints' to aid identification of the dyslexic child, and to give advice in intervention.

Identification of the dyslexic child will probably start as it did in the 1970s – Hickey's signs and symptoms are still valid indicators. However, there is wide consensus that dyslexic pupils will have language difficulties centred around phonology rather than meaning. Many observers, including Hickey, point to poor ability in memorising common sequences like months of the year or multiplication tables; this indicates a difficulty with verbal learning. Experimental studies into word-finding difficulties, rapid naming of familiar objects, and repetition of non-words, report that dyslexic children have specific difficulties with recalling phonological information from long-term memory. Other studies point to specific difficulties in processing sound; the dyslexic pupil's development is delayed in a whole range of sound-processing tasks, such as segmenting and blending syllables and sounds, detecting and generating rhyme, and holding sequences of sound in short-term memory in order to 'play' with them (for example, making spoonerisms such as 'par-cark' – commonly produced by accident, but hard for them to produce at will). This knowledge affects both assessment and intervention, and the Hickey programme needs to make explicit links with phonological awareness training (see Chapter 3, and Further information on Chapter 7, p. 87–8)

How to Detect and Manage Dyslexia, by Philomena Ott (1997), is an excellent resource for parents, Special Educational Needs teachers and classroom teachers working to get the best deal for the dyslexic in a school setting.

Dyslexia, Speech and Language: A Practitioner's Handbook (Snowling and Stackhouse 1996) presents current ideas on the relationship between spoken and written language difficulties.

Overcoming Dyslexia: A Practical Handbook for the Classroom (Broomfield and Combley 1997) deals with the problems experienced by the dyslexic child with word-finding difficulties.

Chapter 2
The pupil's need for simultaneously seeing, hearing, speaking and writing when learning the written language skills

Reading and writing are neurological functions. Eyes, ears, mouth and hand movement need to be integrated in the development of literacy skills. Poor ability to sequence sounds is associated with dyslexia. Traditional approaches ('look and say' and 'phonics') are not effective. Dyslexic individuals need a multisensory approach that enables them to use strengths and excercise weak areas. The reading cards and spelling cards are used to provide a routine that trains automatic recall of visual, auditory and kinaesthetic aspects of each letter-sound link. The routine for introducing each phonogram is described.

The constitutional basis of learning the language skills

Naidoo (1972) states that learning to read and spell depends upon the ability of a child to form automatic and permanent associations between what he sees, hears, says and writes, and that failure lies in the inability to do this. If we analyse the complexity of the task a learner faces when using the language skills, we shall see that what is required is, in fact, a multisensory activity.

In reading he must see symbols, identify them by their shapes, distinguishing between similar shapes, and recognise their visual sequences. He must hear and identify the symbol–sound correspondences, distinguishing between similar sounds, and hear their correct sequences. He must say the words, either aloud or internally, in the correct sequences, understand the meanings of the words and follow the ideas contained in their sequences.

In *writing* he engages in a converse activity. He must construct the words and use them in the correct sequence. The ingredients of this process are obtained from his knowledge of words, knowledge of the letters or combinations of letters that represent sounds, combined with his experiences of putting words together in sequences.

In *spelling* he must either remember what whole words look like so that he can reproduce or construct them from previous experience, or be able to appreciate the sound–symbol correspondences and build parts into whole words whether he has seen them before or not.

The formation of the permanent associations that enable the learner to give automatically correct responses is the result of the complex interaction of all these activities, which is made possible by adequate constitutional endowment in sense-perception systems.

When such analysis presents a picture of multisensory activity, in normal use of the skills, it is self-evident that this is the kind of experience the dyslexic learner needs in order to succeed, because without deliberate practice his constitutional endowment does not function well enough for such a complex interaction to take place between his seeing, saying, hearing and writing.

When a pupil fails to learn to read and write, it is usual to look for emotional causes, some form of deafness or short sight, deprivation or intellectual defects. These may indeed be causes of failure and an effort should be made to exclude them. Nevertheless, as reading, writing and spelling are aspects of the learning activities of the brain via the use of the required senses, it would seem that observation of the manner in which a pupil learns should be part of the initial investigation and, while this is being conducted, a multisensory learning approach tried so that time is not wasted while waiting for the results of investigations.

The sensory systems required for the discrimination of sound symbols and for arranging these in sequential order, are visual, auditory, tactile-kinaesthetic and oral-kinaesthetic. They are interdependent and it seems that they must interact simultaneously. If one or more is 'out of step' dyslexia in some form is the result.

Various researchers have added to our knowledge by investigating the nature and function of these sense-perceptual pathways and sensorimotor activities. In the main, the sensory systems have been researched individually and knowledge of their interaction in brain activity is slight. Teachers occasionally receive psychologists' reports on pupils which include such observations as 'poor visual discrimination', 'poor auditory sequencing' and 'poor results obtained on tests of motor skills'. If there is a deficiency in the development or functioning in a particular sense-perceptual system, it will result in failure of harmonious linkage with the other sensory systems to give correct automatic reactions.

It seems that most of us have our own particular approach to perceiving the graphic symbol–sound relationships, some relying more on their visual and others on their auditory ability. Both types must be able to put into sequential order what they see and hear.

Naidoo (1972) said that the results of her research indicated that the patterns of the disability varied but that there was evidence to suggest that a sequencing disability may underlie reading and spelling retardation. Many pupils find difficulty in putting the elements of written language into sequential order. An example of a sequencing disability when spelling a word is given below. It describes an incident which took place when a highly motivated intelligent pupil was learning to spell words beginning with two blended consonants followed by a short vowel and ending with two blended consonants. He could not do this by visual practice. The incident illustrates his great difficulty in first getting the letters in the correct order and then retaining the order for transferring the word to a blackboard.

Teacher said the word 'crisp'.
Pupil repeated aloud 'crisp' listening to the sound-sequence of the letters /k/, /r/, /ĭ/, /s/, /p/ then spelt aloud <u>c</u> <u>i</u> <u>r</u> <u>s</u> <u>p</u>.

Teacher repeated 'crisp' slowly emphasising the blended <u>cr</u>.
Pupil repeated 'crisp' and spelt <u>c</u> <u>r</u> <u>i</u> <u>p</u> <u>s</u>.

Teacher repeated 'crisp' emphasising the blended 'cr' and 'sp'.
Pupil repeated 'crisp' and spelt correctly, aloud, 'c, r, i, s, p' then naming each letter correctly as he wrote, said '<u>s</u> <u>p</u>' but wrote <u>c</u> <u>r</u> <u>i</u> <u>p</u> <u>s</u>.

He finally wrote the word correctly, once the principle of blend–vowel–blend was established and he was then able to spell and write other similarly constructed words.

Even without clear-cut, observable lines of perceptual function from the sense organs to the brain activity, the behaviour of dyslexic pupils is observable. In presenting the schematic, contrasting diagrams representing the variations in activity between normal and dyslexic pupils, the writer is attempting the demonstrate her way of looking at the problem as the result of observing a learner's reactions when attempting to bring into use, simultaneously, all the sensory modalities required for discrimination and ordering symbols in reading, writing and spelling (Figures 2.1. and 2.2.)

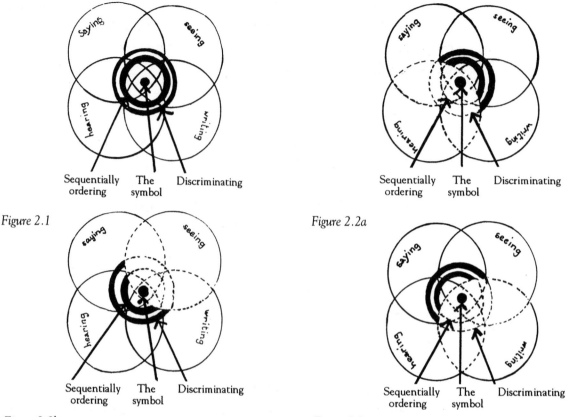

Figure 2.1

Figure 2.2a

Figure 2.2b

Figure 2.2c

Figure 2.1 Normal constitutional functioning for effectiveness in the language skills. Complete simultaneous interaction between the sensory systems results in the ability to discriminate between, and correctly order, the sound-symbols when the pupil is engaged in reading, writing and spelling

Figure 2.2 Abnormal constitutional functioning resulting in ineffectiveness in the language skills. The broken line indicates possible incomplete interaction.

(a) Poor auditory ability in discriminating (hearing) and sequentially ordering the sound-symbols result in its weak interaction with other required sensory systems when the pupil is engaged in reading, writing and spelling. A pupil with this weakness might get a 'flash' impression of a word but fail to associate its component parts with their corresponding sounds and put them in sequential order. He

might read or write 'gril' for 'girl'.

(b) Poor visual (seeing) ability in discriminating and sequentially ordering the sound-symbols results in its weak interaction with other required sensory systems when the pupil is engaged in reading, writing and spelling. A pupil with this weakness might hear all the sounds and attempt to put them into sequential order, but get the visual spellings wrong. Such a pupil might write 'fotowgraf' for 'photograph'.

(c) Poor motor co-ordination for writing, discriminating and sequentially ordering the shapes of the symbols results in its weak interaction with the other required sensory systems when the pupil is engaged in reading, writing and spelling. A pupil with this poor motor co-ordination would have difficulty in writing sound-symbols correctly, and would probably scan inaccurately when reading.

Multisensory learning is diagnostic of the particular type of difficulty the pupil is having. He can be seen to react confidently, but usually inaccurately, in his stronger areas of activity and falter in his weaker or seldom used ones.

The 'look and say' approach

If we critically examine this method, we can see why some dyslexic pupils fail to make progress with it. The pupil looks at a word and cannot say it until he knows the meaning. He is given a picture to illustrate the word. Soon he is expected to identity it without a picture, but the printed word has made no impression on his visual-perceptual system; therefore, he does not remember the word when he sees it in isolation or in context. If the context suggests the word, he may say it correctly. For example, if the sentence to the read is, 'The girl put her money into her purse', he may be able to read purse, but if the sentence is, 'The girl carried a purse', then the context may not help recognition. We do not know what a poor visualiser sees.

The phonic approach

In may instances this approach is taught in the same way as the 'look and say'. The pupil is told that 'sh' sounds /sh/. A poor visualiser may not recognise the 'sh' again and if he has poor auditory ability, he will not remember which sound to associate with the symbol. We do not know what a poor auditor hears.

Multisensory learning for reading and writing

The value of multisensory learning is that it enables individuals to use their own approach to the tasks through utilising their strong areas and at the same time exercising their faulty ones. The aim is for the pupil to acquire, for permanent automatic response, the names–sounds–shapes of phonograms and an ability to put them in the correct sequential order. His visual, auditory, tactile-kinaesthetic and oral-kinaesthetic perceptual systems must interact sufficiently to make learning so secure that he can produce any aspect of the phonograms when needed whether for reading or spelling. When the pupil is given:

- the name(s) of the letter(s), he must be able to recall the clueword, the sound, the appearance of the symbol for reading and the feel of the shape for writing.
- the sound, he must be able to recall the clueword, the appearance of the symbol for reading, the name for spelling and the shape for writing.
- the writing shape, he must be able to recall the name, clueword, sound and relate it to the printed shape for reading.
- the clueword, he must be able to recall sound, name and shape of the letter(s) for reading, writing and spelling.

Note: the sounds are written in slanted brackets with their markings; the letters to be read by name are in single quotation marks or inverted commas, thus /ĭ/ sound, 'i' name of letter.

The tools for training a learner to read and spell by using all the required senses are the Reading Cards and Spelling Cards. Each one is made by the teacher and pupil as required throughout the training course. As each new sound is introduced in Part II, the face and reverse of each card is shown. The details that belong with each card are listed on pages 152 and 153.

The Reading Cards consist of 84 cards, size 5 cm × 8 cm. On the face of each is a phonogram (a symbol representing a spoken sound) printed in lower case letters. At the bottom right-hand corner of the card is its capital form in a smaller type size acting as a reminder to the pupil that capitals behave in the same way as the lower case letters for sound blending.

Face

Reverse

Figure 2.3
The Reading Card.

On the reverse of the card is a picture of the clue to the sound of the phonogram, the 'clueword' and the representation of the sound. The written form of the sound should become familiar to the pupil as he progresses. For example, the letter 'i', which is the first letter in the Language Training Course, is represented by the picture of an igloo, the clueword 'igloo', and the sound /ĭ/ which is heard at the beginning of the clueword. It is not necessary for the pupil to be able to read the cluewords. Vowels are distinguished by drawing two bars across the top, or by using a different coloured card. Figure 2.3 is a representation of both sides of the Reading Card with the phonogram 'i'.

The cards are self-checking. They are introduced one at a time and the pack is gradually completed. As each card is added, the pupil's reading skills are built up and his knowledge of the English language broadens. The routine practice for using the Reading and Spelling Cards needs to be studied carefully by the teacher. Expertise will come with use.

The Reading Cards should be used by the learner alone for practice at least once a day and whenever he has a spare moment. When he is with his teacher, he should handle his own cards under observation so that the correct responses are checked and maintained.

When the teacher presents a new card, he should go through the 'Introduction to a new phonogram' and 'The stimulus response routine (SRR)' on pages 21–25.

The learner working alone or under observation picks up the first card in the pack, looks at the phonogram, says the clueword and sound 'igloo /ĭ/', turns the card over and places it face down, checks by the picture(s) that his response is correct and looks at the next card. If he has made a mistake he looks at the phonogram again, repeats the cluewords and sounds and places the card back in the pack so that he can re-read it. He must have an awareness of the need to increase his speed.

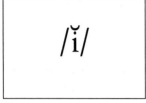

Face

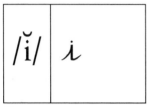

Reverse

Figure 2.4 The Spelling Card.

When revising with the teacher, if the learner gives an incorrect response to a phonogram, clueword and/or sound, the teacher may have to repeat the stimulus response routine until secure. The pupil should be encouraged to make a note of the phonograms he finds difficult to remember and, when presenting himself for a lesson, to tell his teacher. Alternatively, he can separate them from the pack so that revision is concentrated on them.

With each phonogram, the learner has multisensory practice for reading:

Visual	– He looks at the letter 'i'.
Kinaesthetic	– Uses his spatial ability to see the letter is alone on the card, its direction, the relationship of its parts and figure ground.
Auditory	– Listens to himself giving the clueword and sound /ĭ/ for the letter 'i'.
Oral-kinaesthetic	– Repeats and relates the clueword to the sound and feels the position of his teeth, tongue and lips in reproducing it.

The Spelling Cards consist of 51 cards of size 5 cm x 8 cm. The purpose is to present the written sounds so that the learner can listen to them and spell them, if necessary, in their several possible ways. Figure 2.4 gives a representation of the spelling card of the sound /ĭ/.

The pupil looks at the face of the card and says the sound /ĭ/. He then names the letter 'i' before writing it in his book. He then turns the card over to check the spelling. Only the spelling choices which he has learned will be on the card. Later the second spelling choice will be added.

The pupil has multisensory practice for spelling:

Auditory	– Listens to a sound.

Oral	– Speaks the sound aloud, links it to the name(s) of the letter in its possible different spellings.
Kinaesthetic	– Uses movement to write correctly the spelling alternatives naming each before writing.
Visual	– Sees the spellings he has written and is learning their different positions in words or their order of probability in words.

Introduction to a new phonogram

Continuing with the same example (the letter 'i'), the steps below, which have been found to work with many pupils, should be followed for introducing each of the phonograms.

Step 1: recognising its appearance and name from the printed letter

He is shown his first Reading Card 'i'. He is already familiar with the capital 'I' in his alphabet work. He is reminded of this and shown its relationship to the lower case printed form on the card. He is told that this is the one he will find in words in his reading book. He picks out capital and lower case letters in a book in order to gain familiarity with the difference between them. He is asked to name the letter 'i'.

Step 2: discovering its short sound and learning its relationship to the clueword

Ask the learner to discover its sound by giving him objects with names beginning with the sound, words which begin with the sound to listen to and pictures and/or objects beginning with the sound to look at. Then give him the clueword and ask him to listen to it and discover its initial sound. If a learner has difficulty in making a sound, he can be helped to become aware of the position of his teeth, tongue and lips in producing it by watching himself and the teacher make the sound in the mirror.

Step 3: learning to write the hand-written symbol

1. The teacher makes a faint line on a large surface, e.g. blackboard, whiteboard, flip chart etc.
2. The teacher places a small cross on the line at the point where the approach stroke to the letter begins:

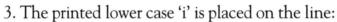

3. The printed lower case 'i' is placed on the line:

4. The pupil is shown how to lead from the cross to the point where the letter begins, how to write over the letter and how to lead off:

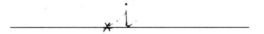

The pupil says the sound /ĭ/ and names the letter 'i' as he writes. Stage 4 is repeated as many times as necessary in order for the flowing movement to be thoroughly learnt.

5. The pupil then attempts the letter on his own beside the teacher's model.

6. Both are then erased and the pupil writes the letter from memory remembering to say the sound and name before writing.
7. Finally he writes the letter with his eyes closed, feeling his way through the shape, making the sound and naming the letter as before.

Copy the writing practice sheet (Figure 2.5) for practice.

This is usually a fascinating part of the procedure for the pupil and he will often continue to do this for pleasure. Tracing decreases the need for copying letter shapes and is a more certain way of securing the image. The learner must make the sound first and name the letter before writing so that a permanent relationship is established between the sound–name–shape of the phonogram.

Step 4: the stimulus response routine

The stimulus response routine (SRR) shown in the table (see p. 25) will help the pupil to become aware of all his senses for learning and remembering. He should know that the teacher's intention is to cultivate this awareness. He is asked to focus his attention on the different aspects of the phonogram to be learnt.

After the phonogram has been introduced and has become familiar only SRR no.4 (Reading Cards) and SRR no.8 (Spelling Cards) need be repeated regularly. If the pupils finds any aspect difficult, the SRR should be repeated.

When the first phonogram is secure, the second Reading Card can be given and the pupil goes through the same process of 'Introduction of a letter'. He gradually builds up his pack of phonograms, learning each one in the same way until his response to it is automatic.

1. Written letter for pupil to *trace* over, sounding and naming it aloud before writing	2. Space for pupil to *copy* the written letter, sounding and naming it aloud before writing
3. Space for pupil to *write* the letter *from memory*, sounding and naming it aloud before writing	4. Space for pupil to *write* the letter *with eyes closed*, sounding and naming it aloud before writing

Figure 2.5 The writing practice sheet. (Photocopying of this sheet for use with pupils is permitted.)

Stimulus Response Routine (SRR)	
What the TEACHER does (stimulus)	**What the LEARNER does (response)**
1. *Visual stimulus:* shows the learner the reading card 'i' and asks him to respond with the <u>name</u> of the letter.	*Visual–spatial and oral response:* sees the letter, discriminates its shape, names 'i'.
2. *Visual stimulus:* shows the learner a picture of the clueword (igloo) and asks for the <u>sound</u> heard at the beginning of its name.	*Visual–spatial, auditory and oral response:* sees the picture, says the word, listens to the sound, says /ĭ/.
3. *Auditory stimulus:* says the <u>name</u> of the letter and asks for the <u>clueword</u> and <u>sound</u>.	*Auditory and oral response:* hears the name of the letter and says 'igloo, /ĭ/'.
4. *Visual stimulus:* shows the learner the reading card 'i' and asks for the clueword and <u>sound</u>.	*Visual–spatial, auditory and oral response:* sees the letter, links shape to clueword, links this to sound and says 'igloo, /ĭ/'.
5. *Auditory stimulus:* says the sound /ĭ/ and asks for the clueword and the <u>name</u> of the letter.	*Auditory and oral response:* hears the sound , links it to the clueword and says 'igloo /ĭ/'.
6. *Auditory stimulus:* says /ĭ/, asks the learner to repeat the sound and <u>name</u> the letter that represents it.	*Auditory and oral response:* hears the sound, repeats it, relates to the letter and says /ĭ/, 'i'.
7. *Auditory stimulus:* says the clueword 'igloo' and asks for the <u>sound</u> and the <u>name</u> of the letter.	*Auditory and oral repsonse:* hears the clueword 'igloo' and says /ĭ/, 'i'.
8. *Auditory stimulus:* makes the sound /ĭ/ and asks learner to repeat the <u>sound</u>, <u>name</u> and <u>write</u> the letter.	*Auditory, oral, kinaesthetic and visual repsonse:* hears the sound, repeats it, names the letter, writes in cursive style ⅃
9. *Visual and kinaesthetic stimulus:* writes the letter 'i' in the air or on some surface (e.g. on learner's back) and asks for <u>clueword</u>, <u>sound</u>, <u>name</u> of letter.	*Visual, kinaesthetic, auditory and oral response:* sees the movement, feels (follows) the shape, relates to its name, clueword and sound, says igloo /ĭ/, 'i', hears own voice.

As the Reading Cards are self-checking and small enough to go into a pocket, the pupil can take them home and practise them. He should be encouraged to do this whenever he has a quiet spare few minutes. Later he can do the same with the Spelling Cards. Some parents may be able to supervise the practice. The complete list of phonograms for the Reading Cards is given on pages 152–3. The complete list of sound spellings for the Spelling Cards is given on pages 154–5. The instructions for introducing each phonogram are given in detail in the Language Training Course.

Further information

The past two decades have seen an explosion of research into the biological bases of dyslexia. Genes implicated in the development of dyslexia have been identified. Advances in technology have allowed researchers to study differences in the brains of living subjects, so that cognitive tests can also be carried out. CAT scanning uses X-rays; MRI uses magnetic fields; PET scanning involves the use of radioactive chemicals and can provide three-dimensional images of the areas of the brain involved in a range of language processing tasks. They have produced strong evidence of differences between the neurological functioning of the dyslexic and non-dyslexic brain.

See *Dyslexia: Biology, Cognition and Intervention* (Hulme and Snowling 1997), which brings together recent advances in understanding the biological bases of dyslexia, its presentation in different cognitive styles, and the efficacy of different interventions.

Chapter 3
Taking Hickey into the twenty-first century

The educational needs of the dyslexic pupil are increasingly being met within the inclusive mainstream classroom. In most primary schools in the country, teachers are using the National Literacy Strategy (NLS) Framework to achieve the targets set out in the English National Curriculum. The teaching takes place in a designated Literacy Hour. This method of delivery has many advantages for dyslexic pupils, but in order to achieve their full potential, most of them will need additional support. The Individual Educational Plan (IEP) on p.41 indicates the gap; there is often a need for extra help in moving information up the learning hierarchy and achieving multisensory mastery of concepts and knowledge explained and understood, but not generalised. The Hickey Language Course is an excellent, well-tried programme for filling this gap. Individual Education Plans suggest ways of fitting the Hickey programme into current classroom organisation at Key Stages 1 and 2.

Experience and knowledge from research gained since earlier editions of the Hickey need to be taken into account. Games and activities to develop phonological awareness, and integrated approaches to reading and writing, are described in detail.

This chapter includes information about resources for educational assessment and intervention, and discusses use of computers and word processors.

Implementing the National Literacy Strategy for the dyslexic child in the primary school

Primary schools are expected to devote a formal hour to the teaching of literacy. The NLS Framework suggests a practical structure for classroom organisation and time management, and lists the details of what should be taught. The first quarter of the hour is whole class teaching of shared reading or shared writing. The second quarter is whole class teaching of focused word work at Key Stage 1, and a balance of word work or sentence work at Key Stage 2. The next 20 minutes allocates differentiated tasks to groups, enabling the children to work at an independent level. The teacher spends the time working with groups in turn on guided reading or writing. The last 10 minutes is a plenary session, reviewing, reflecting and consolidating the work covered that day, acknowledging and celebrating achievement. First sight suggests a rigid structure, which might make it difficult to cater for the needs of the dyslexic pupil in the primary school, but the NLS Framework can be implemented quite flexibly; OFSTED teams check that children with special educational needs receive their full entitlement to the English National Curriculum, but they also recognise that there is a wide range of needs in different schools, and the organisation of the Literacy Hour can reflect this variety. The NLS Framework has real advantages for the dyslexic child:

- It is based on best practice culled from a wide range of teaching, including approaches developed for dyslexic learners.
- Reading and writing skills are directly and explicitly taught.
- It provides a structured, detailed, sequential programme.
- Its framework allows successful class teaching.
- It promotes an approach that integrates phonic skills with whole language.
- Its range is wide, including phonological awareness training.

- It allows for uneven abilities within the individual.
- It includes simple, searching assessments.
- It encourages modelling of expressive language, spoken and written.

However, it only works for children with special needs if its implementation is flexible:

- Dyslexic children will need help in accessing difficult texts that they can appreciate and enjoy, but not read independently. Parents or Support Assistants can be given Shared reading texts in advance, or extra time given during the week, so that the dyslexic child can work on tricky words or unusual language registers.
- Independent activities do not have to link in with the shared text, so there is time to implement useful programmes within the skills level of the dyslexic child. Use any suitable published materials that can be completed independently.
- Hickey groups may have to be taught outside the Literacy Hour. Make sure that they still receive the full National Curriculum to which they are entitled, so any lesson missed regularly will be changed after a specified period, and provision made for extra 'catch-up' work in core subjects.
- If dyslexic children have to be withdrawn from any part of the hour, their IEP needs to specify that this is going to happen in order to fulfil an identified purpose.
- Group guided reading is not enough for most dyslexic children. They usually need individual reading time aimed at giving help in generalising and 'owning' new strategies (silent reading time, often taking place in schools straight after lunch, is a good time for this).
- Setting is working well in some schools, though differentiated work still needs to be provided. Remember – not all SEN children benefit from being placed in lower sets (e.g. dyslexic

children, visually impaired children, children with emotional and behavioural difficulties (EBD)).

- Use the framework flexibly. A dyslexic child in Year 6 could be using the framework at an age appropriate level in text level work, and still need sound processing activities taken from the Year 1 objectives.

Some schools are setting their children for Literacy Hour. Although the dyslexic children may have poor skills, the bottom set is not necessarily the best place for them – the Hour works best when the children are in a group that pitches the oral work at the right level. A child who can understand and enjoy a difficult text will be able to enjoy and learn from a shared reading session where better readers can permit access to the text, and the poor reader can contribute to oral work. Delivery of the Literacy Strategy can be very flexible, and can accommodate the special needs of the dyslexic child.

The NLS Framework is intended for Key Stages 1 and 2 children, but is feeding through into Key Stages 3 and 4, as secondary school teachers dip into the Framework to provide continuity and appropriate teaching for a range of educational needs.

Developing phonological awareness

There is strong consensus that the phonological difficulties are a core deficit in dyslexic children (e.g. Snowling and Stackhouse 1996), and that specific training in phonological awareness increases the effectiveness of literacy teaching (e.g. Hatcher 1994). The shaky foundation of phonology, on which the literacy skills need to be built, must be strengthened. The Hickey Course trains the learner to develop the links between sounds and letters or letter clusters; it introduces the phonograms and the concepts and rules to fit them into words and sentences; it involves recall and recognition at a level that involves eyes, ears, mouth and hand movement.

For thousands of pupils, the Hickey approach, as it stands, has been the key to success. But many pupils have struggled unnecessarily with the early stages. If they cannot use the sounds they learn to segment a simple word into phonemes for writing, or blend them together for reading, the routines become fruitless. Until they can accomplish the sound discrimination and manipulation tasks in spoken language, it is going to be impossible to build fluency into the next stage of mapping letters onto the sounds. Assessment of the pupil's phonological awareness and sound processing ability, leading to a suitable intervention programme, needs to be built into the Hickey Language Course. This chapter includes some ideas for games and activities that work well, and some ideas for other useful resources. As well as providing development in phonological awareness skills, the games and activities can foster listening skills, concentration, working memory, expressive language, social inter-action, and self-esteem. Chosen appropriately, they can be used as part of the Literacy Hour, music or dance sessions, or small group work for those following the Hickey programme.

Games and activities to foster phonological awareness

Awareness of rhythm

The English language has a pattern of stresses that underpins knowledge of word boundaries and syllable segmentation. Dyslexic children often have speech that is weakly emphasised, and can improve their ability to repeat longer words by rhythmically tapping out the syllables.

Pass the message

Aim: To encourage ability to develop rhythmic movement, combined with speech patterns.
Number of players: 4 – 12

How to play: Sit in a circle. Leader starts a series of rhythmic claps – for example, claps hands together, then taps legs. The rest of the group join in. The leader calls the name of another member of the group, who establishes a new pattern. The rest of the group join in.

What time is it, Mr Wolf?

Aim: To encourage ability to develop rhythmic movement, combined with speech patterns.

Number of players: 4 – 40

How to play: A leader is chosen to be 'Mr Wolf'. Mr Wolf marches round the hall or playground. The rest of the group chant, 'What time is it Mr Wolf?' Mr Wolf will stop, turn, and say a time – one o'clock, two o'clock – and the group will stop and listen. This goes on until the response is 'DINNER TIME!'. Then the group will turn and run, and Mr Wolf will chase and catch someone to take over as Mr Wolf.

Cookie jar

Aim: To encourage ability to develop rhythmic movement, combined with speech patterns.

Number of players: 4 – 40

How to play: Sit in a circle. Say the words of the chant very rhythmically. Mark each syllable with a clap – alternately clap hands together, then slap thighs.

All: Who stole the cookie from the cookie jar?

Leader: (Chooses a name, e.g. Louis) stole the cookies from the cookie jar

Louis: Who, me?

All: Yes, you!

Louis: Couldn't be!

All: Then who stole the cookies from the cookie jar?

Louis: (Chooses, e.g. Oscar) Oscar stole the cookies from the cookie jar . . .

The man with the power

Aim: To encourage development of expressive language, awareness of rhythm and social interaction.
Number of players: Two groups (or two individuals)
How to play: Chant rhythmically, clapping or tapping in rhythm.
A. You remind me of a man.
B. What man?
A. The man with the power.
B. What power?
A. The power of Hoodoo.
B. Hoodoo?
A. You do.
B. I do what?
A. Remind me of a man.
B. What man? . . .

Clapping games

Aim: To encourage ability to develop rhythmic movement, combined with speech patterns.
Number of players: Any even number – played in pairs.
How to play: The players face each other, clap their hands together, then clap each other's hands. The pattern can be made more complicated (e.g. together, right, together, left, together, both). Say a simple rhyme in time with the claps. A well known example is: 'A sailor went to sea, sea, sea, To see what he could see, see, see, But all that he could see, see, see, Was the bottom of the deep blue sea, sea, sea . . .'
Chanting 'raps', poems and phrases, playing musical instruments,

aerobics, dance: activities like this can develop rhythmic ability in pupils of all ages.

Awareness of rhyme

Recognition of rhyme the basis for use of analogy in reading and spelling. It is particularly important in reading; there is time to think out a word for spelling, but speedy recognition of letter clusters that represent sounds is a crucial skill in fluent reading.

Children need to enjoy rhymes and poems together. Most Key Stage 1 children have access to high quality books with poetry and verse that lead to an appreciation of rhyme. Shared reading sessions will draw attention to words that rhyme, and to the patterns of letters that make the rhymes.

Alphabet arc (group or individual activity)

Use the white board and magnetic letters to lay out the arc. Provide a relevant rime (e.g. 'ark') – it can be taken from the shared reading text. Ask the children to use the letters to make words. The words can be put on cards for snap, rummy, pairs etc.

Guess the rhyme (group activity)

Copy or adapt a simple poem, omitting the rhyming word. Ask the group to supply a word that rhymes. For example, you could ask young children to fill in the gaps:

> 'Tinky Winky went for a walk,
> Laa Laa came and started to . . .'

Ask the children what colours the characters like – they could even provide illustrations:

> Mr Down likes . . . Mr Hoo likes . . . Mr Head likes . . . Mr Mean likes . . . Mr Mink likes . . . (You can give the first sound as a clue.)

Rhyming pairs

Aim: Word finding, identification of rhyme.

Number of players: 2, 4 or 6

How to play: Provide pictures of rhyming pairs (e.g. mug, bug; fan, pan; hen, pen; flower, tower). Discuss each one, and make sure that the labels are understood and agreed (e.g. 'flower' not 'daisy'; 'mug' not 'cup'). Practise speedy naming of each one. Then lay the cards out, face down. The first child turns up two cards, and names the object on the card. If they match, the child can keep the card and have one more turn. The next child then follows on. The one with the most pairs is the winner.

Older pupils could be given poems with words blanked out, and fill them in by writing. Discuss and choose together the most suitable word, and compare it with the original – they might prefer their own.

Phoneme awareness

Guess the word (individual or small group activity).

Teacher says, 'What am I thinking of?' and says the sounds of the word slowly, separating each phoneme. If the child can't guess, give a clue. For example:

'p – i – g. It's an animal. p – i – g.'

When the pupils are able, they can have a turn to stretch out the word for you to guess.

What does Sammy like? (group activity – initial sound)

Make or acquire a snake puppet – call it Sammy. Have a bag full of small objects. Sammy will only like the ones that start with 'sss'. (Start with easy sounds that can be drawn out and exaggerated – 'sss' or 'fff' rather than 'b' or 'd'.)

Educating Eddie (group activity – final sound)

Eddie is a puppet who finds it difficult to pronounce words properly. Take an object out of a bag, and ask the children to name it (e.g. 'cup'). Ask Eddie what it is, and have him call it 'cut' or 'cuff'. The children have to teach Eddie to say the word properly – they will repeat the word, emphasising the last sound, thus increasing their own phoneme awareness.

Sound boxes (group activity)

Give each child a strip of card marked into a row of five boxes. Say a word with two, three or four sounds in it. Each child in turn will slide a counter into a box to represent each sound. All the children will then check by repeating the word, and chanting the sounds together.

Familiar games

Games such as 'I Spy' are always popular – younger children might need to limit the game to sounds only, and to choosing from a collection of objects or pictures on a page. Use also packs of cards for sorting into categories – same initial, middle or end sound.

Integrated approaches to reading and writing

Multisensory programmes are about training and skills acquisition. Many dyslexic pupils achieve well in cognitive tests, and have a good knowledge of the world, an understanding of language, a receptive vocabulary, and a grasp of new concepts in a wide range of subjects. Skills training is their pre-eminent need, but it is not enough. Users of the Hickey Language Course know from bitter experience that it is possible for hard-won skills to remain in a separate capsule. Many dyslexic pupils can demonstrate use of a full range of literacy strategies. Handwriting may be satisfactory, spelling may be weak but good enough for communication, and good enough to register improvement on spelling tests, yet they find it impossible to express themselves in writing. They may demonstrate use of context, knowledge of sight vocabulary, ability to decode words, good listening skills, but they cannot orchestrate these strategies into fluent reading of connected texts. The dyslexic pupil will need an integrated approach in order to generalise the new skills into reading and writing.

Reading

The National Literacy Strategy Framework adopts the 'Searchlights' model of reading. Readers use a range of strategies to get at the meaning of a text, and these strategies can be depicted as a series of searchlights. As each one is used appropriately, light is shed on the text, and meaning emerges. The learner uses different 'searchlights', even within the same sentence, relying on:

- Word recognition and graphic knowledge – automatic and speedy recognition of letters, words, and punctuation.
- Phonic knowledge – the ability to link a letter or a group of letters with a sound, and to use this sound as a clue to accessing the word.
- Use of context – a word can be intelligently and speedily 'guessed' by use of context or a swift glance at the picture.
- Use of grammatical knowledge, or sentence structure.

The shared and guided reading and writing sessions involve direct teaching of techniques and strategies. The dyslexic child will benefit from this approach, but most of them need individual help in gaining personal ownership of the techniques. The Hickey Lesson Plan (pages 148–149) has been modified to include individual reading sessions.

Choosing a book

A feature of dyslexic children is their ability to enjoy and learn from materials that cannot be tackled independently. Do continue to read aloud to the dyslexic learner, but make sure that there are readable texts available. To check readability, ask the pupil to read aloud, explaining that you are not going to help or teach, just check for the difficulty of the text. Tick every word read correctly. If one in ten words are wrong, the text is too hard. Make sure that the reader gets plenty of practice, especially the confidence-building exercise of re-reading a familiar text. For ideas about working with complete non-readers, see Marie Clay's (1993) *Reading Recovery* and Broomfield and Combley's (1997) *Overcoming Dyslexia*.

Introducing a book

It is important to start the book with some expectations of what the book might contain. This primes the mind to use existing experience and knowledge. Look at the pictures, 'blurb', title page and ask the reader to predict what the book will be about. Prepare the reader for any oddities – unusual names, use of first person, archaic language, use of irony, unusual humour. *Reading Recovery* teachers call this 'debugging' the book.

Reading aloud

When the reader leaves an error uncorrected, or refuses a word, encourage use of appropriate strategies. Different questions call into play different strategies. When use of *context* is required, ask the reader to read the whole sentence and guess what the word might be, or encourage use of the picture. Some words can be worked out by using *phonic analysis* – encourage the reader to say the sounds in turn, thus exercising skills taught in their Hickey programme. Some words (like 'fantastic' or magnetic') require a combination of strategies – 'first syllable and guess'.

Encourage *reading for meaning* by asking the reader to re-tell the story so far covered, or discussing what might happen next, or recalling incidents from real life that connect with the text.

Develop *sight vocabulary* by photocopying a page or a current book for scanning – ask the reader to quickly scan the text, highlighting and repeating the chosen word (for example, 'when', 'want' or 'went'). Keep a pack of words being worked on, and give regular practice of them in the Hickey sessions.

Encourage *active learning* by drawing attention to strategies used in reading. Ask the reader how they managed to work out difficult words, or comment on their success with a word not known the day before. Summarise what has been covered in a session, and point out the main strategy to be exercised in class work and homework.

Writing

Although there is consensus that dyslexia is so much more than a reading disability, teachers and parents still get exasperated at the dyslexic's 'refusal' to write. We are beginning to realise that the inability to write can be almost as crippling as the inability to read, and the techniques of writing demand attention.

The National Literacy Strategy recognises that spelling and handwriting are only two of the many techniques that need to be taught. The Framework for Teaching (DfEE 1998) advocates shared writing – the teacher uses texts they have shared for reading to provide ideas and structures for writing. Together, the class composes a story, poem, play, account of experience, or piece of non-fiction. The teacher models the writing process, demonstrating layout, presentation, use of punctuation, grammatical points, and use of appropriate language. The dyslexic child can benefit from the oral work, and can make useful contributions to such compositions. Right from the start, the Hickey structure covers correct sentence formation and use of punctuation to convey meaning and emphasis.

It will be helpful for teachers working with dyslexic children using the Hickey programme to make use of the concepts being covered in the classroom, making explicit links between the two. Classroom teachers need to know when a dyslexic child has mastered the use of a new concept so that the dyslexic pupil can be given an opportunity to shine in shared writing sessions.

Developing written expression: special needs of the dyslexic learner

Dyslexic children are finding it very helpful to have the secrets of writing made more explicit. If they are having the skills training they need, so that they have acquired a reasonable vocabulary of high frequency words, and can use fluent 'invented' spelling (Broomfield and Combley 1997), they are able to tune into the classroom guidance and produce independent writing. Meanwhile, spelling choices can be gradually added at an appropriate rate and generalised into their writing. 'Getting Started' (DfEE 1999) provides a training programme for Additional Literacy Support workers who will work more closely with small groups. Many of the needs identified generally in children's writing apply also to dyslexics – getting the 'feel' of a sentence, marking it with punctuation, adding descriptive words and phrases, varying sentence structure, learning how to use the conventions for various sorts of writing. Dyslexic children often have a particular difficulty with:

- getting started – where does the writing begin? what is worth writing about?
- word-finding
- simplifying and organising a plethora of ideas.

They often need help in articulating ideas before writing, and gaining ownership of the concepts and ideas demonstrated to the whole class.

Individual Education Plan: John Smith (age 9y 7m)				
Special Concerns: John is dyslexic, and his problems with reading and writing are affecting confidence and self-esteem, and jeopardising his relationships with his peer group. His educational programme will ensure success, which should increase his confidence. All staff will be made aware of John's special needs, and help to provide support. Circle time and co-operative games will be used to strengthen peer relationships.				
Priority areas	**Targets**	**Staffing**	**Frequency/timing**	**Materials/resources**
1. Development of reading	1. Comprehension: enjoyment of stories, reading for information	Class T	Daily shared reading	Big Books; range of texts
		Class T	Weekly guided reading	Group readers, Red Level
		Parents	Three times a week, home reading programme	Oxford Reading Tree readers, level 6; library books, use of tape recorder
		Specialist teacher	Twice weekly	Range of appropriate texts
	2. Word attack skills: build in phonic skills in decoding unfamiliar words; use of suffixes (ing, ed, er)	Class T	Daily shared reading	Big Books; range of texts
			Weekly guided reading	Group readers
		Specialist teacher	Twice weekly	Hickey's multisensory structured programme
2. Development of phonological awareness	Auditory segmentation skills, recognition and generation of rhyme and rhythm	Class T	Weekly	Drama, music
		Specialist teacher	Twice weekly	Hickey's multisensory structured programme
3. Development of writing and spelling skills	1. Increase knowledge of common spelling patterns	Class T	Weekly	Shared writing
			Small group time	PAT level 2
	2. Improve fluency through use of 'invented spelling'		Classroom writing tasks	Broomfield and Combley, Chapter 7; 'Clicker' software
	3. Develop awareness of reader; match style to listener		Guided writing, literacy hour	
	4. Teach cursive writing, increase automaticity in sound/letter links	Specialist teacher	Twice weekly	Hickey's multisensory structured programme

Use of technology

Some dyslexic children, particularly those with related dyspraxic difficulties, will flourish with use of word processors and computers. Software has been developed that enables learners of all ages to improve their written communication. The Clicker range (Crick Software) starts with programmes that allow young children to build up text by clicking on pictures or words supported by good quality speech, and extends to programmes that give students access to thousands of words and phrases categorised in topics, subjects or alphabetic lists. The machine can't do all the work; getting thoughts into order is the most difficult aspect of writing, and encouragement and support from a teacher or parent may be the first step on the way to independent writing.

Spell-checkers are useful once the pupil has reached a stage of being able to write phonic approximations that can be recognised.

A-level students and older dyslexics who have begun to specialise in a subject may find the voice-activated computers a boon. They are not easily accessible and, for younger children, only the most committed primary school teachers can find the time to help the child 'train' the computer to react to the individual voice, and they need a quiet space, not commonly available in small schools

Individual help can also be given with use of a tape recorder. Use the guided reading text (the shared reading text might be suitable when it is quite familiar). Older learners should use a text at the independent reading level. After initial training, the tape can be used independently. The focus can be:

- listening to the taped passage, checking for accuracy;
- listening to the passage whilst thinking about expression – responding to punctuation, reading in a more lively manner;

- checking for hesitations, making sure that the re-taping will be more fluent;
- preparing a poem or short story to entertain other class members – ideal for a shy child who is afraid of reading aloud in public.

Individual Educational Plan

Learners working through the Hickey Language Training Course are usually being given help on an individual bases within the school or with a private tutor. Learners do not benefit much from a separate capsule of skills, and it is vital that the range of adults working with dyslexic children are fully aware of the different strands of their education. School children with Special Educational Needs will be working through an Individual Educational Plan (IEP) drawn up and co-ordinated by school's SENCO. The IEP (see page 41) demonstrates the way in which the different strands can be brought together.

The role of the specialist teacher mentioned in the IEP might be taken by the class teacher working closely with a trained child care assistant or an additional support assistant. If the multisensory structured programme is being led by someone outside the school, they will need to provide the school with a copy of the structure, and detailed information about skills and concepts covered – which sounds have been mastered for reading and/or writing, which will be targeted for the next period. The class teacher can then notice which skills are being generalised into reading and writing within the classroom, and reinforce with comment and praise.

Further information

Links with Literacy Hour

Phonological awareness assessment and training

Snowling and Stackhouse (1996) gather together recent research on the links between phonological awareness and literacy skills, plus excellent suggestions for intervention. Broomfield and Combley (1997) have a teacher's view of language and literacy links, and some ideas games and activities to improve phonological awareness. Wilson's (1995) PAT materials programme are useful resources. Hatcher's *Sound Linkage* (1994) provides a wide ranging and thorough programme of assessment and intervention, and positively bubbles with ideas to develop sound awareness in finely discriminated categories. Quilliam's (1980) *Bright Ideas: Language Development* provides a good source of verse and rhymes with ideas for using them.

Integrating skills into reading and writing

More ideas for connecting skills and whole texts are found in the National Literacy Strategy Framework of Teaching (DfEE 1998). Although this applies to children aged 5–11, young people in secondary school will also find the principles applicable and easy to adapt for the older learner. See Reason and Boote (1994) for suggestions for intervention. See Broomfield and Combley (1997), and Clay's (1993) *Reading Recovery* for ideas for development of whole language approaches to reading and writing, including emergent writing.

Information technology

Get a catalogue from Crick Software, Tel 01604 671691, Fax 01604 671692 for information about their range of Clicker programmes.

Chapter 4
The Language Training Course

Chapter 4 points out the relationship between reading and spelling. The two entail different learning processes and require teaching approaches that take this into account. This chapter stresses the importance of a structured approach to skills training. The pupil needs to be presented with the regularities of the English language and to be taught the appropriate vocabulary of language.

A comprehensive plan for the systematic acquisition of reading, writing and spelling

In school, a pupil is often taught skills related to reading and is then expected to produce written work, correctly, by using the same kind of practice in order to spell. This may be very confusing because, in reading, the emphasis is on helping him to recognise and differentiate the visual appearances of the units of sound from symbols which are before him. This does not apply to spelling. If the approach is suitable it does sometimes improve his reading, but may have little, or no, impact on his spelling ability. The difference between teaching the phonograms and syllables for reading and spelling is explained fully in separate chapters on the two skills which are like the two sides of the same coin.

When devising or purchasing materials for teaching a particular part of a word, because the pupil needs practice in a certain area, it is frequently overlooked that the content of the rest of the material involved may be beyond the pupil's experience.

For instance, if a teacher wishes to teach the suffix '-ing', he obtains a piece of apparatus for teaching this. Having learned about adding '-ing' to words the pupil gets that part of the work correct. For example he is asked to add '-ing' to the word 'play'. If the word 'play' is placed before him he can copy 'play + ing'. If asked to spell 'playing' without a copy he may write 'plaing', because he has not learnt about the 'ay' part of 'play'. When adding '-ing' to 'hope', unless the pupil knows the spelling rule he will probably write 'hopeing' or 'hopping'. A common error in writing the word 'hoped' is 'hopt' or 'hopet', because the pupil may not have been taught that the suffix '-ed' may be sounded /t/. He may have been taught that 'i' comes before 'e' except after 'c', but when he has to write a word, how is the pupil to know that the word begins with 'c'? Why not 's'? He is then given words such as 'receive' to spell; he may write 'receiv' because he has not been taught that 'v' is never written at the end of a word without an 'e'.

In order to read and spell, a dyslexic pupil needs a complete system of language training which is based on a definite ordered sequence.

The regularities of the language are rarely given sufficient consideration. The several languages brought to England with the different invasions, each one making its impact on our mother tongue, have caused many teachers to feel that there are few rules for guidance in the teaching of spelling; the skill has to be 'caught because it cannot be taught'. A pupil with dyslexia cannot 'catch' spelling. The regularities are there and can be presented to the pupil in a way in which he can learn them.

About 85 per cent of words conform to patterns of letter sounds. These regularities can be taught step by step so that they gradually accumulate and build into a comprehensive whole. A clear distinction needs to be made between what can be relied on as regular and what has to be learned as irregular. The 15 per cent of irregular words can be added to the pupils vocabulary in a clearly defined way. As teacher and pupils proceed through the Language Training Course, they will find that words which are regular for reading may not be regular for spelling. When this becomes clear, it will be seen that a systematic approach is the only sensible one, particularly for a confused pupil.

The vocabulary of language must be learned as the pupil progresses. New concepts will be acquired and given their correct names, and learned just as the vocabulary of mathematics or music is learned. As each phonogram is introduced, he can learn to identify the terms consonant, vowel, long vowel, short vowel, the simple dictionary markings such as breve (˘), macron (⁻) and stress (/). Syllables are given their distinguishing names, closed, open, regular final, suffix and prefix. He will learn to distinguish voiced and unvoiced sounds, stressed and unstressed syllables. This precise use of the correct vocabulary and the common dictionary markings reduces the pupil's confusion, because it helps to identify sound–symbol relationships exactly and to provide the tools for learning spelling with the same exactitude.

The position in which phonograms are commonly found in words is taught. The pupil is trained to expect to find a particular one at the beginning, middle or end of the word, and to know how to expect it to behave according to its juxtaposition to other letters.

When he has reached only his second phonogram, he can learn that the letter 'i' will sound /ĭ/ when a consonant comes after it in the syllable, and that he will not expect to find it at the end of words. The spelling rules by which any phonogram might be governed are taught when it is introduced, as is appropriate to the pupils age and stage of development. By the time the first 12 phonograms have been covered, the pupil will be able to recognise and say the sound for each letter so far covered – many teachers are happy to recognise this as 'knowing' the sounds. With multisensory learning, the pupil will also be able to listen to the sound, recall the correct letter, write it in relaxed cursive writing, sequence it into words, and use it in sentences. In addition, a whole raft of concepts and spelling rules will have been covered by some pupils. Table 4.1 lists some of these.

Further information

The National Literacy Strategy Framework for Teaching includes a glossary of linguistic terms intended for teachers. It also includes them in the detailed teaching framework – for example, a child in Year 3, Term 2 will be taught terms such as adjective, collective noun, singular and plural, comma. The Hickey approach of using correct terminology fits in happily with this. The timing may be different, but this should present no problems; Hickey's terms are welded with the concepts being taught on an individual basis, and thus will provide revision of past work or preparation of work to come.

Table 4.1 Early language concepts

Letter order	Concepts and rules that may be introduced
i	• a letter is a symbol that represents a sound (or sounds) • it can be presented in a range of fonts • it can be upper or lower case • it represents a vowel – movement of air from the lungs with no obstruction from tongue, lips or teeth. Every syllable must contain a vowel
t	• letters can be sequenced together into words which have meaning • some letters are consonants • consonants can be voiced or unvoiced • consonant are formed by movements of muscles of the mouth and throat
p	• the sequence of the letters can utterly change the meaning ('tip', 'pit')
n	• words with the same rime can rhyme ('in', 'tin', 'pin')
s	• the same letter can have two sounds ('is' and 'sit') • 's' can be a suffix that makes nouns plural ('tins'), or puts verbs into third person singular ('sits') • contractions can be introduced (e.g. 'it's', 'isn't') • two consonants can be blended together to make a sound ('spin', 'snip', 'its')
a	• words can have two syllables ('instant', 'pippin', 'insist') • simple sentences can be used to introduce punctuation - start with a capital letter, end with full stop or question mark. ('It is a tin.' 'Is it a tin?') • apostrophe + 's' to denote possessive ('Stan's tin')
d	• 5 of the 10 high frequency words that make up 20 per cent of the English language can be mastered ('and', 'a', 'in', 'is', 'it')
h	• another of the top ten high frequency words ('that')
e	• high frequency word 'the'
c	• spelling rule 'c' is the first choice for the /k/ sound at the beginning of words and syllables
k	• spelling choice: for the /k/ sound, choose c at the beginning of words and syllables, unless the following vowel is 'i' or 'e'
ck	• spelling choice for /k/ at the end of words and syllables: choose 'ck' at the end of one syllable words with one short vowel (e.g. sack, neck, pick). Choose 'k' to follow another consonant (e.g. desk, task). Choose 'c' in longer words (e.g. plastic, picnic)

Chapter 5
The alphabet and dictionary

It is important for the dyslexic pupil to have a comprehensive grasp of the alphabet. They need to understand that the 26 letters of the alphabet are the basis of all written language, and alphabetical order is the basis of most of our reference systems. They need to be able to recall the name and sound of each letter, and to have automatic mastery of alphabetical order. Alphabet activities using wooden or plastic letters teach understanding of stress in spoken language, and provide a foundation for use of a dictionary.

The alphabet

The importance of the alphabet in education is that it is the basis of the English language. The thousands of words we use are all made from one or more of these letters.

The dictionary, which is the organisation of words into alphabetical order, is our reference for identifying the pronunciation, spelling, meaning and origin of new words. Yet, the teaching of the alphabet to a pupil, naming the letters in sequential order, has been neglected and thought to be old-fashioned or an end in itself with no reference to his educational needs. In spite of this neglect, he is expected to use dictionaries, encyclopaedias and other alphabetised lists efficiently. A school might teach him to 'sing' alphabet songs, but this does not help as the song remains a song and has no real application to the use of the alphabet.

The dyslexic pupil needs help in understanding that the letters in the alphabet are symbols representing speech sounds which are the ingredients of words. They are the tools of language in the same way that numbers are the tools of mathematics. Both sets need to be learnt by name and in sequential order so that they can be located when needed.

Learning sequentially to order the letters of the alphabet

This is extremely important for a dyslexic pupil. An inability to learn to do this with a reasonable degree of facility usually accompanies written language disorders. He may need a long period of regular and frequent practice before he becomes proficient in the practicalities of its use for reference to alphabetical lists and other activities requiring a knowledge of the sequence of the letters.

In order to build his skill, after he has learnt the total sequence, the pupil will need practice in finding his way backwards and forwards in the alphabet. He needs to know which direction to go from M to find G, or from L to find I and so on, so that when using a dictionary he knows which way to turn the pages to find the word he needs. It is important to remember that many dyslexic children have directional problems and the term 'backwards' and 'forwards' may be difficult to understand and therefore interpret correctly.

Each lesson needs to be carefully organised to build up these skills. Five minutes each day is sufficient, but it may be a long time before he becomes proficient in using a dictionary. The following suggestions for helping towards efficiency in alphabetising and using a dictionary may be useful for teachers.

The capital form of each letter needs to be presented to the pupil first. In due course each one can be associated with its lower case character, because the block capital is the form of the letter which remains the most stable. Once the relationship between the capital and lower case is established, if in doubt about the identification of the lower case letter, the pupil can be referred back to the capital.

Wooden or plastic letters are suitable for introducing the alphabet. In order to identify each letter, the pupil can pick it up, feel it with eyes open or closed and name it. In this way the visual, auditory, oral and tactile-kinaesthetic channels of learning are all interacting.

Alphabet activities

These can be devised when a teacher is aware that a pupil finds difficulty in learning the alphabet. These should be challenging in order to encourage him to improve his skill. Self-correcting activities are, of course, preferable not only for competent learning but also for helping to economise on teaching time. The guiding principles for devising such activities are that they should give practice in familiarising the pupil with:

1. *The name and shape* of the capitals, lower case printed and written forms of the letters. Sorting and matching.
2. *The sequence of the letters*, putting out cut-out letter shapes, words on cards in alphabetical order, saying in sequence, writing in sequence and using alphabetised lists.
3. *The position of each letter in the alphabet* and its relationship to the other letters. Finding missing letters, going backwards and forwards in the alphabet from any letter to find another.

Initially, the pupil needs to learn that there are 26 letters in the alphabet forming a whole. He can gradually work through the stages below. At first he puts out each letter, naming it aloud, picking it up in sequential order until the letters form an arc. It may take several weeks before he can do the whole of this (Figure 5.1).

Figure 5.1 Forming an arc from letters of the alphabet

Stress

The ability to identify the stressed syllables of words is important for both reading and spelling. Unstressed syllables often have an indeterminate vowel sound (e.g. velvet, magnet) and present problems for spelling. Meaning is affected as the stress changes (e.g. 'inval'id' is not valid; 'in'valid' is a disabled or sick person).

For spelling it is particularly important when adding a vowel suffix to a two-syllable word ending with one vowel and one consonant. If the stress falls on the first syllable, the final consonant of the word will not be doubled, e.g. lim'it - lim'iting. If the stress falls on the second syllable, the consonant will be doubled, e.g. begin' - begin'ning.

All one-syllable words are stressed, e.g. cat', bridge', page'.

In the majority of words with two or more syllables, the stress falls on the first syllable of English nouns (stu'dent, can'didate, el'ephant). The stress changes when words have prefixes (nouns: ob'ject, con'duct; verbs: object', conduct')

In compound words, each syllable keeps its stress. Therefore both syllables are stressed equally, e.g. lip'stick', hay'stack'.

Before learners can successfully break words into syllables for spelling, it is helpful to give practice in tapping out rhythms and emphatically stressing selected beats. This can begin with the alphabet.

The teacher begins the rhythm and the pupils join in: clap, tap, or use any other means of identifying the rhythm.

1. AB' CD' EF' GH' etc.

2. A'B C'D E'F G'H etc.

3. A'BC D'EF G'HI J'KL etc.

4. AB'C DE'F GH'I JK'L etc.

Pupils can be asked the following questions:

1. How many letters in each group?

2. Where is the strong beat (or stress)?

3. Can we think of a word or name with that rhythm?

  e.g.   AB' – begin', Denise'

       A'B – mar'ket, Jan'et

       A'BC – lim'ited, Jenn'ifer.

The dictionary

Learning how to apply the alphabet to the use of a dictionary

This can take place concurrently with activities in learning the alphabet. As soon as the pupil has an appreciation of the wholeness of the alphabet, and the sequence of its letters, he should be given practice in giving the number of letters in the alphabet, 26 in all. He then names the first and last letters (A and Z) and practises finding the mid-way point and naming the two middle letters (M and N). He discovers the number of letters in each half, and puts out the alphabet in two halves:

A   B   C   D   E   F   G   H   I   J   K   L   M

N   O   P   Q   R   S   T   U   V   W   X   Y   Z

Figure 5.2 Two sets of thirteen letters.

He then learns that each half of the alphabet corresponds to each half of the dictionary and learns to open the dictionary in the middle and find that he is likely to turn up 'M'.

The four quartiles of the alphabet are found by dividing each half of the dictionary. If this is done well, the letters will divide thus:

A   B   C   D
E   F   G   H   I   J   K   L   M
N   O   P   Q   R
S   T   U   V   W   X   Y   Z

Figure 5.3 The four quartiles of the alphabet.

Activities for learning the sequence and content of each quartile can be devised. The pupil should have practice in naming the first and last letters of each quartile, knowing how many letters in each one and locating any letter in a quartile.

Dividing the dictionary into four quarters for speedy location of words

The four quartiles, or stages, in the alphabet correspond to the four quarters of the dictionary. A pupil should learn to halve the first half of the dictionary and find 'D' and halve the second half of the dictionary and find 'S'. The three letters dividing the dictionary into four quarters will be 'D', 'M' and 'S' as in Figure 5.4.

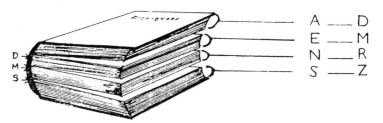

Figure 5.4 The dictionary open at the four quarters – the quartiles.

When dividing the dictionary into four, logically it should divide at 'M' or 'N' for the middle, 'D' or 'E' for the first quarter and 'R' or 'S' for the final quarter.

The histogram in Figure 5.5. represents roughly the distribution of the letters of the alphabet in the dictionary. It was worked out by a 13-year-old dyslexic boy who had good mathematical ability.

Clearly it can be seen that when dividing the dictionary, because there are more words beginning with 'D' than 'E', the letter which will turn up more regularly will be 'D'. Although 'M' and 'N' are equally in the middle of the alphabet, the letter more likely to be turned up will be 'M' because there are more words beginning with 'M' than 'N', and for the last quarter, 'S' is more likely than 'R' because 'S' has more words than 'R'.

When the pupil arrives at the stage of working with a dictionary, he can have this histogram before him as a reference. Work on the quartiles is well worth while. It is useful for a pupil to be fully conversant with each quartile, not only the number of letters in each, and its beginning and end letters, but also the amount of the dictionary likely to be taken up by words beginning with each letter. This enables him to be economical with his time when using a dictionary to find a word.

Alphabet games and activities for using a dictionary to find words can be devised by the teacher to further the pupil's interest in his knowledge of the dictionary.

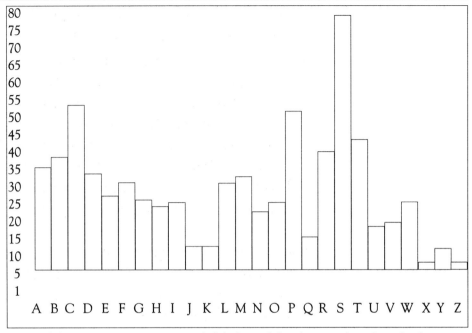

Figure 5.5 Approximate proportional alphabetical distribution of words in the dictionary except when using dictionaries with specialised vocabularies.

When the pupil can divide the alphabet into quartiles and the dictionary into quarters, in order to familiarise himself with the letters contained in each quarter, he can then play the challenge game of finding any word in five moves.

Finding a word in five moves can be played with any number:

1. The pupil is challenged to find the word PAT. He looks at the quartiles marked in the histogram, finds that 'P' is in the middle of the third quartile and tries to open the dictionary at this letter: but perhaps the word which he has found is PIN.
2. He must go back (towards his left hand) to find PAT because 'PA' is before 'PI'. With constant practice he can eventually decide roughly how many pages to turn back. He makes his judgement and turns back getting PAIN.

3. He keeps the places for PIN and PAIN because he knows that PAT must be trapped between the two.

4. He again makes his judgement and goes forward (towards his right hand) again but goes too far and gets PATRON. He now knows that the word is trapped in a smaller area between PATRON and PAIN, so he holds those two pages.

5. The chances are that his next division will turn up PAT because he will probably know that he must turn back one page from PATRON because PAT begins that word. He has found his word in four moves only so he scores a point.

Success in this game gives a sense of real practical achievement. A pupil will be willing to practise when given sensible guides, and challenges, and knows that he can play the game on fairly equal terms with other people.

A useful way to gain practice in familiarising the position of letters in the alphabet, and in the quartiles, is to give the pupil the alphabet letters jumbled and ask him to place the letter as it turns up where it should be in the alphabet, first in an arc and then in the quartiles (Figure 5.6 a and b).

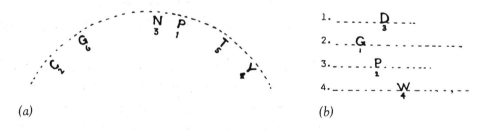

(a)   *(b)*

Figure 5.6 (a) Putting out jumbled letters in an arc: the first one is 'P' – he places it at its approximate point; next 'C', next 'N', then 'Y' and so on until he has completed the alphabet. *(b)* Putting out the jumbled letters in quartiles: the first one is 'G' – he places it in its approximate position in the second quartile; the next is 'P' – he places it in position in the third quartile. He continues to give them their correct positions as he turns them up.

Putting words in alphabetical order

Ten words on cards are given. The steps for learning the skills are as follows: give ten cards all beginning with different letters. Ask the pupil to place them out so that he can see all the first letters. He says 'A' and looks to see if he has a word beginning with 'A', if not he says 'B' and looks for a word beginning with 'B'. If there is one he puts it out. He then says 'C'. If there is a word, he puts it out, if not he goes on to 'D' and so on.

When he can put out ten words with their first letters in alphabetical order, the next group of words he is given will include two or three all beginning with the same letter, so that he has to begin looking at the second letter on these cards and finding the alphabetical order of the second letter. When he can do this he is given ten cards with two or three where the first and second letters are the same and he must look at the third letter in these words, and so on, until he can put any number of words into alphabetical order with the task becoming gradually more difficult.

Further information

Hickey was ahead of her time in advocating the teaching of letter names. The letter sounds are used for reading, and the link between letter/s and sound (grapheme phoneme link) is a key to successful decoding and fluent reading. The letter names are also important because there are many variables in the use of letters in words – each letter can represent a variety of sounds, and have a variety of fonts. The letter name collects together under one banner all these variables, and defines a finite task in that there are only 26 of them. Studies have pointed to knowledge of letter names as a significant predictor of later success in reading. *Beginning to Read: Thinking and Learning about Print* by M.J. Adams (1990) includes a lucid and searching review and analysis of current information about the importance of the alphabet.

Chapter 6
Handwriting

Handwriting for young children

The dyslexic pupil needs to learn joined handwriting in order to compensate for confusion with sequential order and laterality. It is an easily taught skill for all except those with severe motor disability. The style described is simple and unornamented. Every letter follows the same routine, starting from the base line. The printed form is embedded in the written form, ensuring a natural development.

In the same way that reading and spelling are separate but interrelated skills, so are printing and handwriting. Printing is for reading, handwriting is for transferring speech to the writing surface.

Although an ability to print is a difficult skill to acquire, very young children are traditionally taught to reproduce the printed forms of letters they have learned to recognise in their reading books. Usually, when it is considered that they have had sufficient practice at this skill, they are then asked to learn joined writing, thus creating another major task because the first shapes have become established in the kinaesthetic or motor memory and may not be correct. Young children have great difficulty in unlearning one habit and forming another. It is both unnecessary and undesirable to put them to all this trouble. In fact it is much easier for them to learn the letters initially, with the connecting strokes attached in readiness for joining them as soon as possible. The shape is a flowing form which gives aesthetic pleasure, being one sweeping movement.

The dyslexic pupil

Joining the letters is desirable for all but essential for the dyslexic pupil. He is likely to confuse any printed shape, so in teaching him to make separate printed shapes his problems are increased.

When making the printed form, the pencil sometimes has to be lifted within the letter, e.g. in k ,f and x. This broken rhythm increases the tendency to reverse or confuse letter shapes. When making a printed letter with first a stroke, then the semicircle added, the pupil may make the stroke and add the semicircle anywhere. Thus p may become 9, d or b.

Separating the letters within words adds to his problems. In many instances his writing looks disjointed and all over the place, even when spelt correctly; magic , topic are common among young children. The older dyslexic pupil will find it even more difficult than a young one to beak an established habit. Spacing between words is often a problem for him so that he may write Once upon a time thus: On ceup cnat ime or leave no spaces at all.

A cursive or joined form of handwriting is the one most suitable for a pupil who confuses or reverses letter forms and has problems of direction and sequential order. Many difficulties can be avoided if handwriting is taught from the beginning. Even for a dyslexic pupil, unless his motor disability is severe, handwriting is one of the most easily taught skills if begun early and regular practice given.

The simplest form for him to learn in order to link reading with writing is the printed form with the connecting strokes attached, as discussed above and reproduced in Figure 6.1. When the letters in a word are joined they make a sensible whole unit and a natural break is made before the next word begins. The techniques for teaching writing are described in 'Introduction to a new phonogram' (pages 21–25) where it is explained that the pupil is shown how to arrive at the written form over the printed form. In this way each letter is securely learned and the association between the reading book and written work made. In addition, there is no confusion between the printed letter and the handwritten letter. Nor will there be any necessity for a 'handwriting scheme to right these wrongs'.

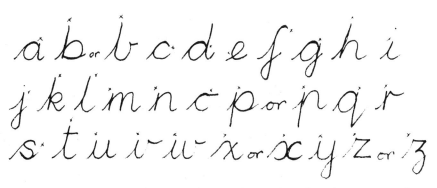

Figure 6.1 The written forms of the letters with their approach and carry-on strokes and their beginning points marked. The *x* is crossed like a t, after the word has been written.

Some schools object to 'loops' in handwriting. The reason for the objection is not clear, but if letters are to be joined, the loops cannot be avoided on those letters which come down below the line. There are only five of these: *f*, *g*, *j*, *y*, *z*. Ascenders do not have to be looped in order to join.

It is helpful to have the beginning points of the letters clearly illustrated. They are indicated by a small cross in Figure 6.1. Each letter needs to be approached from the line of writing with an approach stroke which goes to the beginning point of the letter. The letter is then written in one flowing movement. The carry-on stroke leaves the letter where it finishes and is ready to become the approach stroke of the next letter. In most cases the carry-on stroke leaves the line of writing except for *b*, *o*, *r*, *v* and $\mathcal{w}$ where it comes off the top of the letter and makes a bridge to the next one. These letters need extra attention.

Some letters follow the same pattern of movement and for a pupil who has a severe kinaesthetic problem it is useful for him to practise these letters in their groupings. He might need to verbalise directions to himself as he writes (Figure 6.2).

The 'over and back' letters: there are seven of these.	*a c d g q o s*
The 'off the top' letters where the 'carry-on' stroke or bridge to the next letter comes off the top of the letter: there are five of these.	*b o r v w*
The 'up down, up again, over and off' letters: there are five of these.	*h k m n p*
The 'up down off' letters: there are five of these.	*i j l t (x)*
The 'up down, up again, down again' letters: there are three of these.	*u w y*
Letters with tails: there are five of these.	*f g j y z*
Letters which need special practice: there are eight of these.	*f k g r s e x z*
Alternative written styles: there are four of these.	*p b x z*

Figure 6.2

Either form $\mathcal{f}$ or f is acceptable providing it joins and is made in one movement. The one the pupil finds easier to write might be the better one to use. f can be joined to the next letter with its crossed stroke but there is a break in the movement if the tail is not continued to the next letter. The written forms of b and d do not present the same confusion as the printed form.

Artificial aids such as specially printed exercise books are not particularly helpful in developing good handwriting. The pupil should be helped to find his own slope, size and speed. One way is to give him ordinary exercise paper, because this is what he is expected to use, and rule a faint pencil line above the writing line so that he begins to understand the uniform height of the lower half of the letters. Place a mark on the writing line to show the pupil where to begin. The following sentence contains every letter of the alphabet.

A quick brown fox jumps over the lazy dog.

When his writing shows some ease and uniformity, change to a dotted line, giving less support.

A quick etc.

As soon as he writes evenly and confidently, gradually reduce the number of dots. Should he still feel the need for guidance tell him to put a dot here and there along the line himself whenever he wishes.

A quick etc.

A timer can be used to increase his speed of writing. The alphabet joined and the sentence of 'A quick brown fox ...' are useful for speed practice. At intervals he can try to beat his own time record and at the same time keep up his standard of legibility.

Further information

The NLS Framework (DfEE 1998) suggests that children in Reception Year should be taught to 'write letters using the correct sequence of movement'. In Year 1, Term 1 they should learn to 'form lower case letters correctly in a script that will be easy to join later'. By the end of Year 4, Term 1, they should be taught to 'use joined handwriting for all writing except where other special forms are required'. Hickey's routines fit in very well with this, and could be easily adapted as a whole class approach (see also pages 21–25 for an account of the multisensory introduction to a phonogram).

Chapter 7
Reading

Hickey points out the inadequacy of the traditional methods of teaching reading – a sentence or whole-word approach, backed up by training in sound blending. Dyslexic pupils with good ability can 'get by' in reading in the early stages, especially if the emphasis is phonic rather than 'look and say'. The dyslexic pupil needs a structured, cumulative approach, using Reading Cards to build in automatic responses to phonograms, involving all modalities – looking, translating into sound, then into speech. The phonograms systematically build into syllables, then words, then sentences, then into continuous prose. Syllables are classified into six categories, and appropriate techniques are described that will enable the pupil to develop the skills to analyse unfamiliar words.

Traditional methods

The majority of children in school can learn to read by the use of traditional methods. These are usually based on a sentence and/or whole word approach, sometimes supported by the use of phonic material which requires the teacher to give training in sound blending. Apparatus providing practice in matching and sorting, word to word, word to picture, sentence to picture may be part of such an approach. Sometimes there are accompanying work-books.

Some dyslexic children of good ability, who can make intelligent use of context, do learn to read by the use of such methods, more often where the emphasis is on a phonic rather than a 'look and say' approach. In may cases, it is because their teachers themselves learnt to read by sound blending and are able to understand the pupils' needs. In general, teachers who use phonic material do so only in the early stages of learning to read, after which either their pupils' needs outstrip the teachers' familiarity of word structure in the language, or the pupils are thought not to be in need of further help. A beginning approach with analytical phonics is unsuitable for a pupil who needs to build sounds.

Unfortunately, many pupils and in particular the seemingly successful dyslexic readers merely 'get by' in reading and seldom reach their full potential. They are extremely fortunate if they become sufficiently competent to enjoy books, because the process is a laboured one for them. They often have to guess at, or leave out, words which they cannot recall or build, and therefore acquire only a general feeling for the ideas presented in the text.

Many such children think of reading as something they learn in school. They are not helped to understand that it is just one aspect of their total language function, or that reading is written speech for communication.

A systematic cumulative approach using multisensory learning

Learning the phonograms and building words from them

Many pupils need a structured, cumulative approach such as is presented here, in which reading, writing and spelling go hand in hand and where skill in reading is built up by systematically blending letter sounds into syllables, syllables into words, words into sentences and sentences into continuous prose. It is essential that teaching is given at regular, frequent intervals. Familiarity with the Reading

Cards of 84 phonograms (sound spellings) representing 51 different sound responses is the basis of the pupil's reading skill. He practises looking at a phonogram, translating it into sound and reacting automatically in speech. He is made familiar with all forms of a letter, capital and lower case, printed and hand-written and helped to acquire the skill of sound blending for word building.

The regular word pack

As the pupil learns each new phonogram in the Language Training Course in a multisensory way, and practises blending it to the ones he has already learned, he builds up a store of words. Words can be printed on separate cards and practised regularly. New word cards should be added to this pack as fast as he can take them. The more efficient he becomes in sound blending, the more rapid become his responses to the words. The pack should be re-shuffled for each lesson.

This pack is known as the regular word pack because it contains only words which he can work out for himself by blending the sounds.

The irregular word pack

Irregular words may be introduced only when they contain phonograms the pupil has learned. For instance, with the introduction of the seventh phonogram in the Language Training Course, which is 'd', he will have learned to read, write and recall for spelling the letters 's', 'a', 'i' and 'd', and therefore may be given the word 'said', which is his second irregular word, 'I' being the first one. He can begin to build a separate irregular word pack. He is taught that he will not be able to sound blend irregular words but must learn to read and spell them by frequent oral and written practice. These are gradually incorporated into his reading material. As soon as there are enough words in a pupil's pack to make phrases and/or sentences he can begin to read connected words. Examples which indicate how simple phrases and sentences can be extended when only a few letters have been learnt:

1. Using three letters   – tip it
2. Using four letters   – tip it in
3. Using five letters   – spin it, sit in it
4. Using six letters   – spin a tin
5. Using seven letters   – did I spin a tin?

Much of the difficulty experienced by a poor reader is in breaking down multisyllabic words which he has not met previously. A pupil taught in this systematic was will learn to identify regular patterns of vowels and consonants in words, and the way in which the patterns can be divided into separate syllables.

Syllables for reading

A teacher should be certain that a pupil understands what is meant by a syllable. Every separate beat in a word is a syllable; each beat usually has a vowel sound. Practice can be given in tapping out words and giving the correct number of syllables. Once this is established the pupil will need to be able to distinguish between the different kinds of syllables. There are six:

1. Syllables which are also words.
2. Closed syllables.
3. Open syllables.
4. Regular final syllables.
5. Suffixes (usually a syllable).
6. Prefixes.

Syllables which are also words

Some syllables are basic words, such as 'me', 'hot'. Many one-syllable base words are irregular such as 'through', 'search'. Later, when learning to add suffixes a pupil may be confused when the addition of a suffix does not add another beat. Words such as 'stayed' with a one-syllable basic word and suffix, should not be taught until the three different reading sounds of the suffix -ed are familiar.

Closed syllables

These are introduced into the Language Training Course with the second phonogram 't': 'it' is a closed syllable; its vowel is short. In a closed syllable the vowel is closed in by a consonant; the vowel is short. *Examples:* ĭt, sĭt.

Open syllables

These have no consonant following the vowel. If an open syllable is stressed the vowel has its long sound. Examples: bē', hē', mē', wē', sō , gō , ā'/corn, tā'/ble, stā'/tion.

Vowels in open unstressed syllables need attention 'e', 'i', 'o' and 'u' will keep the long sound, but the pronunciation is less distinct. *Examples:* de scribe', di rect', o mit', u nique'. 'a' tends to have an indeterminate /ə/ sound. *Examples:* a dorn', a dore'.

Regular final syllables

These are described in their name. They are discussed individually in detail as they arise in the Language Training Course. Examples of syllables found regularly at the end of words are: ble, kle, dle, fle, tion, sion and cian.

Suffixes

Definition: a suffix is a letter or a group of letters added to the end of a base word to change the way in which that word may be used in a sentence.

>   *Example:* jump + ing, -ed and -s - I can jump, I am jumping, I jumped, He jumps.

Prefixes

Definition: a prefix is a letter or a group of letters placed at the beginning of a base word (or root) to change the way in which the word may be used. *Example:* port meaning carry: with prefixes re, de, ex.

>   We must report this *or* Have you written a report?
>   We will deport him.
>   We will export this car *or* This beer is for export only.

Stressing the correct syllable

Before the pupil learns to divide words into syllables, he will need to understand that, in words of two or more syllables, at least one will be stressed more than the other(s). He will have been learning about stress in his alphabet work. The concept now begins to have some significance in word reading. The stress mark in his dictionary should be discussed and applied to words (example: ban'/dit). Oral practice should precede written. It can be related to the stress patterns in the alphabet work (example: A'B = ban'/dit). Activities can be given where he claps word patterns, his own and his friends' names, bringing out the stress. He will need practice in changing the position of the stress so that after dividing the syllables in words he can place the stress mark on the appropriate syllable(s).

Syllable division patterns for reading

In learning how to divide words into syllables for reading, isolated word examples are given with no context, so that children can practise the skills without having to worry about the meaning of a passage. Vowels and consonants in words fall into patterns. The patterns divide and the syllables can be read separately.

Words with the pattern <u>VC/CV</u> – *two closed syllables*

With the principle of 'closed syllable' already familiar, early in the Language Training Course a pupil can be introduced to words with two closed syllables. This is the time to begin teaching how to divide syllables for correct word reading. At first the number of words which can be given for syllable division practice will be limited. As new phonograms are introduced, further practice can be gained from an increasing number of words.

His first syllable division pattern is <u>VC/CV</u> (vowel–consonant/consonant–vowel). He will learn to call this 'the <u>VC/CV</u> pattern'. Words regularly divide between two consonants unless there are digraphs or blends. If the order of the Language Training Course is followed, the pupil will not yet have the problem of blends or digraphs. The word to be divided should be written twice; this is because it can be sounded in two ways – with either the first syllable or the second syllable stressed.

1. Write a word twice, one below the other.	bandit bandit
2. Place the syllable division pattern <u>VCCV</u> over the top one, beginning with the first vowel.	<u>V C C V</u> b a n d i t b a n d i t

3. Place a line through the two Cs (consonants) in the pattern and down through the consonants in both copies of the word.

$$\frac{VC|CV}{}$$
b a n|d i t
b a n|d i t

4. If necessary, place the short mark over the vowels They are both closed syllables.

$$\frac{VC|CV}{}$$
b ă n|d ĭ t
b ă n|d ĭ t

5. Place the stress on the first syllable in the first word, and on the second syllable in the second word. Say both words, emphasising the stressed syllable.

$$\frac{VC|CV}{}$$
b ă n'|d ĭ t
b ă n|d ĭ t'

6. Decide which one sounds correct and place a tick beside it.

$$\frac{VC|CV}{}$$
b ă n'|d ĭ t ✓
b ă n|d ĭ t'

Plenty of practice should be given with this type of word, with either of two syllables stressed so that the pupil has opportunities of trying it both ways and deciding on the correct version.

When the stress is on the second syllable, the first one is usually a prefix but he may not, at this stage, have been taught prefixes as such. As he becomes familiar with shifting the stress from one syllable to another in words out of context, he will build up the habit of doing this when engaged in reading. He will not, of course, be expected to mark out every word he meets with two closed syllables, but he will be alerted to what is required. Expertise will come with practice. Later he will divide automatically as his eyes move along the word and he sees the two consonants together.

Words with pattern <u>VCV</u> – two closed syllables

The next syllable division pattern he will learn will also be in words with two closed syllables but with only one consonant between the two vowels. Such words are: cabin, debit, edit, satin, robin, baton, topic, with the stress on the first syllable. The pattern is VC/V (vowel, consonant/vowel). These words divide after the consonant. The pupil proceeds in the same way as for the VC/CV pattern. Because these words create a difficulty and are less frequent than those with VC/CV patterns, it is helpful to place them in a separate VC/V pack as they arise in the pupil's experience and treat them as irregular.

Words with one open-accented syllable and one closed syllable

Words with the VCV division pattern may not be two closed syllables. After the pupil has been introduced to a stressed open syllable where the vowel is long, he should be given words such as basin, taken, item, open; the pattern is the same but the words divide before the consonant, V/CV. The teacher should only present words which have the first syllable stressed and tell the pupil this is so. This time the marking will be different.

	V/CV	V/CV
Write a word once. Divide before the consonant. It has an open syllable and a closed syllable. Mark the vowels. Mark the stress on the first syllable. It is open, stressed and therefore long. The word can now be read.	ī' t ĕm	stā'mĕn

Words with the VCV pattern dividing before and after the consonant

The pupil should now be given words with the VCV pattern which are a mixture of both types of words, dividing either before or after the vowel. Some with two closed syllables and some with an open and a closed syllable. The words should be presented twice because they may be pronounced in two different ways: two possible kinds of vowel sound and two possible positions for the stress.

The pupil divides one before the consonant and one after. After marking all the vowels and trying both, he reads them.

$$\frac{V\,|C\,V}{c\,\bar{a}\,|\,'b\,\breve{i}\,n} \qquad \frac{VC\,|V}{c\,\breve{a}\,b\,|\,\bar{i}\,n} \checkmark$$

Words with this pattern may also have open unstressed syllables and closed unstressed syllables. When the pupil is far enough in the programme he will be learning indeterminate vowel sounds.

He should be given the pattern four times, as the words may be sounded four ways:

$$\frac{V\,|C\,V}{\begin{array}{l} p\,\bar{i}\,'|\,v\,\breve{o}\,t \\ p\,\bar{i}\,|\,v\,\breve{o}\,t\,' \end{array}} \qquad \frac{VC\,|V}{\begin{array}{l} p\,\breve{i}\,v\,'|\,\breve{o}\,t \\ p\,\breve{i}\,v\,|\,\breve{o}\,t\,' \checkmark \end{array}}$$

The pupil needs to become familiar with the concept of 'trial and error'. The above exercises will give the pupil strategies to deal with longer words, and a range of things that can be attempted, so that complex words like 'distrust' or 'diphtheria' can be approached with an active attitude.

Words with the pattern <u>VV</u> dividing between two vowels that are not vowel digraphs and vowel blends

Two adjoining vowels in the same syllable usually represent one sound. They are vowel digraphs. Two adjoining vowels in the same syllable are sometimes vowel blends.

Examples: Vowel digraph b<u>oa</u>t   Vowel blend c<u>oi</u>l

The latter are strictly diphthongs but the concept of a vowel blend will be more easily understood by a pupil who is already familiar with the concept of the consonant blend. They can be underlined to indicate that they are not to be separated. Multisensory learning of words with regular vowel digraphs and vowel blends must be given at the appropriate stage in the Language Training Course so that the pupil has already had practice in reading them in familiar words before coming to syllable division for this pattern.

When a vowel ends a syllable and is followed by one beginning the next syllable, the syllable division pattern is VV (vowel, vowel). The first vowel sound is nearly always long in a two-syllable word, but the rule for the sounds of vowels in open unstressed syllables should be borne in mind when pronouncing the word because, in longer words, the stress varies.

Words in which two adjoining vowels are heard in separate syllables. *Examples*: dū/al, prī/or

No words should be given which contain phonograms that have not already been presented. A pupil needs practice in dividing these VV words so as to be able to spot them when reading. Words should be presented in pairs and the pupil should work through the following routine.

1. Place the pattern above the vowels, divide through the words between the vowels, mark the vowels if necessary, try the stress on both syllables and tick the correct one.

V | V		V | V	
d i'	ăl ✓		r ū'	ĭ n ✓
d i	ăl'		r ū	ĭ n'

2. Pairs of vowels which can be expected to divide: ia, io, iu, ao, eo, ua, uu and ua are vowel digraphs with the letters reversed.

   Examples: di/ary, vi/olet, tri/umph, a/orta, pe/ony, virtu/ous, vacu/um, du/al

3. Pairs of vowels which usually form digraphs but which sometimes divide are: ai, ea, ei, eu, oa, oi, oo and ui.

   Examples: prosa/ic, re/ality, de/ity, nucle/us, bo/a, co/incide, co/operate, ru/in

Few words with divided pairs which are normally vowel digraphs are to be found in the reading material of children at Key Stages 1 and 2. Once a pupil has been alerted to the possibility of these combinations dividing, it is helpful to regard them as irregular and put them into a separate pack for reading and spelling practice.

Some vowel digraphs which the pupil will have been taught are frequent word endings and can be expected to divide when found in the middle of words.

Examples: ue, oe, ie

du/et, po/etry, di/et

Words with regular final syllables
Fluent reading demands that the reader's eye can quicky identify common chunks of words. It is helpful for children to have their attention drawn to regular syllables which frequently appear at the ends of words. There are common ways of spelling word endings

which are often a suffix combined with a previous consonant (e.g. 'ure', as in 'picture', 'pressure'; 'ion' as in 'explanation', 'extension'). For fluent reading, it is not necessary to investigate the exact linguistic root of every syllable. Point them out to the pupil, and develop strategies for dealing with them. The aim is speedy recognition. They are introduced one at a time in the Language Training Course when their letters have been learnt and the pupil is ready for the concept. They are first introduced in packs, if necessary with cluewords.

One common set which comes first in the Language Training Course is as follows: ble, cle, kle, dle, fle, gle, ple, stle (silent t), tle and zle. A regular final syllable is unstressed. Words in isolation can be given for practice. The pupil divides the syllable from the rest of the word, reads the first part and then the final syllable. For syllable division practice, first give words with a closed, stressed syllable and a regular final syllable. Present the word once only. The following routine is observed.

Divide off the regular final syllable, mark the remaining closed syllable, place the stress on the first syllable and read the word.

Examples: tŭm'/ble cǎn'/dle

Next present words with an open syllable and a regular final syllable.

Divide off the regular final syllable, mark the remaining open stressed syllable and read the word.

Example: tā'/ble bī'/ble

When a pupil can comprehend that dividing off the regular final syllable may leave a closed syllable with a short vowel, or an open syllable with a long vowel, words of both kinds should be presented together to give practice in spotting the difference and reading the different pronunciations. In more advanced reading, he can be introduced to multisyllabic words with regular final syllables. First divide off the final syllable, then divide the rest of the word, if necessary, with syllable division routines using the patterns. The remaining syllables may be a mixture of open, closed, accented and unaccented syllables.

1. Divide the regular final syllable,
    place the pattern on the remaining
    part of the word, divide, mark the
    vowels, place the accent, read the word

    Examples:

VC	CV
m ŭ l'	t ĭ /p l e
s ŏ l'	ū /b l e

2. Adverbial regular final syllables, bly, fly,
    gly, ply, etc. divide off easily

    Examples:
    si m'/ply, ā'/bly

    bŭ b'/bly

Other regular final syllables

These are also compounded suffixes which can be conveniently divided off for reading and spelling, and will therefore be regarded as regular final syllables; they are: tion, sion and cian, pronounced /sh'n/. These occur very frequently in words. The <u>ti</u>, <u>si</u>, and <u>ci</u> at the beginning of the syllables usually sound /sh/. These letters are compounded with many other suffixes.

Regular final syllables where the final consonant sound in the base word combines with the first vowel of the suffix to form the sound /sh/. Some are infrequent.

Examples: tion, tian, tial, tious, tient, tiant, tience, tiance, sion, sian, sial, sious, sient, siant, sience, siance, cion, cian, cial, cious, cient, cience, ciance, ciancy, ciency

Sometimes the way the regular final syllable is sounded is dependent on the sound produced by the last sounded consonant in the base word and the first vowel in the suffix.

The suffix 'ure' may produce five differently sounded final syllables stressed or unstressed.

/yo͞or'/	as in manure	/ger/	as in figure
/cher/	as in picture	/sher/	as in pressure
/zher/	as in measure		

The V-e pattern is expected to have the long vowel sound and frequently, in words of two or more syllables, it forms a stressed final syllable.

Words of two and three syllables with regular pronunciations.

Examples: dē/cī de', cŏm/plē te', ĭn/sīde'

Sometimes a final syllable does not conform to the expected pronunciation.

1. Final syllables with pronunciations which might be expected to be pronounced with a long /ī/ sound but have the short /ĭ/.
   Examples:
   -ĭce (ĭss) apprentice   -ĭte (ĭt) definite
   -ĭne (ĭn) genuine   -ĭve (ĭv) detective

2. Other irregular pronunciations.
   Examples:
   -age pronounced (ĭj) village
   -ogue pronounced (ŏg) prologue
   -ique pronounced (ēēk) unique

Others will be found but most of them are introduced in their place in the Language Training Course and dealt with more fully there. A pupil can be taught to identify and divide them off before reading the rest of the word.

Words with suffixes for reading

These will be dealt with individually in the Language Training Course. A particular suffix is introduced when a pupil has learned the letters it contains and when he is ready for the concept of suffix. Therefore he will have learnt its form and meaning before he meets it in reading continuous prose. In reading a word with a suffix, the same routine is followed as for a regular final syllable. Suffixes beginning with a consonant will seldom give trouble. Most vowel suffixes are pronounced with their preceding consonant. The pupil divides off the suffix, divides the rest of the word, if necessary using the syllable division patterns, marks the stress, then reads. (It is better to divide with the preceding consonant or use syllable division rules.) The suffix would seldom be accented in long words.

Suffixes change the way in which the word may be used. Therefore, it might be expected that the context would suggest that the suffix needed to make sense and help in a word being read correctly.

At first give words with one syllable and the suffix. Divide off the suffix with the preceding consonant. Mark the remaining syllable, mark the stress, read the word.

Examples: hŏp'/pĭng   hō'/pĭng

Words with prefixes for reading

A pupil meets with prefixes in his reading material before he needs to understand their significance. They are first introduced as groups of letters which are frequently found at the beginning of words and may be introduced into the Language Training Course as soon as the letters contained in them have been learnt in a multisensory way. When the teacher decides that they should become meaningful, they can be introduced in a pupil's work as prefixes. Before teaching the meaning of prefixes, teachers are asked to read carefully the section on prefixes in Chapter 8 on spelling. At some stage, and this is indicated in the Language Training Course, the pupil will benefit by knowing the definition: a prefix is a letter or a group of letters placed at the beginning of a base word (or main syllable) to change the way in which that base word may be used.

The particular meaning of a prefix must be understood if a word is to be read correctly. Skill in understanding and reading words with prefixes will increase if the following routine is observed.

Distinguish the prefix, divide it off, read the rest of the word. *Examples:* ex'/port, de/port', re/port'

A base word having more than one syllable, after the prefix has been divided off, may need to have the syllable division rules applied to its remaining part. Observe the following routine if necessary:

1. Cut off the prefix	ex/planation
2. Cut off the regular final syllable	ex/plana/tion
3. Apply the syllable division pattern to the rest of the word	$\underline{vc/v}$ ĕx/plăn/ā/tion
4. In this case either division line serves and this is frequently the case in words of more than three syllables. The stress must be tried on different syllables.	$\underline{v/cv}$ ĕx/plă/nā/tion

Although context helps pronunciation, the pupil is encouraged not to rely on it for accurate identification of stressed syllable. He should practise moving it from one syllable to another. An additional reason for his recognising the prefix is that it does not always have the same sound.

The consonant following a prefix is sometimes pronounced with its last letter and the sound of the prefix is changed because the stress changes.

Examples:
base word   – grade
prefix de   – dē/grāde'
but   – dĕg/radation

Some similarly spelt words which have alternative pronunciations are nouns and verbs

The accent and sometimes the vowel sound changes from one syllable to the next with change of use.

Examples:
cŏn'/dŭct   – noun   cŏn/dŭct'   – verb

ŏb'/jĕct   – noun   ŏb/jĕct'   – verb

Some prefixes ending with consonants have their final letter changed before certain consonants for easy enunciation. These are listed in full in Chapter 8.

Final letter of the prefix changed for ease of speech.

Examples:
n̲ becomes m̲ before p̲
prefix i̲n̲ + basic word p̲o̲r̲t̲
in/port becomes import

The pronunciation of a final consonant in a prefix may begin the next syllable. This again points to the importance of recognising the prefix.

A word in which the sound of the final consonant of the prefix is heard at the beginning of the base word.

Examples:
Prefix d̲i̲s̲, base word 'agree' = disagree
pronunciation: dĭ/sa/grēe'

Placing the stress on the correct syllable in longer words

By the time he is required to read longer and more complicated words, the pupil may be assisted by the context but because a dyslexic pupil often reads multisyllabic words incorrectly and 'makes do' with the ones he can read, he gets only the general drift of a passage. If he is to read for information, correct word-reading is essential. The summary of the routine is as follows:

- Prefixes, suffixes and regular final syllables are divided off.
- Blends and digraphs are identified and underlined. The division is made between two consonants which are not digraphs or blends.

- Where there is only one consonant between two vowels the division is tried on either side of the consonant.
- A decision is made as to whether the syllables are open or closed, how the vowels are sounded, and where the stress should come.

The ability to read a word correctly will depend on an ability to stress the correct syllables. In some cases the context and a natural ability to do this will help but most pupils need practice in articulating stress patterns which can be applied to words.

1. Part of this skill can be acquired with the use of the alphabet or numbers.

   Examples:
   A' B C D   A' B
   en'/er/gi/sing   rab'bit
   A B'   A B' C
   inside'   com/men'/cing
   1 2 3'   1 2 3' 4   1 2' 3 4' 5
   lemonade',   educa'tion   unapp'eti'sing

2. In words of more than one syllable it is usual for a final, closed, stressed syllable ending with one vowel and one consonant to double the final consonant before a vowel suffix.

   Examples:
   re/but' – re/but'/ting
   double t because <u>but</u> is stressed
   mar'ket – mar'keting
   single <u>t</u> because <u>ket</u> is unstressed

3. A final 'l' is always doubled regardless of accent.
   Example: tra'vel – tra'velling

A pupil should always be encouraged to spot the double consonant before a suffix and accent the last syllable of the basic word except in the case of <u>ll</u>. The <u>l</u> is not doubled in the USA.

Further information

Only very recently has there been a convergence of research from a range of disciplines, and significant advances in understanding the reading process. When Hickey was forming her educational ideas, the key controversy was still 'phonics versus look and say' (Chall 1967). At that time, children were usually given graded readers. Some limited the range of phoneme/ grapheme links, using only short vowel sounds and single consonants, then proceeding to consonant blends, consonant digraphs, long vowel sounds, soft c and g, etc. Others used a whole word approach, but the vocabulary and language structures were limited.

The focus of discussion in staff rooms began to be 'top down' or 'bottom up'. 'Top down' entailed starting with a whole text, looking for meaning from contextual clues, then using them to work down to the level of print on the page. Clay (1972), Goodman and Burke (1972), and Holdaway (1979) emphasised the part played by understanding and knowledge of language structures in becoming a fluent reader. Reading was described as a sophisticated 'guessing game' that brought together knowledge of letters, whole words and language structures. The 'story book', or 'real book' approach was advocated, with an emphasis on meaning and the use of contextual cues. 'Bottom up' approaches taught the reader to decode letters and words, and work upwards towards the meaning of the whole text. The 'bottom up' approach, which used phonics or key vocabulary as a base, was seen as mechanistic and sterile.

MJ Adams's (1990) *Beginning to Read* became an overnight classic, bringing together a hundred years of research into reading. Her lucid analysis proposes an integrated model of reading. The key to this model is not the dominance of one process or form of knowledge, but the co-ordination and co-operation of them all.

The National Literacy Strategy's Framework for Teaching adopts a model of reading similar to the one proposed by Adams. The attention of teachers is drawn to the various 'Searchlights' that can be used to shed light on text. Successful readers can use them all, and can orchestrate them at speed in accessing meaning. The dyslexic child tends to be weak in using phonics, and in building up a consistent and wide vocabulary of sight words. Hickey's structured phonic approach fits in well with this model. Hickey assumed that teachers would root new skills into real reading and writing, but this is not explicit in the programme; its focus is on teaching the missing skills, and pays little attention to the need to 'orchestrate' a range of strategies. The Hickey lesson plan (pages 148–149) has been modified to reflect an integrated approach to reading and writing. Chapter 3, which has been added to this edition, will give users of a Hickey programme guidance in fitting the Hickey skills training into the structure of the Literacy Strategy, and in rooting the skills into whole language activities.

Chapter 8
Spelling

Individuals have different learning styles, and these need to be taken into account when teaching spelling. Learning to spell is a major hurdle for the dyslexic pupil. The skills necessary for reading are not the same as the skills used for spelling. Even avid readers can be poor spellers. This chapter describes a method of teaching irregular words (simultaneous oral spelling) and discusses the importance of vowels and the effects of stress on spelling multisyllabic words. The concept of 'spelling choices' is introduced, and the long vowels are collected into a frame that demonstrates these choices. Rules and generalisations that govern the different types of syllables are clarified.

Words in the English Language are formed by blending sequences of sounds into meaningful wholes. By the manipulation of only 26 letters of the alphabet, 44 sounds are produced. Some letters have more than one sound, and combinations of letters produce further sounds. This in itself presents a problem for poor spellers, but in addition they must contend with 100 or so different ways of spelling these 44 sounds. These sound spellings will be referred to as phonograms in the text.

The manner in which individuals react to creating or recalling the word for spelling depends upon the way they process language. When required to spell a word one person may attempt to recreate in the 'mind's eye' a picture of the whole word. He is relying on his visual–perceptual ability probably with unconscious use of his powers of sound association. Another may attempt to sequence the sounds he hears into syllables and build these into whole words. He is relying on his auditory–perceptual ability probably with unconscious use of his ability to visualise the correct sound spellings. Either type of speller must use his kinaesthetic or motor ability to get the letters and syllables in the correct order. Those who spell without difficulty seem able to combine visual and auditory perception efficiently with the power to feel their way through the ordering of the phonograms and syllables.

In a dyslexic pupil, these perceptual systems seem to be 'out of step'. If the visual speller is dyslexic, he may react to the general shape or 'see' all the letters in a word but confuse the order when writing them down, because he does not sequence the phonograms correctly. It is common for such visualisers to write <u>paly</u> for <u>play</u>, <u>form</u> for <u>from</u>, <u>gril</u> for <u>girl</u>. The auditory speller may use the sounds, and even sequence them correctly, but he may make incorrect choices of phonograms because he does not visualise them. For example, he may write <u>fowtograf</u> for <u>photograph</u>. All the sounds are there, in the correct order, but with the wrong spellings.

When multisensory techniques are used in teaching the alternative spellings of a sound, simultaneous use is made of all the perceptual areas. The pupil looks at the symbol, listens to its sound, feels its shape, repeats it sound and names its letters at the same time. He is thus helped to make more efficient use of his strong perceptual pathway to learning because these are being supported by the re-education of his weaker ones.

It is important for teachers to be aware of the difference between teaching phonograms for spelling and phonograms for reading. These two interrelated skills need different kinds of practice, although both skills depend on a person's ability to absorb, sustain, process, order and store sound symbols. Spelling is a process of recalling or creating and depends only in part on the ability to read which is deciphering seen symbols.

Spelling is the dyslexic person's main difficulty. It is erroneous to think he can 'catch' spelling when he has been taught to read. He may be an avid reader but produce written work which is indecipherable. Because a word has no tangible form until it is written down, in order to recall or create it, several skills are involved. Taking as an example the word 'edge', a pupil must be able to :

1. Differentiate between similar sounds
   Examples:
   /ĕ/ and /ĭ/

2. Appreciate the vowel spellings
   an /ĕ/ spelling is 'e' or 'ea'

3. Know what the choices are for use in a particular position
   a /j/ spelling is 'j', 'ge' or 'dge'

4. Sequence them in the correct order
   /ĕj/ = /ĕ/ + /j/ = 'e' + 'dge' = edge

5. Make the correct shapes for writing
   /ĕj/ = *edge*

Learning the different spellings of a sound

Multisensory learning of the phonograms takes place in every lesson through the use of the Spelling Cards. As the pupil learns a new spelling for a sound, it is added to his choices on his spelling card.

1. For the sound /j/ he first learns 'j'. He says '/j/', names the letter
   and writes ___*ʄ*___. He can then write words beginning with 'j'.
   Examples: jam, jump.
2. 'ge' is added next: he now says /j/ 'j', /j/ 'ge' and writes ___*ʄ ge*___.
   He can then write words with a final ge. Examples: cage, huge.
3. 'dge' completes his spelling card; he now says /j/ 'j', /j/ 'ge', /j/ 'dge'
   and writes ___*ʄ ge dge*___. He can now write words ending 'dge'
   after one short vowel. Examples: edge, bridge, badge.

He continues to practise making decisions about which choice to
use in a given situation.

Word spelling for regular words

Learning the sound spellings is a preparation for sequencing sounds
correctly to make words. The routine for spelling words is the same
as for spelling the sounds, but now the pupil has to link the sound
spellings together to make a complete word. He has learned to read,
spell and write the phonograms 'i', 't', 'p', 'n' and 's', and has been
learning to blend sounds together from the first two sounds, naming
each letter /ĭ/ + /t/ = 'i' 't' = it. Soon he is having longer words.

The example is <u>spits</u>. The teacher says '<u>spits</u>'. The pupil listens to
the word <u>spits</u>. He repeats it slowly, listening to himself. (He is men-
tally connecting the sounds he hears to the names of the letters.)

He spells the word aloud naming the letters, then writes it naming each letter he is about to write. He then reads <u>spits</u> to be sure he
wrote what he meant to write: ___*spits*___.

The habit of proofreading should be developed from the time
when the pupil has his first word for spelling. As he adds further
spellings of the same sound to his Cards, he must spell words where
he has to choose from several spellings of that sound, as in the
example <u>edge</u> explained earlier.

Word spelling for irregular words

When the seventh phonogram 'd' in the Language Training Course has been reached, the pupil will have his first irregular word, 'said', because he will have been introduced to all its letters and have learnt to write them. The routine for learning to spell 'said' and other irregular words will be different from that of learning to spell regular words which can be sound blended. He must be told that he cannot do this; he must learn to recognise the word for reading. It starts his irregular pack which can now be used for spelling.

The most reliable method for dyslexic and many other pupils to learn the spellings of irregular and tricky words is simultaneous oral spelling (SOS).

1. Print the word clearly for the pupil to read:

said

2. Pupil reads the word.
3. Pupil writes over the word, naming each letter aloud as he forms it in a joined style.
4. Stage (3) is repeated as many times as necessary.
5. The word is covered. The pupil says the word and writes it, naming the letters aloud as before.
6. Pupil checks his attempt carefully with the original model.

The vowels: their importance

Accurate spelling

This depends on the pupil's familiarity with common patterns of vowels and consonants, and when to expect them to occur in words. These patterns, in turn, are dependent upon the vowel sounds. The sound of the vowel may be long, short or indeterminate. The ability to distinguish between them is one requisite for accurate spelling.

Most of us who do not have problems with written language react automatically to the value of a vowel sound and have a built-in ability to couple it with the correct pattern of consonants. A pupil with poor auditory discrimination may need much practice in discerning the difference. In a spelling lesson where there is reference to long and short vowels, the teacher should make certain that pupils fully appreciate and can react to the difference between the sounds.

Games and activities can be devised for practice. A tape-recorder is a valuable aid for self-learning and for testing the accuracy of a pupil's responses. A random list of one-syllable words containing long and short vowels can be recorded by the teacher.

1. Teacher records words having long and short vowels:	hat,	home,	sit,	mop,	hut,	time
2. The pupil listens and writes 'l' for long, 's' for short:	s,	l,	s,	s,	s,	l

Spelling the vowel sound

This usually presents difficulties. When a pupil has learned to appreciate one sound and recognise its variety of spellings, how does he choose between these when he needs to write a word? Most poor spellers make a wild guess, but it is possible to give a firm directive. If the Language Training Course is followed, teachers will find that the vowel spellings are presented in such a way that the pupil has an opportunity to become familiar with the use of each one before a new one is introduced.

The effect of stress on the vowel-containing syllable

This gives the vowel its full value whether it is long or short. When it is unstressed it loses its full value and may become indeterminate. The number of consonants following a vowel may be decided by whether the syllable containing the vowel is stressed or not, for example:

A short vowel in a final stressed syllable of a base word ending with a vowel and a consonant will have its final consonant doubled before a vowel suffix.

upsĕt't ing   remĭt't ed   but   ben'efit ed

Consonants following vowels

These are sometimes voiced and sometimes unvoiced according to whether the vowel is long or short. For example:

'th' may be unvoiced or voiced.
bath; th after the short vowel (unvoiced)
bathe; th after the long vowel, voiced (V-e pattern)

The position of the vowel in a syllable or word

This is significant for spelling. Having learned a particular spelling of a vowel, the pupil must learn where it is likely to occur in a word or syllable. A poor speller will usually write the first which comes to mind, example stayble for stable. When he reaches the appropriate point in the Language Training Course, he will learn that for the sound /ā/ he need to write only 'a' where he has written 'ay' because of its position in the syllable. The spelling 'ay' is normally used in the final position.

Regular spelling of the short vowels

This must now be studied in detail. Early in the Language Training Course, the pupil will be helped to become familiar with the concept of *vowel*. Next he learns to react to the short vowel sound. A sound is always linked to its clueword. The short vowels are illustrated as /ă/, /ĕ/, /ĭ/, /ŏ/, /ŭ/ and /o͝o/. They can be spelt in several ways.

1. /ă/ has one spelling, 'a' as in ant
2. /ĕ/ two spellings, 'e' and 'ea' as in egg and tr<u>ea</u>sure
3. /ĭ/ two spellings, 'i' and 'y' as in igloo and jell<u>y</u>
4. /ŏ/ two spellings, 'o' and 'a' as in orange and wasp
5. /ŭ/ three spellings 'u', 'o', 'ou' as in g<u>u</u>n, w<u>o</u>n, c<u>ou</u>ple.
6. /o͝o/ two spellings, 'oo' and 'u' as in h<u>oo</u>k and p<u>u</u>t.

'a' and 'e', if unstressed, often have an indeterminate sound /ə/ as in canary, totem, velvet.

Spellings of the long vowels

These are learnt in the same way. Because they have an even greater variety of spellings than the short ones, it is essential that the phonograms are presented to the pupil one at a time in systematic order and multisensory techniques of training used. Word spelling with emphasis on its position in the word should follow each newly introduced vowel spelling. This in turn should be followed by its use in dictated sentences and then in sentences composed by the pupil. He should say his sentence aloud listening to it before writing. Regular spellings are those most frequent in the language. The pupil learns to regard these as his first choices.

> When a long vowel sound ends a stressed syllable write one letter only for the vowel sound.
> *Examples:* **re**' cent, **ta**' ken, **i**' tem, **mu**' sic, **ro**' bot

Using the same method as for learning the short vowels, the spellings of the long vowels can be put into a framework for reference. Given a blank frame, when the pupils learns his first long vowel spelling, he places it in his frame and learns where it is used in a word (Figure 8.1).

Figure 8.1 The pupil's frame when he has learnt the long vowel spellings 'e', 'i' and 'a' only.

Long vowel sounds	Regular spelling of the long vowels			
	Open syllables	First choice in one syllable words	Word ending	Endings in longer words
/ā/	a			
/ē/	e			
/ī/	i			
/ō/				
/ū/				

The next long vowel spelling to be introduced will have the *vowel–consonant–e* pattern. This is pipe /ī/ 'i–e' with the 'e' silent. The pupil learns that when he writes a one-syllable word with the long vowel sound followed by a consonant sound, this is the spelling he must consider first. It applies to all the long vowel sounds except /ē/ where 'ee' is his first choice for one-syllable words. No alternatives are given at this stage.

> When a word of one syllable has the long vowel sound followed by a consonant sound, write the 'V–e' spelling (*vowel–consonant–'e'*) except when the vowel sound is /ē/ then write 'ee'.
> *Examples:*
> cake – write 'a-e', feet – write 'ee', pipe – write 'i–e',
> mole – write 'o-e', cube – write 'u–e'

The few one-syllable 'e-e' words should be grouped together and learned separately. Were, where and there are irregular because they do not sound blend.

One-syllable words with the 'e–e' spelling pronounced /ē/.
Examples: these, scene, scheme, theme, sphere, mere, sere, here, eke, gene, peke, eve.

When 'ay' is reached in the Language Training Course, the pupil learns that when the last heard sound in a word is /ā/ its most common spelling is 'ay'. The other final long vowel spellings are /ē/ 'ee', /ī/ 'y', /ō/ 'ow', /ū/ 'ue'.

Words ending with long vowel sounds have these regular spellings.

Examples:
pay – write 'ay', crow – write 'ow', fee – write 'ee'
due – write 'ue', try – write 'y'

As the pupil learns the regular long vowel spellings for open syllables, one-syllable words and word endings, he will place them in his frame. The complete frame for the regular spellings of the long vowels will look like Figure 8.2.

Figure 8.2 The pupil's frame when he has added the long vowel spellings in given situations.

Long vowel sounds	Regular spelling of the long vowels			
	Open syllables	First choice in one syllable words	Word ending	Endings in longer words
/ā/	a	a–e	ay	
/ē/	e	ee	ee	e–e
/ī/	i	i–e	y	
/ō/	o	o–e	ow	
/ū/	u	u–e	ue	
/o͞o/	u	oo	ue	

Irregular spellings of the long vowels

These are the second and further choices. As the phonograms occur in the Language Training Course, words containing them can be put into packs of cards and practised regularly at first for reading only. They can be used in spelling games and other activities for consolidation. When the pupil is ready to use an irregular long vowel spelling for writing, it should be placed in his frame in the appropriate place and word spelling routines for irregular words used.

The phonogram 'ai' is the second choice for the long sound /ā/ in words of one syllable and should be placed below 'a–e' in the frame. It is the second choice because whereas any consonant follows the /ā/ in 'a–e' words, only certain ones can follow 'ai'. The most usual are 'l', 'n', 'r' and a few with 't', 'd' and 'm'. Any other letter is rare. It is helpful to tell the pupil this. Practice should be given with pairs of words having the two types of spelling.

Pairs of words with 'a–e' and 'ai' spellings.
Examples: pale – pail, stare – stair, pane – pain

The phonograms 'ea' for the sound /ē/, 'oa' for the sound /ō/ and 'ew' for the sound /ū/ are common second choices to 'ee', 'o–e' and the ending 'ue' and should be placed in the frame in their appropriate places and treated in the same way as other irregular spellings. As the less frequent choices arise in the Language Training Course the same techniques can be used. They should be placed in the frame in descending order of frequency. When a pupil has worked through the Course and added the irregular spellings his frame might look like that in Figure 8.3.

Figure 8.3 The pupil's frame when he added the irregular spellings of the long vowels in given situations.

Spellings of the long vowels				
Long vowel sounds	Open syllables	Choices in order of frequency of main syllables	Word endings	Other endings in longer words
/ā/	a	a–e ai ei eigh ea	ay ey eigh	a–e
/ē/	e	ee ea ie c–ei e–e	ee ey ie	e–e
/ī/	i	i–e igh y–e	y ie igh	i–e
/ō/	o	o–e oa ow	ow oe	o–e
/ū/	u	u–e eu	ue ew	u–e
/o͞o/	u	oo ou ui	ue ew	u–e

Spelling the different types of syllable

The concept of syllable must be established before any discussion of spelling the different types of syllable begins. Some review of the vocabulary to be used should always precede the lesson. The teacher must be sure that the pupil understands the meaning of the words *syllable, open, closed, short vowel, long vowel, consonant, stress,* in relation to language. This is the 'language of language'.

The task of reproducing a syllable for spelling does not depend upon remembering its visual image, although an ability to do this will contribute to final success. Training in achieving this is part of multisensory learning. When writing words, the pupil must be aware that they may be made up of one or more syllables, and that each vowel sound he hears represents a new syllable. A warm-up to a lesson might be for him to beat out the number of syllables he can hear in his name or the teacher may ask: 'How many syllables or beats are there in the word car, in carpet, in carpeted? Which is the first syllable, the middle syllable and the last syllable?' He can then watch the teacher write words, syllable by syllable. All the beats (vowel sounds) must be present in the final word. He can count the vowels or vowel combinations in the written word to make sure he can hear the same number of beats.

Types of syllables

In order to spell correctly, the learner must understand the significance of syllables in words. In Chapter 7, the six types of syllables have been set out. They are repeated here for spelling:

1. *Base word syllable:* the syllable which is also a word, e.g. port.
2. *Closed syllable:* the vowel sound heard is short, it is closed by a following consonant or consonants, e.g. ĭp, ĭst.
3. *Open syllable:* the vowel sound heard ends the syllable, and is long if accented, e.g. tā', bē'.
4. *Regular final syllable:* groups of letters regularly found at the end of words. It can be spelt correctly once the pupil has learned to react to its sound, e.g. ble, tion.
5. *Suffix:* there are definite rules of spelling for this, e.g. ing, ful.
6. *Prefix:* this may have a change of spelling in its final letter, e.g. ad, con.

Base word syllables may adhere to the rules and be part of the 85 per cent of regular language. Many are irregular and spelling them will be the most difficult task a learner will meet, as they may be represented by a variety of spellings which are incapable of being sound blended. The word spelling routine for spelling irregular words must be used. The learner may need a special pack of irregular one-syllable words for practice.

Words with closed syllables are the first to be learnt. The learner should begin with words consisting of one closed syllable. If the Language Training Course is followed the first word he will be asked to spell will be 'it'. This is a closed syllable. He should be trained to listen for the short vowel and close it with the 't'. With the addition of 'p', 'n' and 's' to his Spelling Cards, his spelling vocabulary will be extended to include further closed syllable words and he will be able to spell words such as pin, tin, snip, spit using the word-spelling routine: listen, repeat, spell, write, read.

Putting syllables together for spelling

This is the opposite of syllable division for reading.

Spelling words with two or more closed syllables – pattern <u>VC/CV</u>

The first ones to be introduced should be those where the two closed syllables can be clearly heard. Longer words composed of clearly heard closed syllables are fairly easy to spell when the learner is trained to listen to sounds and sequence them orally before writing. The words can be built up by listening and sound blending.

1. Words where two closed syllables can be clearly heard.
   Examples: băn/dĭt, kĭd/năp, nŭt/mĕg

2. Longer words with three clearly heard closed syllables.
   Examples: hŏb/gŏb/lĭn, făn/tăs/tĭc

Words with two similar consonants between vowels – pattern <u>VC/CV</u>

These are more difficult to spell. These are words such as 'rabbit', where the consonant ending the first syllable matches the one beginning the second syllable. The pupil learns to listen to the first short vowel /ă/. He knows that it must have a following consonant, although he cannot hear it, because the syllable must be a closed one – 'răb/'. He can only hear the 'b' in '<u>bit</u>', the second syllable. What he can hear he must write. He must also write what he knows must be there, although he cannot hear it. So he arrives at ra(b)bit. In word-spelling practice the first consonant is bracketed by the pupil to indicate that it cannot be heard but is needed to close the first syllable. He will be quick to acquire this skill if his practice in spelling such words is accompanied by practice in dividing closed syllables for reading with the <u>VC/CV</u> pattern.

> Words with a double consonant between two vowels making two closed syllables.
> *Examples:* ra(b)bit, ca(r)rot, pu(f)fin

Words with two closed syllables with the <u>VC/V</u> pattern

Words such as rŏb/ĭn, căb/ĭn which also have two closed syllables, but the <u>VC/V</u> pattern, should be treated as irregular, placed in a separate pack if necessary and learned in games and other activities.

Words with open stressed syllables

These have long vowel sounds. After 'e' is introduced in the Language Training Course the pupil will meet the word 'be'; soon he will be able to use <u>me</u>, <u>he</u>, <u>so</u>, <u>go</u>. He will learn that these words are also open syllables. At this time he will need practice in listening to the long vowel sound ending the syllable. When he hears the word, he writes the consonant and one long vowel letter only. This activity should be well practised before going on to open stressed syllables in words with two syllables.

Words with open and closed syllables – <u>V/CV</u> pattern

These are the next to be taught, where the first syllable is open with a long vowel stressed, and the second one is closed and unstressed. Words of this pattern are not difficult for spelling, but they must be dictated for practice with the vowels in each syllable clearly enunciated and the first one stressed. The pupil must be reminded to write one letter only for the long vowel sound ending the syllable, because what he can hear is an open, stressed syllable.

At this stage, the short vowel in the second syllable should be clearly enunciated by the teacher, so that the learner writes the correct letter, which, being unstressed, may be indeterminate or obscure sounding.

Words with an open stressed syllable and a closed syllable: pattern <u>V/CV</u>.
Examples: tū'/lip, crō'/cus

The learner will be dividing words with this <u>V/CV</u> pattern for reading concurrently with spelling practice. Words such as rab/bit with two closed syllables and ba/sin with an open and a closed syllable can be given in pairs, so that he has practice in listening to, and differentiating between, the two types of words. The habit of reacting to different types of syllables for spelling is best started early in the Language Training Course, as soon as enough phonograms are available to construct a few suitable words, and then continued as new phonograms are added, with much over-learning.

Words with vowel-consonant-e spellings

These are taught with the introduction of i–e pipe /ī/ (Figure 8.2).

1. Words with a V–e spelling in an accented second syllable may begin with open or closed syllables.
   Examples: ĭn/sīde', dē/bāte', rē/sīde'

2. A common final syllable is e–e (e–consonant–'e') in longer words.
   Examples: interfere', ath'lete, impede', intervene'

Regular final syllable spelling practice

This will have been taking place for some time with the isolated syllables: ble, cle, kle, dle, fle, gle, ple, stle, tle and zle. Teachers may include them in the Reading and Spelling Cards. The pupil will have been reading words with regular final syllables, dividing them off before reading the remaining part of the words. He is now ready to use them in words for spelling. The first words given will be those with a clearly heard closed syllable and a regular final syllable.

Words with a closed syllable and a regular final syllable.
Examples: căn/dle, jŭm/ble, pĭm/ple

The next words to be given will be those where the consonant ending the first syllable matches the one beginning the regular final syllable, so that there is a doubled consonant to be considered, only the second of which will be heard. As with words such as rabbit, the consonant sound in the middle of the word will be heard in the final syllable. The regular final syllable must remain intact, and added complete. The first syllable will be closed with a consonant because the vowel is short. It should be bracketed in words for practice.

Words with a doubled consonant; the first, unheard one, is bracketed.

Examples: c ă(t)'tle, b ŭ(b)'ble, snŭ(g)'gle

The next words given will be those with an open stressed syllable and a regular final syllable. There is little difficulty in spelling words of this pattern because the long vowel in the open stressed first syllable can be clearly heard.

Words with an open stressed syllable and a regular final syllable.

Examples: bī'/ble, lā'/dle, bū'/gle

Following separate practice with the two kinds of words, words such as căt'/tle and bī'/ble can then be mixed. When put together for practice, it can be clearly demonstrated how the spelling of such words is differentiated.

Pairs of words: a closed syllable and regular final syllable; an open stressed syllable and regular final syllable.

Examples: nō'/ble but nŏb'/ble, gā'/ble but găb'/ble

Further regular final syllables

Those common in the language are tion, sion and cian, introduced in this order in the Language Training Course. The pupil will be familiar with them for reading and will have been writing them on the Spelling Cards for the sound /sh'n/. They are suffixes compounded with the last consonant of the base word but, for purposes of spelling, are best treated as a unit of sound which can be heard as a syllable /sh'n/. The different ways of spelling them must be understood by the pupil.

He will need to learn the function of the word in order to decide whether the /sh/ part is spelt 'ti', 'si' or 'ci'. Such words are frequently verbs or adjectives converted to nouns. The '-an' at the end of cian is probably a contraction of man. The explanation magic-man, music-man appeals to the pupil and gives a clue to the spelling. Educate becomes education; 'ti' is used because the last consonant in the verb is 't'.

1. Some verbs ending in 'it' have the 't' changed to 's' and sion added, giving a double 's'.
   Examples: permit but permission
               remit but remission

2. When /sh'n/ follows 'l', 'n', 'r' or 's' in the base word, it is usually spelt sion.
   Examples: ma*ns*ion, expu*ls*ion, imme*rs*ion, mi*ss*ion.

3. The voiced sound /zh'n/ is spelt sion.
   Examples: televi*sion* = /zh'n/
               explo*sion* = /zh'n/

When these three common spellings for /sh'n/ and /zh'n/ are securely understood, the pupil may go on to other endings beginning with ti, si and ci sounded /sh/. These are ent, ant, ence, ance, al and ous, ancy and ency. They make nouns and adjectives of base words and are listed in full under regular final syllables in Chapter 7. All the variants of these regular final syllables are best practised by the use of separate word packs, which should be built up as such words occur in a pupil's reading or spelling experience.

Irregular final syllables

These sometimes have a different pronunciation and these must become familiar out of context and classified as irregular because they do not conform to the regular sound patterns, but they occur frequently enough to be practised as a group. The pupil will have been learning to divide them off in reading practice but he must become accustomed to hearing and isolating the unconforming sound for spelling. He can do this with spelling practice.

Among the final syllables are: ice, ine, ite and ive which when accented in one and two syllable words, are pronounced with a long /ī/ but in longer words may be unstressed and pronounced with a short /ĭ/.

1. What is sometimes heard is /ĭss/ as in pract<u>ice</u> – written 'ice'.
2. What is sometimes heard is /ĭn/ as in genu<u>ine</u> – written 'ine'.
3. What is sometimes heard is /ĭt/ as in defin<u>ite</u> – written 'ite'.
4. What is sometimes heard is /ĭv/ as in detect<u>ive</u> – written 'ive'.

'Age' is an unstressed syllable when added to multisyllable words and pronounced /ĭj/. It is strictly a suffix but because it combines with the previous consonant it is best taught as a regular final syllable for spelling in the following way.

1. '-age' should be taught as the regular spelling for the sound /ĭj/ at the end of multisyllabic words.
   Examples: village, cabbage

2. '-ege' pronounced /ĭj/ is irregular.
   Examples: privilege, college

3. /äzh/ is irregular
   Examples: garage, corsage

/ĭj/ spelt 'idge', regular in one-syllable words, is uncommon at the end of longer words. Among the few existing words are porridge, partridge, cartridge, which will present no problem in reading but must be put among the irregulars when required for spelling if 'age' is the more regular; 'ogue' may be pronounced /ŏg/ occasionally, as in catalogue; 'que' at the end of a word is sounded /k/ with a preceding 'i' sometimes sounded /ē/ an in unique. Others will be found and should be added to the pupil's irregular pack if necessary.

Suffixes for spelling

The concept of suffix

This concept for spelling is taught when the pupil is ready for it even though he may already have been using suffixes because the letters contained in them have been learnt in a multisensory way. So far it has been sufficient for the pupil to know that words frequently end with these groups of letters. The word suffix has not necessarily been used.

Before any discussion of spelling words with suffixes is undertaken, the teacher must be sure that the pupil understands what is meant by a suffix. He will have been reading and spelling a few base words. When he is taught the first suffix plural -s, the terms 'base word' and 'suffix' can be explained together. He could then learn to define first a base word and then a 'suffix'.

Definitions

Base word: a word to which suffixes may be added.
Suffix: a letter, or group of letters, added to the end of a base word to enable the base word to be used in a different way.

The meanings of suffixes

The meaning, as taught to the pupil, can be demonstrated by taking the first three suffixes in the Language Training Course as examples. As each suffix is introduced, its meaning must be made clear to the pupil. When learning the first one, plural -s, he must practise adding it to words. The next suffix will be -ing. This is used early and frequently in children's reading books. The words which the teacher uses to explain its use will depend on the age and ability of the pupil. He must learn to spell it and add it to words. The next suffix 'ful' is the word 'full' with one 'l' dropped (probably because the rule of doubling 'l' at the end of a one-syllable word no longer applies). He can be told this.

1. Suffix plural 's' – meaning 'more than one'.
   Examples: pins, tins

2. Suffix '-ing' added to doing or action words (verbs) – present tense.
   Examples: resting, listing, packing

3. Suffix '-ful' – meaning 'full of'
   Examples: restful, helpful

The pattern of vowels and consonants

In base words and suffixes this pattern will later have significance for spelling words with suffixes.

Identification of the two types of suffix

This can take place with the introduction of the first suffix plural '-s'. The pupil learns that it is a consonant suffix because it begins with a consonant. When '-ing' is introduced he learns that it is a vowel suffix because it begins with a vowel. He now has two types of suffix, consonant suffixes and vowel suffixes. Practice can be given in putting C for consonant and V for vowel over the first letter in the suffix whenever he learns a new one. the first three suffixes in the Language Training Course are used to illustrate his practice routine.

Consonant suffix: -s; vowel suffix: -ing, consonant suffix: -ful

Identification of the patterns at the end of base words

This can take place from the beginning, so that the pupil is familiar with the skill when it begins to have significance for spelling words. He can begin to identify the patterns of vowels and consonants by placing V for vowel and C for consonant over the letters in a word and then naming the pattern. He begins with the first vowel in the syllable to which the suffix is to be joined. The only patterns he will have learnt up to this point will be VC and VCC.

1. The vowel-consonant pattern – VC

   Examples:

   VC   VC

   p in   t ip

2. The vowel–consonant–consonant pattern – VCC

   Examples:

   VCC   VCC

   t int   p ick

As the pupil increases his list of suffixes he can engage in extending his vocabulary by adding suitable suffixes to base words. He begins with base words where the suffix joins without any alteration to the spelling. Words with the VCC pattern are suitable, not VC words.

Changing words by varying the suffix added to the base word.

Examples:

Base word		Suffix		Complete Word
VCC		V		
pr ess	+	ing	=	pressing
VCC		V		
pr ess	+	ed	=	pressed
VCC		V		
pr ess	+	es	=	presses

In order to help him remember the suffixes he has learnt, he might rule an on-going framework in his notebook for listing them as they are learnt.

The spelling rules for adding suffixes to base words

Adding a suffix to a base word

This may change the spelling of that word. These changes are difficult for poor spellers to learn. A dyslexic pupil is utterly confused by the whole concept which seems to provide no stability. The rules can be simplified and structured by being put into a framework for reference. The complete frame illustrated in Figure 8.4 is presented here for the teacher's benefit. The pupil should be given a blank frame. He can place the rules in position as he learns them (Figure 8.4).

Figure 8.4 Rules for adding suffixes : teacher's frame

Definition of a base word: A word to which suffixes may be added.
Definition of suffix: A letter or group of letters added to the end of a base word to enable that word to be used in a different way.

Two kinds of suffixes 1. A consonant suffix which begins with a consonant.
2. A vowel suffix which begins with a vowel.

Adding a suffix to a base word often affects the spelling of the end of the base word. Action may be taken in one of four ways: *just add* without any change, *double* the last consonant, *drop* the final 'e' or *change* a final 'y' to 'i'.

	Rule	Base word pattern	Suffix pattern	Completed word
Just add	You may *just add* a suffix without change of spelling when: 1. Adding a consonant suffix 2. The base word ends in one vowel and two consonants 3. Two vowels and a consonant 4. A long vowel spelling (except 'ue' and 'ie') (see Figure 7.4): 'ee' when suffix begins with 'i'	$\breve{V}CC$ $\overline{VV}C$ $\overline{VV}$ $\overline{VV}$	C V V V i	restful wishing looking playing seeing
Double	When adding a vowel suffix to a *one-syllable* word with one vowel followed by one consonant, *double* the final consonant before adding the suffix. The vowel will be kept short, the pattern becomes the same as required for *just add*	$\breve{V}C{+}C$ $\breve{V}CC$	V V	hop(p)ing hopping
Drop	1. When adding a vowel suffix to $\bar{v}$–e syllable, *drop* the 'e' before adding the suffix. These are long vowel words – the vowel remains long 2. Words ending in 'ue' and 'ie' drop the 'e' before adding a vowel suffix	$\overline{V}C\not{e}$ ue	V hoping V	hop~~e~~ing su~~e~~ing
Change	1. When adding any suffix to any word ending in consonant + 'y', *change* the 'y' to 'i' before adding the suffix. When the suffix begins with 'i' – do not *change* the 'y' 2. When a word ends in 'ie', *change* 'ie' to 'y' before adding a suffix beginning with 'i' 3. When adding a suffix beginning with 'i' to a one-syllable word ending in 'y' it sometimes changes to 'i'. It seems to be optional	Cy	C V i	happ^{i}~~y~~ + ly happ^{i}~~y~~ + est pitying t~~ie~~^{y} + ing tying but tied drying and dryer, but dries and ties

When spelling a word with a suffix

For this the pupil may take action in one of four ways. He many: *just add* the suffix without changing anything, *double* the last letter of the base word, *drop* the silent 'e' at the end of a word or *change* a final 'y' to 'i' or 'ie' to 'y'.

Adding suffixes

The spelling practice routine must be carried through in spelling words with suffixes: train the pupil to stop and consider – 'Do I add, double, drop or change?'

Adding consonant suffixes

This is the first rule to be taught: *Just Add 1*. The pupil considers the suffix to be added. Is it a consonant or vowel suffix? He may add a consonant suffix to any word. *Examples*: helpful, hopeful.

Adding vowel suffixes

It is sometimes possible to do this without altering the base word. If the suffix begins with a vowel, the pupil considers the pattern ending the base word, beginning with the first vowel in the final syllable. There are three patterns to which he may just add a vowel suffix. By the time he reaches the suffix '-ing' in the Language Training Course, he will be reading words with the pattern <u>VCC</u> (examples: help, rest, pant). He practises adding '<u>ing</u>' to such words.

A vowel suffix may be added to a word ending in the pattern <u>VCC</u> (vowel–consonant–consonant): <u>Just Add 2</u>

Examples:

	VCC		V		
h	elp	+	ing	=	helping
	VCC		V		
r	est	+	ing	=	resting
	VCC		V		
p	ant	+	ing	=	panting

When he has reached the phonograms 'oo' and 'ee' in the Language Training Course, he learns the third *'Just Add'* rule. The pattern at the end of the base word is <u>VVC</u> (vowel–vowel–consonant).

A vowel suffix may be added to a word ending in the pattern <u>VVC</u> (vowel–vowel–consonant).

Examples:

```
  VVC        V
l ook    +   ing  =  looking

  V VC       V
p e e l  +   ing  =  peeling

   VVC       V
scr e en +   ing  =  screening
```

When a pupil reaches 'ay' in the Language Training Course, he learns the fourth *'Just Add'* rule: when the pattern at the end of the word is <u>VV</u> (vowel–vowel) (except 'ue' and 'ie'; 'y' and 'w' at the end of words used as vowels). The 'ee' ending can have suffixes beginning with 'i' added.

A vowel suffix may be added to a word ending in the pattern <u>VV</u> (vowel–vowel)

Examples:

```
  VV         V
p l a y  +   ing  =  playing

  VV         V
s e e    +   ing  =  seeing
```

Adding vowel suffixes by doubling the final letter of the base word

This is used when the pattern at the end of the one-syllable base word is <u>VC</u>; the final consonant must be doubled before adding a vowel suffix in order to keep the vowel short. <u>VCC</u> is a short-vowel pattern – see *Just Add 2*

Before a vowel suffix is added to a one-syllable word ending in the pattern <u>VC</u> (vowel–consonant), double the final consonant.

Examples:

VC		C		V		
s it	+	t	+	ing	=	sitting

VC		C		V		
b an	+	n	+	ing	=	banning

VC		C		V		
d ig	+	g	+	ing	=	digging

Adding vowel suffixes by dropping the final 'e'

This is used when the pattern is <u>V–e</u> (vowel–consonant–'e'). Drop the final 'e' before adding the suffix. The vowel remains long. The patterns <u>VCC</u> and <u>VC+C</u> have short vowels. The drop V– ¢ rule is a natural progression from those. The difference between *double* for <u>hopping</u> with the short vowel and *drop* for <u>hoping</u> with a long vowel should be pointed out. Pairs of words such as 'hopping' and 'hoping' could be given for practice using packs of cards, games and programmed activities.

Before a vowel suffix is added to a word ending in the <u>V–e</u> (vowel–consonant–'e' pattern), drop the final 'e'. The vowel remains long.

Examples:

VCe̸		V		
hope̸	+	ing	=	hōping

VCe̸		V		
take̸	+	ing	=	tāking

VCe̸		V		
line̸	+	ing	=	līning

Drop also applies to words ending in 'ue' and 'ie'. They are exceptions to the *Just Add* words ending in <u>VV</u>.

When a word ends in 'ue' or 'ie' drop the 'e' before adding a vowel suffix (see also under '*Change 2*' below).

Examples:
value̸ + ed = valued, rescue̸ + ing = rescuing
die̸ + es = dies, lie̸ + ed = lied

Adding vowel suffixes by changing a final 'y' to 'i'

This has no link with the first three rules. *Change* has three rules. They are concerned with words ending in 'y' and 'ie' (the sounds /ĭ/ and /ī/), and includes words of one or more syllables, and both consonant and vowel suffixes.

Change rule no. 1

Change 1 applies to words ending in 'y' preceded by a consonant. The 'y' is changed to 'i' before adding any suffix, except when the suffix begins with 'i'. Two 'i's are not written together in English words.

Before a suffix is added to a word ending in 'y', change the 'y' to 'i' except when the suffix begins with 'i'.

Examples:

happ~~y~~i +	est	=	happiest
marr~~y~~i +	ed	=	married
hurr~~y~~i +	es	=	hurries
but pity	+	ing =	pitying

Change rule no. 2

Change 2 applies to words ending in 'ie'.

Words ending in 'ie' change 'ie' to 'y' before adding a suffix beginning with 'i' (see also under *Drop*).

Examples:

t~~ie~~y +	ing	=	tying but ties
l~~ie~~y +	ing	=	lying but lied
d~~ie~~ +	ing	=	dying but died

Change rule no. 3

Change 3 applies to words of one syllable ending 'y'. Sometimes the 'y' changes to 'i' when followed by a suffix which does not begin with 'i'. It seems to be optional. These words should be put into an irregular pack for practice as the need arises.

Sometimes change 'y' to 'i' in words of one syllable ending in 'y'.

Examples:
dry – drier *or* dryer
fly – flier *or* flyer

Words ending with the regular final syllables, ble, dle, fle etc. have the 'le' changed to 'ly' when adding the suffix 'ly'. Some pupils may find it a simple matter to regard the whole syllable as a regular final syllable for spelling as in reading; 'able' become 'ably', 'simple' becomes 'simply', 'bubble' becomes 'bubbly'.

Spelling words with prefixes

The concept of prefix for spelling

This is not introduced until the pupil is fairly advanced in the Language Training Course. He will have been reading words with prefixes for some time before there is any discussion of them as such. When it is decided to introduce the prefix for spelling, the teacher much be sure the pupil understands the concept. Much oral practice needs to be given. He should learn the definition.

Prefix: a letter or group of letters placed at the beginning of a base word to enable that word to be used differently.

Each prefix can be introduced with its meaning, but only if the letters contained in it have been already taught for spelling. At first, only words which are complete before the prefix is added should be used. *Examples* are:

Prefix	Base word	Base word and prefix	Meaning
be	side	beside	by the side of
de	press	depress	to press down
in	take	intake	to take in

As he lengthens his list of prefixes the pupil can engage in extending his vocabulary by taking a base word and seeing how many words he can make by adding different prefixes.

Changing the use of base words by varying the prefix:

Examples are:

Prefix and base word	Meaning
<u>re</u>port	to carry again, to carry back
<u>de</u>port	to carry away
<u>trans</u>port	to carry across
<u>ex</u>port	to carry out or out of

When it is necessary to use words which are prefixes added to roots, and more difficult to explain, the latter could be called *main syllables*, as this term may be better understood by a younger pupil. The study of adding prefixes to roots may be difficult even for older, more advanced learners. Sometimes a prefix does not join easily to some base words, and there are changes in spelling that cause difficulty. As in adding suffixes to base words, it is the joining point which needs to be looked at: the final letter of the prefix and the first letter of the base word. The first letter of the base word does not change but it sometimes influences the final letter of the prefix.

When a prefix ends in a vowel, there is no change in the spelling. When the vowel ending a prefix matches the one beginning the base word, there is sometimes a hyphen between the two, but in some words the hyphen is not necessary.

1. A hyphen between a vowel ending the prefix and a vowel beginning a base word.
   Examples: re-entry, co-opt

2. Words used with or without the hyphen
   Examples: cooperation, cooperative, coordinate

For ease of enunciation, some prefixes have their final consonant changed to match the one beginning the base word.

The last letter of the prefix is changed before certain letters beginning base words
Examples:
The prefix 'ad' meaning 'to':
'd' changed to 'c', 'ac' + count = account
'd' changed to 'f', 'af' + fix = affix

The adding of prefixes to base words is best learnt with the aid of a reference framework. The pupil is given a blank frame and adds to it each prefix as he learns it with its meaning, any changes of spelling and examples of completed words. Figure 8.5 shows the beginning of such a frame. Figure 8.6 shows a complete frame.

His first prefix in the Language Training Course will be 'in', meaning in, on, into, towards. *Examples:* inside, into. Also meaning *not* – inability = not able; 'in' becomes 'im' before 'b'. 'm' and 'p' for ease of enunciation, e.g. imperfect = not perfect.

Figure 8.5 Spelling words with prefixes.

Spelling words with prefixes				
The prefix	The meaning	Change of last letter of the prefix	First letter of base word	Examples
in	into, not	n to m	b, p, m	imbibe impure immobile
		n to r	r	irregular
		n to l	l	illegal

Figure 8.6 Frame for teachers spelling prefixes in the Language Training Course order.

The prefix	The meaning	Change of final letter	First letter of base word	Examples of completed words
in	into, not			inside
		n to m	b, p, m	imbile, impure, immobile
		n to r	r	irregular
		n to l	l	illegal
anti	against	none	–	antibiotic
dis	away,			dislike
	not	dis to di	v, g	divert, digress
		s to f	f	different
ad	towards			adjust
		d to c	c	accord
		d to f	f	affront
		d to g	g	aggresive
		d to l	l	allow
		d to n	n	annoy
		d to p	p	appease
		d to r	r	array
		d to s	s	assemble
		d to t	t	attack
ab	from			abase
		becomes a	p, m, v	apart, amend, avoid
		becomes abs	c	abscond
		becomes abs	t	abstain
a	away, on up, out	none	–	arise
trans	across	none	–	transatlantic
en	in, into onto, to make	n to m	b, p, ph	endear embalm, employ, emphasis
be	about	none	–	beside
de	from	none	–	depress
ante	before	none	–	antechamber
per	through	none	–	percolate
pre	before	none	–	present
semi	half, partly	none	–	semifinal
mis	amiss, wrongly	none	when s begins the word, ss	misspent
mal	badly	none	–	malcontent

	The prefix	The meaning	Change of final letter	First letter of base word	Examples of completed words
Figure 8.6 (contd)	post	after behind	none	–	postscript
	com	with	none before	p, b, m	compose, combine, comment
			m to r	r	correct
			m to l	l	collect
			m to n	n	connect
			m to n	d	conduct
			n	f	confide
			n	g	congress
			n	j	conjecture
			n	q	conquest
			n	s	conserve
			n	t	contest
			becomes co	h	cohere
			before	gn	cognition

The spelling rules and the spelling choices

A distinction is made between spelling rules and spelling choices. The spelling rules are used mainly in connection with adding suffixes and prefixes to basic words, or with punctuation to give meaning or a different use to words. The spelling rules are distributed through the Language Training Course. A rule is inserted as the pupil adds a phonogram to his spelling pack, which enables him to understand how to use the rule. For example: when he reaches the 's' he can learn the plural rule.

Plural of simple nouns, add 's'
Example: one pin, two pins

Spelling choices

The term 'spelling choice' is used here to describe a group of alternative spellings of a sound. They are listed in Figure 8.7. The use of each phonogram (sound spelling) is learnt by the pupil when it is introduced into the Language Training Course. Its clueword indicates its use. It is added to his Spelling Pack. He learns where and why each one is used and should be able to give his reason for using it. For the vowel choices, he will be building up his frames. As he finishes all the choices for spelling a sound, he completes his Spelling Card. The choices are set out on the cards either in the order of frequency in which a spelling occurs in words or according to its position in a word.

1. The order of its frequency in words.
   Examples:
   $\overline{oo}$ – the most frequent
   ou – less frequent, ui, least frequent

2. Its position in a word.
   Examples: (k) c, k, ck, ch, que
   'k' – begins words before 'e', 'i', 'y'
   'c' – begins words; it does not end one-syllable words; it ends multisyllable words.
   'k' – ends words after the patterns <u>VV</u>, <u>VC</u>
   'ck' – ends words after one short vowel
   'ch' – B, M or E of a word (irregular)
   'que' – ends words (irregular)

Some spelling choices can be grouped for identification because they form regular patterns. There is a recognisable balance of vowels and consonants. It may be that a 'feel' for this balance is what makes

Consonants		Long vowels		Other vowel spellings	
(t)	't' 'ed'	(ā)	'a' 'a–e' 'ay'	(ow)	'ou' 'ow'
(s)	's' 'ss' 'ce' (unvoiced)	(ē)	'e' 'ee' 'ee' 'e–e'	(er')	'er' 'ir' 'ur' 'ear' 'or'
(d)	'd' 'ed'	(ī)	'i' 'i–e' 'y'		(after 'w') accented in
(k)	'c' 'k' 'ck' ('ch' 'que' irregular)	(ō)	'o' 'o–e' 'ow'		main syllables
(l)	'l' 'll'	(ū)	'u' 'u–e' 'ue' 'ew'	(er)	'er' 'or' 'ar' 'our' 'ure'
(f)	'f' 'ff' 'ph'	(o͞o)	'oo' 'ou' 'ui' and any		unaccented at the end
(j)	'j' 'ge' 'dge'		spelling of the sound (ŭ)		of words
(z)	'z' 's' 'se'			(aw)	'au' 'aw' 'a'
(sh)	'sh' 'ch' 'ti' 'si' 'ci'	**Short vowels**		(oy)	'oi' 'oy'
(ch)	'ch' 'tch'	(ĭ)	'i' 'y'	(ŭs)	'ous' 'us'
(sh'n)	'tion' 'sion' 'cian'	(ĕ)	'e' 'ea'	(ah)	'a'
(zh'n)	'sion'	(ŏ)	'o' 'a'		
(n)	'n' ('kn' 'gn' 'pn' irregular)	(ŭ)	'u' 'o' 'ou' obscure 'a' 'e'		
		(o͞o)	'oo' 'u' 'ui'		

Figure 8.7 Sound spelling with alternatives (spelling choices).

good spellers create the correct patterns. Dyslexic pupils do not react automatically to the balance of vowels and consonants in words.

Teaching the spelling choices

The pupil needs to be given activities which enable him to practise using the alternative spellings in dictated words, phrases and sentences. He should also be asked questions requiring written answers which necessitate the use of the spelling choices. If he is not given opportunities for over-learning each step and using the alternatives in his own writing, progressing from the simple to the more difficult, he will be unlikely to apply his knowledge in stressful situations. Games and activities should be devised to give as much reinforcement as possible.

The unvoiced and voiced sounds of /s/ and /z/

The spellings of unvoiced and voiced sounds /s/ and /z/ present some confusions for the poor speller. As each spelling is introduced into the Language Training Course, suitable lists of words for the reading and spelling vocabularies are given. Some of them will need to be treated as irregular.

Further information

Controversy is presently gathering around 'analytical' or 'synthetic' phonics. Kathleen Hickey points to a simple and lucid difference. If you ask a child to look at a word and say its sounds, sequence the sounds into another sound, say that sound and link it with meaning, the required process is analysis. If you say a word, and ask the child to make the word out of plastic or wooden letters, the process is synthesis. Analysis is required for reading. Synthesis is required for spelling. Nearly all children come first to phonics for spelling (Frith 1985; Stackhouse 1990), then begin to use their phonic knowledge in responding to letter sound links when reading. The dyslexic child, who may have poor working memory, poor sequencing, and poor phonological awareness, will find analysis particularly hard. In synthesis, the child can hold in memory the whole word and link it to meaning. Young learners find it much easier to learn decoding by first tackling encoding, mastering the skill of building up words from letters before attempting to 'sound out' words.

However, a certain level of sound awareness is a necessary foundation for use of phonics, analytical or synthetic. Identification of sounds within a word is necessary for analysis for reading or synthesis for spelling. The ability to segment words into syllables is necessary for production of 'invented' spelling or longer regular words. (e.g. 'fan - tas - tic'). Identification of rhyme is necessary for successful use of analogy in developing fluent reading, and in tuning in to orthographic units in spelling. Hickey's structured multisensory programme has verbal kinaesthetic response at its very core; with hindsight, we can see that this is one of the key reasons for its success. Chapter 3 of this edition includes a selection of useful games and activities to develop phonological processing skill, and lists useful resources.

Chapter 9
Story writing

The dyslexic child may need help in speaking and listening before written self-expression is possible. Training in auditory memory span will help the pupil to carry out his intention. A simple analysis of the components of a story is provided, and its six stages can be gradually expanded and elaborated.

In order to write down his own thoughts a pupil may need much help to state clearly, orally, that which he wishes to write. He may then require training in how to listen carefully and hold the sequence of words long enough to transfer them correctly to the writing surface.

Training in lengthening the auditory memory span

The pupil can be given dictation of gradually lengthening groups of words. He must listen carefully, repeat the group of words after the teacher and remain silent while writing. The dictation should contain only words the pupil has learnt to spell. He should not begin to write until he can repeat the group of words and feel confident that he can retain the sequence.

He can begin with simple phrases, leading up to short sentences, which can be lengthened gradually.

Examples:

The article with a noun	the pit, the bell, a pin, a sack
An adjective is added	a red fox, the big doll
With prepositions	at the window, on a tree
With the verbs	see a red fox, run to the park, the man is at the window

When he has written the sentence he may have made a mistake. He should be shown how to correct his own work by looking at each word carefully, while the teacher reads the sentence again slowly. When the teacher has finished reading, the pupil must be encouraged to re-read and when he spots an error he must underline it and write the correct word above the error. He can be helped to increase his ability to find his own mistakes. After practice he can do his own proofreading, underlining his errors and putting the corrections above. This is necessary so that the teacher can identify the kind of mistakes he makes and decide where most practice is needed. For the same reasons, rubbers should not be used or words crossed out obscuring the error.

Story writing

The following plan for story writing was arrived at by asking a group of children with language difficulties to tell a story. As each point was made, they were helped to analyse that part of the story and decide where it fitted into the completed sequence. Six stages emerged. These are given here in the children's own phrases:

1. Introduce the characters.
2. Describe the place where the story begins.
3. Something begins to happen to start things off.
4. The exciting part: the main part of the story leading to the climax.

5. It sorts itself out – or the solution.
6. Describe the ending.

The shape of the story can be illustrated in diagrammatic form to give emphasis to the rise and fall of the feeling of tension as the story proceeds (Figure 9.1).

Figure 9.1

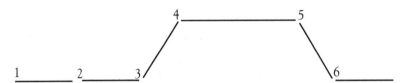

At the beginning of the story there is a state of equilibrium, usually at (1), (2) and (3), but then something begins to happen and there is a rise in expectation. At (4), the middle or 'exciting part' of the story is suspended on a higher level of tension until the climax. Then at (5) the plateau on the diagram ends, the tension is reduced and a return made to (6) – a state of equilibrium, such as existed at the beginning. Here the pupil should be clear than he must describe the situation in which the characters find themselves at the end of the story.

A pupil who has not learnt to work through these six steps in writing stories will often become confused at stage (5) and fail to find a way out of the dilemma, or alternatively the lesson ends and the story cannot be finished. With a feeling of relief, he writes THE END!, when still at the main exciting part of his story.

After working through this pattern of six stages for story *telling* or *writing* a few times, he will become conscious of the importance of stage (5) and he will find it easier to round off his story.

At first, he might invent stories composed of a simple statement at each of the six stages just to get the feel of the sequence and the completeness of the whole. This is best done with his teacher, the pupil giving the ideas and the teacher helping him to put them into suitable English – in other words, helping him to compose sentences. Only one clear sentence at each stage is needed for a complete story, and it can be done with groups of pupils. Members of a group might all be expected to contribute and then the teacher could help them to decide whose idea is the most suitable to be used. The story is then available for a piece of reading material.

The teacher could have large blank sheets of paper clipped together or a flipchart. At suitable points in the story, either the teacher or the pupil could sketch a quick illustration.

Working with a group or class, the use of an overhead projector is an asset. The teacher can face the group who see an enlarged view of the words and pictures on the screen.

In order to get the 'feel' for the six stages established, without having to worry about the composition of written language, a young pupil can compose a story in pictures as follows: give the pupil six pieces of paper which can be stapled or fixed together to make a little book, and ask him to draw a picture on each page. Each page represents one of the stages (Figure 9.2.)

Alternatively, give him a sheet of paper divided into six sections, comic-style, each section representing a stage in the story as in Figure 9.3.

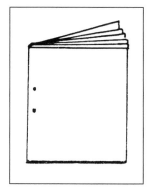

Figure 9.2

Figure 9.3

1.	2.	3.
4.	5.	6.

Next he might try to tell a story in six sentences into a tape-recorder. At this point all he has to concentrate on is *telling* the story. Later he might play back the tape-recorder, using it as a 'dictator' and write down his sentences. Having already completed the composition he will be free to concentrate on his English and spelling. In this way he can gradually build up the skills of inventing a story and producing it in written form so that he and others can read it.

Another way to get the written story started is for the pupil to draw six pictures and write a sentence before each picture, the teacher helping him if necessary. Rule the paper, thus making room for the writing as in Figure 9.4.

Figure 9.4

1.	2.	3.
4.	5.	6.

After the pupil has learnt the pattern of the six stages, provided he can now write a simple sentence, he can begin to compose stories without a picture to guide him, writing only one sentence at each stage. Here is an example of a first story invented by a group of pupils with the help of a teacher.

1. The characters:	One day the twins went out
2. The place:	They came to the woods and began to play.

3. Something happens: Suddenly they saw a rabbit caught in a trap.

4. The exciting part: They tried to open the trap but could not manage it.

5. It sorts itself out: They ran home to bring their father who opened the trap and rescued the poor rabbit.

6. The ending: They took it home and kept it until it could go back to the woods again.

When the pupil manages successfully to think his way through the six steps, putting one sentence at each stage, it can be pointed out that what he has learned to do is to work out the 'skeleton' of a story. Now he has to add some flesh and clothing. He learns how to 'pad out' the 'skeleton' by adding another sentence at each stage, bearing in mind that the new sentences must belong to that stage. Gradually the pupil can be brought to enlarge his six stages to groups of sentences or paragraphs until he feels happy about writing longer stories. The pupil can print, illustrate and bind his own stories into small books.

Figure 9.5 is an example of a story in only 14 words but, because the six stages are there, the story is complete.

Figure 9.5

| Bill | went out. | He met Tom. |
| They played marbles | Tom won. | Bill went home. |

Descriptive writing and writing to provide information

When writing descriptions or pieces of written information, it is useful to help the pupil to try to think in terms of beginning, middle and end. This can be approached in the same way as story writing, at first with a simple sentence at each stage, and then further sentences to 'pad' them out.

1. The introduction
2. The main part
3. The conclusion

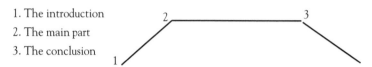

As a beginning to writing essays on different subjects, the same idea of beginning, middle and end can be expanded into six sentences becoming paragraphs. The middle could become three paragraphs covering different aspects of the subject under discussion.

Beginning	1	Introduction
	2	
Middle	3	Discussion of three
	4	different aspects
	5	of subjects
End	6	Conclusion

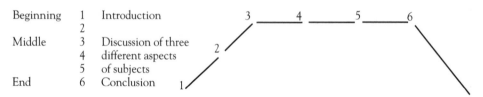

Further information

Hickey's simple analysis of the components of a story still stands as a useful support for the budding writer. The introduction of the English National Curriculum in 1988 gave teachers a framework of expectations, and gathered together ideas that reflected a growing understanding of the stages of development of the writing process. The child is expected to be able to 'undertake a range of chronological writing including . . . stories. . .' (Key Stage 1), and to progress to production of 'stories which are more consciously crafted . . . portrayal of characters and settings . . . elements of suspense or surprise . . . skilfully managed resolution.' Planning, review and redrafting were identified as important parts of the Curriculum. There are now in general use many examples of story planners, pictorial storyboards, flowcharts, 'spider' plans (see Burtis et al. 1983, for a review). During this period, attention has been given to the purpose of writing, and the need to modify the 'voice' to suit the reader.

Information technology

Word processors and computers are now widely available, and good software is being developed and refined. Attention is still given to the development of traditional writing skills, but the Code of Practice urges that information technology should be used where necessary to give access to mainstream curriculum. Chapter 3 includes a section on use of computers.

Chapter 10
Suggestions for self-learning activities in reading and spelling

Games are used to aid learning. They must be carefully structured so that they cover only concepts that have been taught. A bank of game and activities, linked to the structure, can be stored for use of other pupils. Games must be fair, and ensure that they hit the learning targets. Suggestions are made so that familiar games can be adjusted to individual needs, and players at different stages of development can play together to the benefit of all.

A teacher planning a cumulative course of language training must be prepared to devise and make, or otherwise obtain, self-learning and self-correcting materials for his or her pupils' use at each stage in the course. Equally, because the course is based on language structure, the teacher need not spend all his or her spare time making materials for every pupil. He or she can build up a bank of materials and file them under each phonogram, spelling rule or spelling choice. They are then ready for use by various individuals and groups of pupils for consolidation, reinforcement and revision of the skills as they progress through the course.

Points to remember

Practice materials should include only those concepts that have been covered. Each item or answer should be self-checking. When machines are used, pupils must be trained to handle them competently so that lessons proceed smoothly.

Games

There are published games which embody the principles set out here, but they are seldom suitable in content for a pupil following a structured course. Teachers should be sure that the game is teaching what the pupil needs to practise, and also that the players play it in the way it is intended to be played in order to achieve maximum learning. It is possible for children to play games, learn nothing at all and for the teacher not to be aware of this.

Games must be fair. The proportion of skill and luck needs to be balanced between the players. For instance, two players at different stages may need to practise irregular high frequency words. Each one can be given separate packs of words recently introduced and currently being worked upon.

Players of different ages and levels of competence can play together, each being governed by different rules. Taking, as an example, a game of 'Lotto' or 'Bingo' for four players of different ages and stages. Player no. 1 could be the caller and do the checking. Player no. 2 (the least experienced) will be allowed to see the word and use visual checking. Player no. 3 has to listen to the word and find it on his card. Player no. 4 must spell it before he can claim it. Pupils find this way of playing acceptable.

Games can be based on well-known ones but using phonograms, words, phrases or sentences. Useful games are 'Snap', 'Rummy', 'Happy Families' and other card games, 'Snakes and Ladders' and any other boards-and-dice game

Games for learning the alphabet

The essentials for planning alphabet activities will be found in Chapter 5.

Some games which have been devised by teachers working with pupils with written language difficulties are described below. They can all be adapted to teach whatever is needed.

Further information

Hickey's games use the rules of familiar games, making materials that fit the rules and the stage of the structure reached by the pupils. The games are not merely a relief from hard work, but do genuinely provide an opportunity to pleasantly rehearse and practise new skills leading to automatic mastery. However, teachers are finding that the games described are less familiar than they were in the 1970s. It can be a useful (and stress-free) homework activity to ask the dyslexic child to play the games at home so that the rules become familiar. You can also use simpler games. The NLS Framework uses games and game-like activities to aid learning. Additional Literacy Support materials in Modules 1–4 (DfEE 1999) have been developed for those pupils at Key Stage 2 who will not have been using the NLS Framework for teaching in the early stages. They stretch the concept of 'game' to include some very simple activities, but pupils enjoy them very much and learn from them.

Back to base

Purpose To give practice in learning the position of the letters in the alphabet and in spelling words with the regular spellings of the long vowels at the end of words. A *spelling* game.

No. of players Three or more depending on the amount of space available.

Players' alphabet Use pupil's Reading Cards.

Directions The caller holds a pack of word cards, in this case containing words which end with the long vowel sounds spelt in the regular way. The other players each have a set of alphabet letters set out in an arc in front of them. They also have five cards with the long vowel endings. When the caller calls a word, the others take the letters from their alphabet in the order in which they need them and select the word ending. The first one to make the word scores a point. When everyone has completed his word, the caller says 'Back to base', and the first one to get all his letters back into position in the alphabet scores a point.

Caller's words

play	today	display
see	tree	three
spy	fly	sky
show	blow	crow
due	statue	hue

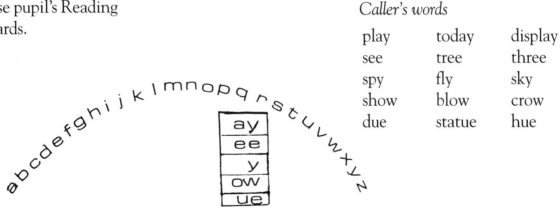

Happy families (the 'families' can be any parts of language)

Purpose Learning the irregular phonograms. A word reading game with oral *spelling* of the phonograms.

No. of players One, three or four.

Directions As in the popular game there can be four in a family but it is possible to have more. The family is a phonogram. This phonogram is placed at the top of each card in the family and below this a picture of the member of the family. The other members of the family are the words listed below the picture. When a player asks for a card he must use the correct formula to get the maximum benefit from playing the game. He must say to his neighbour, 'May I have <u>collar</u> of the 'ar' family?', thus drawing special attention to the spelling of the (er) sound. He can go on asking for cards until he is refused and the next player has a turn. The one who collects the most families has won.

A 'family' of cards

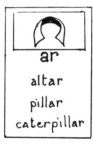
ar

altar
pillar
caterpillar

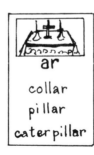
ar

collar
pillar
caterpillar

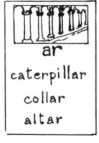
ar

caterpillar
collar
altar

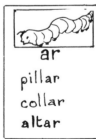
ar

pillar
collar
altar

Rummy (this can also be used for teaching phonograms; words with the same phonogram make a set)

Purpose To practise the phonograms. A *reading* game.

No. of players
Two, three or four.

Directions Players aim to make sets of cards. A set is three cards each having a word with the same phonogram (cat, bat and mat would make a set). Each player is dealt seven cards, the rest are placed in a pile on the table with the first one face up. The player can take the up-turned card or the top face-down card. If he takes one he must throw one away. He must gain the most sets to win, but he must be able to read his set before he claims it.

Completed sets of cards

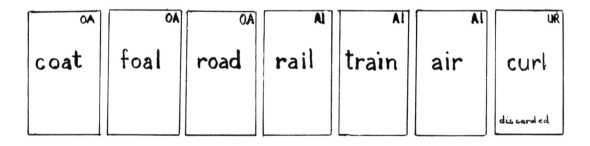

Ladder luck (this game can be adapted to teach whatever the teacher has in mind)

Purpose Differentiating between the short sound of the vowel in words of one syllable, and the long sound of the vowel in vowel–consonant 'e' words of one syllable. It is a *reading* game.

No. of players
Two, three or four.

Directions Ladders of words are compiled with the vowels missing. Each player has two ladders, one with short vowel words and one with vowel–consonant 'e' words. Standing between the players is a folded card as illustrated. Each side of the card has the vowel and numbers so that those on both sides of the table can see it. There is a boxful of small cards or counters with the vowels written on them. A dice is thrown. The player takes a counter as the number he has thrown indicates, puts it into one of his words and reads the word. If he throws a six, he can choose his vowel. The one who finishes his card first or has the most words at the end of a given time has won.

Player no. 1   Player no. 2

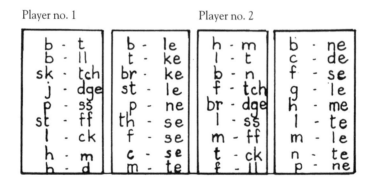

b · t	b · le	h · m	b · ne
b · ll	t · ke	l · t	c · de
sk · tch	br · ke	b · n	f · se
j · dge	st · le	f · tch	g · le
p · ss	p · ne	br · dge	h · me
st · ff	th · se	l · ss	l · te
l · ck	f · se	m · ff	m · le
h · m	c · se	t · ck	n · te
b · d	m · te	f · ll	p · ne

Card and dice   Vowel letters

Snap (this can be played to teach whatever the teacher decides; it is useful to play as suggested)

Purpose To learn the phonograms and the groupings of the spelling of a sound. A *reading* game.

No. of players Two, three or four.

Directions This can be played with the pupils' own reading packs. Two can be mixed together. It is best to play with the vowel cards only or the consonant cards only. 'Snap' is when two cards show which make the same sound, 'a' and 'eigh', 'ow' and 'o–e', 'y' and 'ie' would make 'Snap'.

Examples of 'Snap'

'Snap': both sounds are (ā)   'Snap': both sounds are (ō)

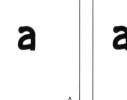

Part II

The course is suitable learners of any age and for a wide range of ability. It can be adapted for individuals, small groups, or classes.

Each phonogram is introduced separately with teaching points, suggestions for visual, auditory and tactile-kinaesthetic discrimination, and activities for reading, writing and spelling. Special attention is given to the development of handwriting and the blending of sounds into words using multisensory techniques.

The vocabularies, derived from the accumulated phonograms, contain most of the available words. All the words are suitable for reading. Some of the words are irregular for spelling – that is, they do not sound blend. It is left to the teacher's discretion to choose words suited to the age, experience and interests of the pupil when devising activities at each step.

The course is not intended as a workbook. The suggestions spread throughout it can be adapted and used with most of the phonograms.

The teacher should keep in mind the stages covered by the learner. Activities should be based on what the learner has learned, so that consolidation and reinforcement can be provided before going on to the next step. In devising activities, remember the difference between reading and spelling. Reading demands recognition and analysis of print; spelling demands recall and synthesis of phonograms.

The use of the Reading Pack, Spelling Pack (pages 18–26) and the word spelling routine (all described on pages 92–93) provide multisensory teaching. Only active and conscious effort from the learner can ensure multisensory learning. Right from the start, the learner should be in charge of the Reading and Spelling packs, physically handling the cards, and being provided always with self-checking activities. Proofreading, self-evaluation of handwriting and content of free writing are essential. LISTENING is the most important teacher skill – individuals need to be aware of the way their own minds work, and to be helped to find a way of remembering that suits them.

Where to start

Teachers often feel that children 'know their letters'. In fact, it usually turns out that they know one or more of the bits of information that collects around a letter – the *name* of one, the *sound* of another, how to *write* a third. The important questions are:

- Has the learner established speedy and automatic multisensory links for recognition, recall, speech and hand movement?
- Can the learner use those links in real reading and writing tasks?

The table on page 49 will remind you of the range of concepts that are covered with the first few letters – if those letters are reasonably familiar to start with, it will make it all the easier for the learner to focus on the new routines, concepts and vocabulary.

For clarity, the first five letters have been presented with a script. The script ensures that the teacher will cover the auditory, visual and tactile-kinaesthetic involved in learning and remembering, and described in the Stimulus Response Routine on page 25. The teacher will adapt the script according to the needs of the learner. Multisensory learning is essential, but the amount of information presented varies with the various needs of the learners. The teacher must decide what is relevant for each individual.

Planning the lesson

The lessons should be up to an hour in length and ideally as frequent as two or three a week, with opportunities for daily self-checking practice of the reading and spelling cards. Children can be given individual programmes within groups of three or four, sharing activities where suitable. Activities should change frequently, but should include a few minutes of each of the following:

1. Some whole language reading, where the learner is encouraged to orchestrate a range of reading strategies. The text can be used

to draw out skills and teaching points that have been covered, or are going to be taught in the rest of the session.

2. Phonological awareness training.
3. Alphabet work, leading to dictionary work.
4. Reading Pack and Spelling Pack.
5. Introduction of new phonogram or concept.
6. Word reading and spelling.
7. Sentence reading and writing.
8. When the learner is ready, free writing – composition of anything from a shopping list to a story, poem or non-fiction account.

The Reading Pack sounds are presented on pages 152–153. The page number shows where detailed information and vocabularies can be found. The Spelling Pack sounds are presented on pages 154–155. The teaching points are cross-referenced in the index. Wherever possible, celebrate the learner's knowledge, and give the learner an opportunity to practise recall rather than recognition of a fact. Before exposition of any teaching point, always make sure that the learner has an opportunity to exercise recall – *request*, rather than *give* information.

Making a Reading Pack

The letter order and clue words are listed in order at the beginning of the programme (pages 152–153).

Look back at pages 18–26 remind yourself how to introduce a new phonogram. The introduction to the first few letters will be described in detail so that the methodology can be reinforced.

1. Decide how you will distinguish vowel sounds from consonant sounds. This volume draws a line at the top of the vowel cards, and leaves them off the consonant cards. Some teachers prefer to put vowels and consonants on different coloured cards.

2. Print the letter/s neatly on the front of the card. Use lower case in the middle of the card, the capital form in the bottom right hand corner. These are reading cards – use the most common PRINTED form, not joined handwriting.

3. On the back of the card, write the clue word and bracketed 'sound picture'.

4. The learner might be able to draw a picture to represent the clue word; if there are problems, give what help is needed.

Using the Reading Pack

Look back at page 25 to remind yourself of the full stimulus response routine (SRR).

Make sure that the learner thoroughly masters the routine described in No.4 – this is the most important one for independent practice between lessons. Do not remove cards from the packs once the learner 'knows' them; the learner needs to exercise the multi-sensory links between eyes, ears, mouth and hand to ensure speedy, automatic responses to the sound–symbol links.

The learner:
- looks at the front of the card,
- says the clue word, and then the sound,
- turns the card over and looks at the picture to check.
  LOOK – SAY CLUE WORD AND SOUND – TURN OVER AND CHECK.

If a mistake is made, repeat the card carefully and correctly, then put it to the bottom of the pack to give it another turn.

Making a Spelling Pack

Once the sound–letter link has been introduced for writing, the Spelling Card can be made (see page 20) so that the auditory and kinaesthetic elements of the stimulus-response routine can be practised.

1. On the front of the card, write the 'sound picture'. This is the bracketed letter/s with the diacritical markings found on the back of the reading card, after the clue word. Use the printed form of the letter.
2. On the back of the card, repeat the printed form of the sound picture, then add the 'answers' – i.e. the learner's response. As a new spelling alternative is learned, the new letter or letter cluster can be added to the Spelling Card. One sound card will gradually collect together all the alternatives for that sound.

The learner:
- listens to a sound,
- repeats the sound,
- names the letter, linking the sound with its possible spellings,
- writes the letter.
  LISTEN – REPEAT – SPELL – WRITE

Supporting handwriting

The sheet on page 24 will give the pupil multisensory practice in learning to spell a new phonogram. Copy it, or draw it onto the white or blackboard, or fold a piece of paper into four. The four stages (trace, copy, write from memory, write with eyes shut) soon become routine. Pupils with problems in organising body movements will need extra kinaesthetic training. Trace the letter with a fingertip, using velvet, felt or sand; make the letter out of plasticine or clay; draw the letters in the air, using a full arm movement; close the eyes and identify the wooden letter by touch.

The Reading Cards (1)

letter/s on card	clue word	sound		page
i	igloo	/ĭ/		156
	iron	/ī/		208
t	ten	/t/		160
p	pot	/p/		164
n	net	/n/		169
s	sun	/s/		173
	rose	/z/		173
a	apple	/ă/		179
	acorn	/ā/		208
	bath	/ah/		179
	canary	/ə/		359
d	dot	/d/		183
h	hat	/h/		186
e	egg	/ĕ/		188
	equals	/ē/		208
	seven	/ə/		391
c	cat	/k/		192
k	kettle	/k/		194
ck	duck	/k/		199
o	orange	/ŏ/		202
	open	/ō/		208
	won	/ə/		350
b	ball	/b/		205
y (c)	yoghurt	/y/		210
r	rat	/r/		212
m	man	/m/		215
y (v)	jelly	/ĭ/		218
	cry	/ī/		218
j	jug	/j/		220

The Reading Cards (2)

letter/s on card	clue word	sound		page
u	umbrella	/ŭ/		222
	uniform	/ū/		222
g	gun	/g/		223
ng	ring	/ng/		228
nk	tank	/nk/		231
f	four	/f/		233
l	log	/l/		235
w	window	/w/		242
v	van	/v/		245
qu	question	/kw/		247
x	six	/ks/		249
z	zebra	/z/		252
th	thumb	/th/		254
sh	sheep	/sh/		257
ch	cherry	/ch/		260
	chemist	/k/		371
	chef	/sh/		372
tch	match	/ch/		260
oo	hook	/o͝o/		265
	spoon	/o͞o/		265
ar	car	/ar/		268
	collar	/ə/		379
er	herb	/er/		271
	hammer	/ə/		271
i-e	pipe	/ī/		274

The Reading Cards (3)

letter/s on card	clue word	sound		page
a-e	cake	/ā/		277
o-e	cone	/ō/		280
or	fork	/or/		284
	mirror	/ə/		
u-e	tube	/ū/		288
ee	teeth	/ē/		290
	tree	/ē/		290
ay	play	/ā/		293
ce	ice	/s/		296
ge	cage	/j/		301
dge	bridge	/j/		301
ow	snow	/ō/		304
	cow	/ow/		321
ue	rescue	/ū/		307
	glue	/ōo/		307
e-e	centipede	/ē/		310
y-e	tyre	/ī/		312
oi	coin	/oy/		314
oy	toy	/oy/		314
wh	whip	/w/		316
ou	house	/ow/		319
au	sauce	/aw/		324
aw	claw	/aw/		324
ea	seat	/ĕ/		327
	treasure	/ē/		330
oa	coat	/ō/		332
oe	toe	/ō/		335

The Reading Cards (4)

letter/s on card	clue word	sound		page
igh	fight	/ī/		337
ai	rain	/ā/		341
ir	bird	/er/		344
ur	fur	/er/		346
ew	new	/ū/		348
	screw	/ōo/		348
ie	shield	/ē/		352
ei	ceiling	/ē/		354
	reindeer	/ā/		354
ph	photo	/f/		356
tion	fraction	/sh'n/		362
ey	donkey	/ĭ/		367
ear	earth	/er/		365
our	colour	/ə/		369
sion	mansion	/sh'n/		376
	television	/zh'n/		376
cian	magician	/sh'n/		376
eu	pneumatic	/ū/		383
ous	dangerous	/us/		385
us	crocus	/us/		385
ui	fruit	/ōo/		387

The Spelling Cards

Sound	Spelling	Cluewords
/ĭ/	i y	igloo jelly
/ī/	i i-e igh y	iron fight pipe cry
/t/	t ed	ten kicked
/p/	p	pot
/n/	n	net
/s/	s ss ce	sun cross ice
/z/	z s	zebra rose
/ă/	a	apple
/ā/	a a-e ai ay	acorn cake rain play
/d/	d ed	dot oiled
/h/	h	hat
/ĕ/	e ea	egg treasure
/ē/	e ee ea e-e ie ei	equals teeth seat centipede shield ceiling
/k/	c k ck ch	cat kettle duck chemist
/ŏ/	o	orange
/ō/	o o-e oa ow	open cone coat snow
/b/	b	ball
/y/	y	yoghurt
/r/	r	rat
/m/	m	man
/j/	j ge dge	jug cage bridge
/ŭ/	u	umbrella
/ū/	u u-e ue ew	uniform tube rescue new
/g/	g	gun
/ng/	ng	ring
/nk/	nk	tank
/f/	f ff ph	four cuff photo
/l/	l ll	log bell
/w/	w wh	window whip
/v/	v	van
/kw/	qu	question

The Spelling Cards (contd)

Sound	Spelling	Cluewords
/ks/	x	six
/o͝o/	oo	hook
/ō͞o/	oo ui	spoon fruit
/th/	th	thumb
/sh/	sh ch ti si ci	sheep chef fraction mansion magician
/zh/	si	television
/ch/	ch tch	cherry match
/ar/	ar	car
/er/	er ir ur ear	herb bird fur earth
/ə/	er or ar our a e o	hammer mirror collar colour canary seven won
/or/	or	fork
/ow/	ow ou	cow house
/oy/	oi oy	coin toy
/aw/	aw	claw
/us/	us ous	crocus dangerous

Reading Card

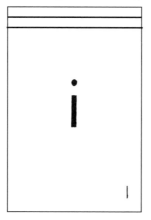

igloo /ĭ/

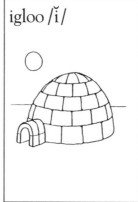

face   reverse

Spelling Card

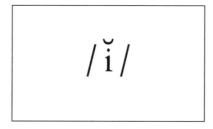

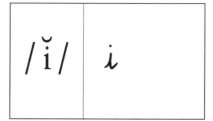

face   reverse

Capital   printed   print to   written
                 lower case   writing   lower case

The Reading Card

1. This is a letter of the alphabet. Its name is 'i'. The lower case is in the middle of the card, the upper case (capital) in the bottom right hand corner.
2. 'i' is a vowel. There is a vowel sound in every syllable. Vowels are made with the mouth open; the air comes straight from the lungs, vibrating the larynx, unobstructed by tongue, lips or teeth. (Choose a vowel card – either distinguish by colour, or by some distinctive mark on the card).
3. On the back of the card, there is a clue word and sound. Can you hear the sound /ĭ/ at the beginning of the word 'igloo'? Say 'igloo /ĭ/'
4. Draw a picture of an igloo.
5. Look at the front of the card. Say the clue word, and then the sound. Turn the card over and look at the picture to check.

Example worksheet at 'i': The letter 'i' can be written and printed in many ways. Look at the letters in the box. Put a ring round every letter 'i'.

i L l *j* i i t ▮ *I* I b i

Example worksheet at 'i': Look at these pictures. Put a counter on each picture that has an /ĭ/ sound in the middle.

Example worksheet at 'i': (Give counters with B (beginning), M (middle), or E (end) on them.) Look at the pictures. Where can you here the /ĭ/ sound, Beginning, Middle or End of the word? Put the correct counters on the pictures.

The Spelling Card

1. Look at the back of your reading card. See the letter in the brackets, with the little mark over the top. The sound is /ĭ/. The little mark is called a breve, and indicates the short vowel sound. Now you are going to learn how to write the letter for that sound.
2. Trace over the printed form. Say the sound, then the name, as you write it.
3. Now make the cursive form from the printed one:

Start at the base line. Write an approach stroke from the base line to the start of the printed letter. Follow the printed letter. Turn up at the base line to form a leaving stroke. This becomes the approach to the next letter. Say the sound, then the name, as you write it.

4. Now follow the TRACE – COPY – WRITE FROM MEMORY – EYES SHUT routine. (See 'Writing the letter' sheet on page 24.)
5. Trace, copy and write from memory the letter in an exercise book (use one with 'tramlines' or draw your own guidelines in an ordinary exercise book).
6. Now you can put that letter on your spelling card, on the back.
7. Practise the spelling routine. (Teacher say the sound /ĭ/. Learner REPEAT – SPELL – WRITE the letter 'i' in its cursive form.)

At this stage, there is one word for reading and spelling – the upper case 'I'.

Reading Card

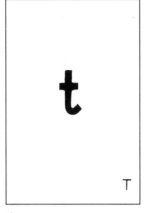

ten /t/

10

face   reverse

Spelling Card

/ t /

/ t /   *t*

face   reverse

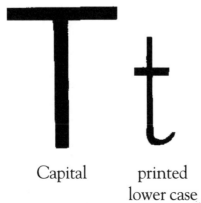
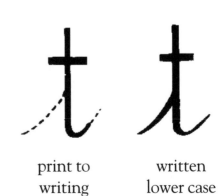

Capital   printed   print to   written
         lower case   writing   lower case

The Reading Card

1. This is a letter of the alphabet. Its name is 't'. Its sound is /t/, not 'ter'. You can hear it more purely at the end of a word – repeat 'hat', 'cat', 'sit'.
2. 't' is a consonant. There are five vowels in the alphabet. All the rest are consonants.
3. On the back of the card, there is a clue word and sound. Can you hear the sound /t/ at the beginning of the word 'ten'? Say 'ten /t/'
4. Draw a picture of the clueword, 'ten'.
5. Put your 't' card with your 'i' card, and practise your reading pack. Look at the front of each card in turn. Say the clue word, and then the sound. Turn each card over and look at the picture to check.

Example worksheet at 't': The letter 't' can be written and printed in many ways. Look at the letters in the box. Put a ring round every letter 't'.

i t T *l* t i t **k** *I* I t t

Example worksheet at 't': Look at these pictures. Put a counter on each picture that starts with a /t/ sound.

Example worksheet at 't': (Give counters with B (beginning), M (middle), or E (end) on them). Look at the pictures. Where can you here the /t/ sound, Beginning, Middle or End of the word? Put the correct counters on the pictures.

Now you can read a word. Put your reading cards together, face up. Say /ĭ/, then /t/. Can you make a word?
Look in a book to see if you can find 'it', as a word, or as an ending. Notice that both letters rest on the line, but the 't' goes into the upper zone.

The Spelling Card

1. Look at the back of your reading card. See the letter in the brackets. The sound is /t/. Now you are going to learn how to write the letter for that sound.
2. Look at the printed form. Notice how it goes into the upper zone. Say the sound, then the name, as you write it.
3. Now make the cursive form from the printed one:

Start at the base line. Write an approach stroke from the base line to the start of the printed letter. Follow the printed letter. Turn up at the base line to form a leaving stroke. This becomes the approach to the next letter. Say the sound, then the name, as you write it.

4. Now follow the TRACE – COPY – WRITE FROM MEMORY – EYES SHUT routine.
5. Trace, copy and write from memory the letter in an exercise book.
6. Now you can put that letter on your spelling card, on the back.
7. Practise the spelling routine. (Teacher say the sound /t/. Learner REPEAT – SPELL – WRITE the letter 't' in its cursive form. Repeat the process using the /ĭ/ card.)
8. Now you can write the word 'it'. See how the leaving stroke of 'i' becomes the approach stroke of 't'. Trace – copy – write from memory.
9. Teacher say 'it'. Learner repeat, spell, (name the letters) then write in joined writing.

Reading Card

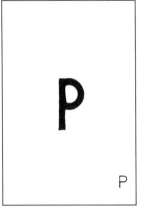

face   reverse

Spelling Card

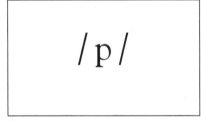
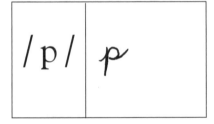

face   reverse

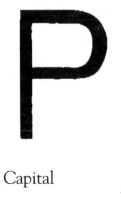

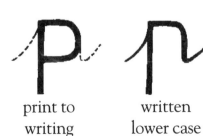

Capital   printed   print to   written
                 lower case   writing   lower case

The Reading Card

1. This is another consonant. Its name is 'p'. Its sound is /p/, not 'per'. The air from the lungs puffs the lips apart. You can hear it more purely at the end of a word – repeat 'lip', 'cup', 'stop'.
2. On the back of the card, there is the clue word and sound. Can you hear the sound /p/ at the beginning of the word 'pot'? Say 'pot /p/'
3. Draw a picture of the clueword, 'pot'.
4. Put your 'p' card with your other two cards, and practise your reading pack. Look at the front of each card in turn. Say the clue word, and then the sound. Turn each card over and look at the picture to check.

Example worksheet at 'p': The letter 'p' can be written and printed in many ways. Look at the letters in the box. Put a ring round every letter 'p'.

i p P *l p* i t **k** *I* P t p

Example worksheet at 'p': Look at these pictures. Put a counter on each picture that starts with a /p/ sound.

Example worksheet at 'p': (Give counters with B (beginning), M (middle), or E (end) on them). Look at the pictures. Where can you here the /t/ sound, Beginning, Middle or End of the word? Put the correct counters on the pictures.

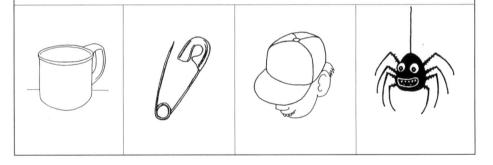

Now you can read a word. Put your reading cards together, face up. Say /ĭ/, then /t/. Can you make a word? Put you /p/ card in front. Can you make another word?

Look in a book to see if you can find any words that end in 'ip'.

The Spelling Card

1. Look at the back of your 'p' reading card. See the letter in the brackets. The sound is /p/. Now you are going to learn how to write the letter for that sound.
2. Look at the printed form. Notice how it goes into the lower zone. Say the sound, then the name, as you write it.
3. Now make the cursive form from the printed one:

Start at the base line. Write an approach stroke from the base line to the start of the printed letter. Follow the printed letter. Turn up at the base line to form a leaving stroke. This becomes the approach to the next letter. Say the sound, then the name, as you write it.

4. Now follow the TRACE – COPY – WRITE FROM MEMORY – EYES SHUT routine.
5. Trace, copy and write from memory the letter in an exercise book.
6. Now you can put that letter on your spelling card, on the back.
7. Practise the spelling routine. (Teacher say the sound /p/. Learner REPEAT – SPELL – WRITE the letter 'p' in its cursive form. Repeat the process using the /ĭ/ and /t/ cards.)
8. Now you can write the words 'pit', 'pip' and 'tip'. Trace – copy – write from memory.
9. Teacher use the words 'pit', 'pip' and 'tip' for dictation. Learner repeat, spell, (name the letters) then write in joined writing.

Awareness of syllables

Part of the daily alphabet work can be a rhythmical recitation of the letters (see page 54): AB' CD' EF' etc. This increases awareness of syllables and accenting in speech. If the learner is ready work at increasing the conscious phonological awareness. A syllable is a beat in a word. Count the number of syllables in each learner's name. To start with, the teacher can tap or clap whilst saying each syllable. Gradually the learners can take over more of the task, and model their own words, or model words for the rest of the group. Move to counting out syllables of things in the room – makes of cars – animals – foods. Let the learners generate words for each other. This underlying phonological development is essential to lay the foundations for sounding out and spelling multisyllabic words.

n N

Reading Card

n

N

face

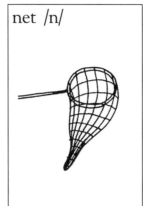

net /n/

reverse

Spelling Card

/n/

front

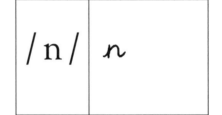

/n/ n

reverse

Capital   printed   print to   written
lower case   writing   lower case

The Reading Card

1. This is another consonant. Its name is 'n'. Its sound is /nnn/, not 'ner'. The air from the lungs goes down the nose. Look in a mirror to see how the lips are parted. You can hear it more purely at the end of a word – repeat 'pan', 'tin', 'when'.
2. On the back of the card, there is the clue word and sound. Can you hear the sound /n/ at the beginning of the word 'net'? Say 'net /n/'
3. Draw a picture of the clueword, 'net'.
4. Put your 'n' card with your other three cards, and practise your reading pack. Look at the front of each card in turn. Say the clue word, and then the sound. Turn each card over and look at the picture to check.

Example worksheet at 'n': The letter 'n' can be written and printed in many ways. Look at the letters in the box. Put a ring round every letter 'n'.

n p N *m p* i N **n** *I* P n p

Example worksheet at 'n': Look at these pictures. Put a counter on each picture that starts with a /n/ sound.

Example worksheet at 'n': (Give B, M, E counters). Look at the pictures. Where can you here the /n/ sound, Beginning, Middle or End of the word? Put the correct counters on the pictures.

Now you can read a word. Put your reading cards together, face up. Say /ĭ/, then /n/. Can you make a word? Put your /p/ card in front. Can you make another word?
Look in a book to see if you can find any words that end in 'in'.

The Spelling Card

1. Look at the back of your 'n' reading card. See the letter in the brackets. The sound is /n/. Now you are going to learn how to write the letter for that sound.
2. Look at the printed form. Notice how it stays in the middle zone. Say the sound, then the name, as you write it.
3. Now make the cursive form from the printed one:

Start at the base line. Write an approach stroke from the base line to the start of the printed letter. Follow the printed letter. Turn up at the base line to form a leaving stroke. This becomes the approach to the next letter. Say the sound, then the name, as you write it.

4. Now follow the TRACE – COPY – WRITE FROM MEMORY – EYES SHUT routine.
5. Trace, copy and write from memory the letter in an exercise book.
6. Now you can put that letter on your spelling card, on the back.
7. Practise the spelling routine. (Teacher say the sound /n/. Learner REPEAT – SPELL – WRITE the letter 'n' in its cursive form. Repeat the process using the /ĭ/, /p/ and /t/ cards.)
8. Now you can write the words 'nip', 'pin' and 'tin'. Trace – copy – write from memory.
9. Teacher use the words 'nip', 'pin' and 'tin' for dictation. Learner repeat, spell, (name the letters) then write in joined writing.

s S

Reading Card

s

s

face

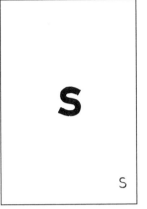

sun /s/

rose /z/

reverse

Spelling card

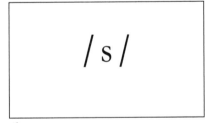

/ s /

face

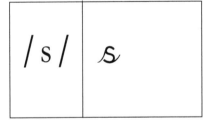

/ s /   ﻭ

reverse

Capital

S

printed
lower case

print to
writing

written
lower case

The Reading Card

1. This is another consonant. Its name is 's'. Its sound is /s/.
2. Look at the back of the card, there is the clue word and sound. Can you hear the sound /s/ at the beginning of the word 'sun'? Say 'sun /s/'
3. Draw a picture of the clueword, 'sun'.
4. Listen to these words. Can you hear the /s/ sound at the beginning, in the middle or at the end? sit – sorry – mess – custard – fussy – snake – slipper – silly – pass.
5. Put your 's' card with your other cards, and practise your reading pack. Look at the front of each card in turn. Say the clue word, and then the sound. Turn each card over and look at the picture to check.

Example worksheet at 's': The letter 's' can be written and printed in many ways. Look at the letters in the box. Put a ring round every letter 's'.

s p **S** *m* *s* i s **n** *I* t s p

(Teacher decide whether or not this information is relevant at this stage.) The letter 's' has another sound. Look at the word 'is'. We pronounce the letter 's' as /z/. Listen to these words – birds – tins – zebras – was. The letter 's' is pronounced /z/. It is a voiced sound. Put your fingers on your throat to feel the vibrations when /z/ is pronounced. There is no vibration when you say the sound /s/. It is an unvoiced sound.

The Spelling Card

1. Look at the back of your 's' reading card. See the letter in the brackets. The sound is /s/. Now you are going to learn how to write the letter for that sound.
2. Look at the printed form. Notice how it stays in the middle zone. Say the sound, then the name, as you write it.
3. Using blackboard or large sheet of paper, make the cursive form from the printed one: Start at the base line. Write an approach stroke from the base line to the start of the printed letter. Follow the printed letter. Turn up at the base line to form a leaving stroke. This becomes the approach to the next letter. Say the sound, then the name, as you write it.
4. Now TRACE – COPY – WRITE FROM MEMORY – EYES SHUT.
5. Trace, copy and write from memory the letter in an exercise book.
6. Now you can put that letter on your spelling card, on the back.
7. Practise the spelling routine. (Teacher say the sound /s/. Learner REPEAT – SPELL – WRITE the letter 's' in its cursive form. Repeat the process using the /ĭ/, /p/, /n/ and /t/ cards.)

Consonant blends

The letter 's' starts more words than any other letter in the alphabet. This is because it can be blended together with so many other consonants. If the sounds are said very purely, without adding an 'er' sound onto the consonant, it is possible to blend even three consonants together. It will be difficult to arrive at 'stop' from 'ser' 'ter' 'o' 'per'. But many learners need extra help with consonant blends. You can make a separate pack of blend cards. Start with 'st', 'sp' and 'sn'. Use them for practice, and for games.

Example worksheet at 's': Look at the picture. Say the word aloud. Write the first two letters in the box (st, sp or sn).

Example worksheet at 's': The letter 's' can be used as a suffix – it is added onto nouns to make more than one (plural), e.g. pip – pips. It can be added to verbs to give third person singular, present tense, e.g. sit – sits. Read the word in the box, and draw a suitable picture. Put a ring round every suffix.

pins	sits	pips
nips	tins	sips

Word lists at at 's'				
regular words	irregular words	with blends	with suffixes	with prefixes
it	it's	spin	(-s to nouns)	insist
pit	isn't	snip	tins	
nit	I	spit	pins	
tit	pint	stint	sins	
is	inn		tips	
tip			pips	
pip				
sip			(-s to verbs)	
in			sits	
tin			spits	
sin			sips	
			nips	
			snips	
			spins	
			tins	

Some of these words can also be used for spelling. Choose only the words which are covered by the spelling pack.

Word spelling procedures

1. Repeat, Spell, Write (for regular words).

Teacher says a word; pupil repeats it, spells it using the letter names, then writes it.

2. (Procedure for children who have weak phonological awareness, and for whom the letter name knowledge is developing slowly.) Repeat, sound out, write, spell.

Teacher says a word, and pupil repeats it, says each sound slowly, then writes it. The word can then be spelled using the letter names, but while looking at the word.

As the learner progresses through the structure, continue to use the Stimulus Response Routine. You need to follow the routines in order to check that the learner has full recognition and recall of each phonogram. Do not be tempted to leave out the cards that the learner 'knows'. Regular exercise of the link between sound and symbol lead to automaticity and the speed that is important in reading everyday texts. Word lists and sentences will be given at every stage to give practice in decoding and encoding. The ideas, games and worksheets given at the various stages of the structure can be adapted and extended according to individual need.

a A	**Reading Card**

face

apple /ă/

bath /ah/

reverse

Spelling Card

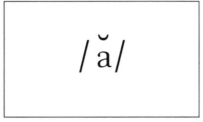

/ă/

face

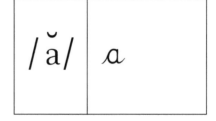

/ă/ a

reverse

Capital

printed
lower case

print to
writing

written
lower case

1. Introduce the reading and spelling cards, using full Stimulus Response Routine; practise the reading and spelling packs.
2. Look in texts to distinguish the different forms of the letter 'a'.
3. Learners with northern dialects may not need the 'bath /ah/' sound on the card.
4. At this stage, most learners will only have the short vowel sound.

Remember to identify this as a vowel card (either by the line, or by a different colour).

Ideas for alphabet work

1. Take out the 'A' and 'I'. Ask the learner to pick up the appropriate vowel as you say the following words: pan, pin, tap, hat, sit, sat, stand, spin.
2. Take out of the arc the letters i, t, p, n, s, a. See how many words the learner can make that end in 'ip' and 'ap'. Use them for handwriting practice.

Word lists at at 'a'				
regular words	irregular words	with blends	with suffixes	with prefixes
an	Ann	span	add suffix 's'	assist
pan	past*	spat	to nouns to	instant
tan	a	snap	make plural,	
at		ant	to verbs for	
pat		pant	third person	
sat		apt	singular	
as				

*Not irregular for some regional accents, or if the /ah/ sound has been added to the 'a' card.

By now there are enough letters to introduce simple sentences for reading. Some of the easier ones will also be suitable for writing. These sentences use only sound/letter links that have been introduced, and the learner can feel confident that they have the knowledge and decoding skills to make the task worthwhile. Whole language reading and writing will draw attention to these links, and the pupil will be encouraged to look out for familiar onsets and rimes, and to decode short words and the first syllables of longer words.

Writing sentences from dictation is a good way of introducing punctuation. Remind the pupil that each sentence will start with a capital letter, and end with a full stop. According to the meaning of the sentence, you can introduce question marks, exclamation marks and commas. In shared, guided and individual reading sessions, apply this growing knowledge of punctuation to a variety of texts, and show how they affect oral expression.

Sentence dictation procedure

Teacher: Keep the sentences short and simple, using only words that contain sounds that have been studied, or irregular words that have been taught. Read the sentence clearly.

Pupil: Listen to the sentence. Repeat then write the sentence.
Listen to the teacher read the sentence again, and proofread your own work. Underline mistakes, and write the correction over the error.

Example worksheet at 'a': Read and illustrate each sentence. Then use the sentence for dictation.

1. Pat has a pan.	
2. Stan is sad.	
3. An ant is in a tin.	

Example worksheet at 'a': Contractions. In speech we often run words together. 'is not' becomes 'isn't', 'it is' becomes 'it's'. The apostrophe signifies a missed letter or letters. Look at the picture, and answer the question. 'It's a . . .' or 'It isn't a . . .'

1. Is it a pan?		
2. Is it a tin?		
3. Is it a tap?		
4. Is it an ant?		

d D

Reading Card

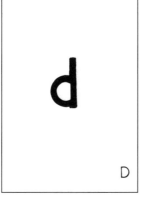

d

D

dot /d/

•

face   reverse

Spelling Card

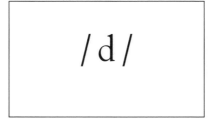   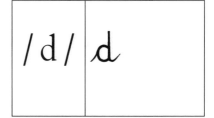

/ d /   / d / d

face   reverse

Capital   printed   print to   written
               lower case   writing   lower case

1. Introduce the reading and spelling cards, using full Stimulus Response Routine; practise the reading and spelling packs.
2. Look in texts to distinguish the different forms of the letter 'd'.
3. Unless the learner mentions it, don't draw the learner's attention to b/d confusion.

Word lists at at 'd'				
regular words	irregular words	with blends	with suffixes	with prefixes
pad	said	and	add suffix 's'	distant
Dad	add	sand		
sad	adapt	stand		
did	didn't			
Sid				
dip				
din				
Compound word: sandpit				

Learning to spell irregular words

The word 'said' is irregular – that is, it cannot be spelled through sound blending. It is also a high frequency function word, and well worth learning for reading and writing. (See page 93 for an account of the simultaneous oral spelling method of learning irregular words. See page 69 for an account of irregular word packs for reading.)

Don't attempt to teach a word for spelling until all its letters have been comfortably mastered for writing.

Speech marks

1. Surround the words actually spoken by inverted commas.
2. Start the speech with a capital letter.
3. Before the final speech marks, use a comma, exclamation mark, or question mark.
4. Look out for speech marks in stories. Use these sentences for reading and writing.

"It is an ant", said Stan.

"Is it in a tin?" said Dad.

"It is in a sandpit", said Sid.

"Ann spits at Pat!" said Nan.

Example worksheet at 'd': How many words can you make? Fill in the matrix, matching the onsets and rimes to make real words.

	ad	and	ip	in
t				
p				
s				
d				

Reading Card

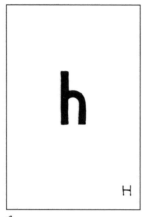

hat /h/

face   reverse

Spelling Card

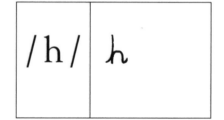

/ h /

/ h /   h

face   reverse

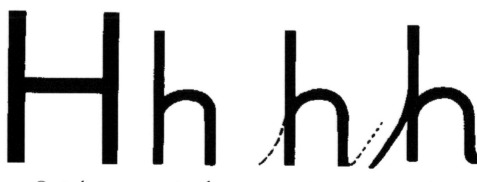

Capital   printed   print to   written
           lower case   writing   lower case

1. Introduce the reading and spelling cards, using full Stimulus Response Routine; practise the reading and spelling packs.
2. Look in texts to distinguish the different forms of the letter 'h'. Compare it with the letter 'n'.
3. Consonant digraphs 'th', 'sh' and 'ch' will be introduced later; however, once the 'h' has been mastered for writing, consonant digraphs can be presented in irregular words.

Word lists at at 'h'				
regular words	irregular words	with blends	with suffixes	with prefixes
had	this	hint	add suffix 's'	
has	that	hand		
hat	hadn't			
his				
hit				
hid				
hip				

Sentences at 'h'
Notice that these sentences include the apostrophe used to indicate the possessive.

1. Pat hid Stan's hat.

2. Ann sits in Pat's sandpit

3. Pip has sand in his hand.

e E

Reading Card

face

egg /ĕ/

reverse

Spelling Card

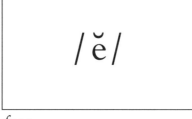

face

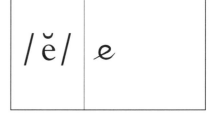

reverse

Capital   printed
lower case

print to
writing

written
lower case

1. This is the only letter that approaches on the diagonal, and cuts through the circle. Look at the mouth in a little mirror, and see how the jaw drops slightly in moving from $/ĭ/$, to $/ĕ/$, to $/ă/$.

2. Older learners could be introduced to the the long $/ē/$ sound (reading only). You can add the long vowel sounds to the existing 'a' and 'i' cards. The responses will be egg, $/ĕ/$, equals $/ē/$; igloo $/ĭ/$, iron $/ī/$; apple $/ă/$, acorn $/ā/$. (See page 208)

3. First make sure that the learner has awareness of syllables in words, and can tap them out and count them. Now you can introduce open and closed syllables. A syllable 'closed' by a consonant has the short vowel sound. A syllable without a consonant at the end is open, and the vowel has the long sound. The long sound is the same as the name of the letter (examples: I, he, she).

Word lists at at 'e'				
regular words	irregular words	with blends	vc/cv words	with affixes
ten	he	end	dentist	add suffix 's'
pen	the	send	pendant	depend
den	she	tend	tennis	dependent
hen	then	spend	pennant	attend
net		sent		independent
set		dent		attendant
pet		spent		
Ted		nest		
		pest		
		test		

Sentences at 'e'

1. Dan has a pet hen.

2. The hen sits in a nest.

3. Ted is in the den.

4. This is the end.

Example worksheet at 'e': Onset and rime. Words with the same ending usually rhyme. Put a dot under the vowel. Put a ring round the vowel and the consonant/s that come after. Write each word in the correct column.

spin   send   pin   spend   sand

end   tin   hand   and

'in' endings	'end' endings	'and' endings

Example worksheet at 'e': Word endings. Look at each word. Mark the first vowel with a 'v'. Mark what comes after ('v' for vowel, 'c' for consonant). Then write each word in the correct column.

spin tent hen spend pan past

in test end and ten sad

'vc' ending	'vcc' ending

Reading Card

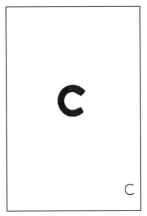

face

cat /k/

reverse

Spelling Card

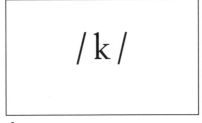

face

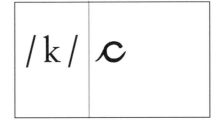

reverse

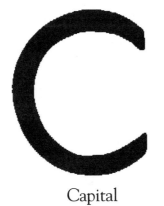

Capital

printed
lower case
print to
writing
written
lower case

1. /k/ is an unvoiced sound, made at the back of the throat. 'cat' starts with the same sound as 'kettle' and 'chemist', so we need the same sound picture for them all – /k/ is the least equivocal.
2. In alphabet work, children will often reach for the letter 's' instead of 'c'. Make sure the learner has practice in responding with the correct names during alphabet activities (see Chapter 5, pages 50–59).
3. Unless the learner mentions it, leave till later work on 'c' saying /s/.
4. Notice the 'ic' ending at the end of multisyllabic words.

Word lists at at 'c'				
regular words	irregular words	with blends	vc/cv words	with affixes
can	can't	scan	tactic	add suffix 's'
cap		scant	picnic	inspect
cat		act	antic	intact
		tact	attic	addict
		pact	hectic	
		cast	distinct	
			intact	
			inspect	
			addict	

Sentences at 'c'
1. Sid's cap is in the sand.
2. 'I can't stand it,' said Dad.
3. The cat spits at the hen.
4. Can I pat the cat?

kK

Reading Card

face

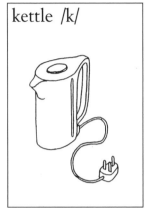

kettle /k/

reverse

Spelling Card

/k/

face

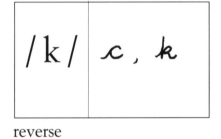

/k/ c , k

reverse

Kkkk

| Capital | printed lower case | print to writing | written lower case |

1. Introduce the reading and spelling cards. Now we have a 'spelling choice' – two ways of spelling the /k/ sound. As time goes on, we will cover the rules and generalities governing the choice. Explain that from now on we will use the name, 'k' rather than the immature sobriquet 'kicking k'. The response to the Spelling Card will now be /k/ 'c', /k/ 'k'.

2. Children often mention that the letter looks like a capital 'r'. Show how to avoid confusion by making sure that only the ascender goes above the writing line.

3. You might want to add 'sk' to the separate blend pack.

Word lists at at 'k'			
regular words	irregular words	with blends		vc/cv words
kid	kind	skid	sink	kidnap
kin	kitchen	skin	pink	catkin
Ken	take	skip	stink	napkin
		kept	tans	
		ask	sank	
		task	spank	
		cask		
Add suffix 's'			

Example worksheet at 'k': Match the beginning and end of the sentences so that they make sense. Draw a line between the two parts. Read the whole sentence. Cover it up, see how much you can remember, and write it in your book. Then check your work before continuing.

Sid the cat	sinks in the sand.
Ted's pet ant	a pink hat.
Pat's tank	sits in the den.
Ann has	is in a tin.

Example worksheet at 'k': If the sound /k/ is followed by /ĭ/ or /ī/, choose 'k'. If it is followed by anything else, choose 'c'.

Example worksheet at 'k': Look at the word endings. Mark the first vowel, and any consonants that come after. Write the words in the correct box.

| ask | desk | kid | cat |
| skin | task | can | skip |

vc endings	vcc endings

Until readers have a fluent and automatic association between letter clusters and their sounds, it can be difficult for them to notice important chunks of words, and they may need a more mechanical method of dividing words into syllables. The next worksheet presents a method that works well, and can build up confidence in tackling a number of common words. Make sure first that the learner knows about vowels, consonants and syllables. Notice that most of the individual syllables are nonsense syllables and give useful practice in the development of word attack skills.

Example worksheet at 'k': Syllable division (two closed syllables). We are interested in the middle of the word, so that we can divide the word into two syllables. Put a 'v' over each vowel. Put a 'c' over the consonants between the two vowels. Say each syllable in turn. Read the whole word. Divide between the consonants.

^{v c | c v}
kid|nap   catkin   hidden

distant   sandpit   pendant

dentist   picnic   attic

intend   happen   insist

ck CK

Reading Card

K

face

duck /k/

reverse

Spelling Card

/ k /

face

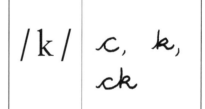

/ k / c, k, ck

reverse

Lower case for reading   Lower case for writing

Introduce the reading and spelling cards. Now we have another way of spelling the /k/ sound. 'ck' are used to spell the /k/ sound at the end of one syllable words. The response to the Spelling Card will now be /k/ 'c', /k/ 'k', /k/ 'ck'.

Word lists at at 'ck'				
regular words	irregular words	with blends	vc/cv words	with affixes
pack kick sack Dick tack neck pick peck tick deck sick heck Nick	trek attack	snack speck stack	ticket picket packet attack	add suffix 's'

Example worksheet at 'ck': Match the onsets and rimes to make real words.			
	ack	eck	ick
t			
p			
n			
s			
d			
h			
k			
st			
sp			
sn			

Example worksheet at 'ck': Think about the spelling choice for the sound /k/. Write the words in the appropriate box. (Teacher dictate: cat, kid, sack, can, deck, pick, kit, cap.)

/k/ = c	/k/ = k	/k/ = ck

Reinforce knowledge and understanding of this spelling choice by looking up words beginning with the /k/ sound in a dictionary. Choose high frequency words, and use a children's dictionary so that the words are not too hard to find. Try looking up /k/ words on an electronic spellchecker.

Reading Card

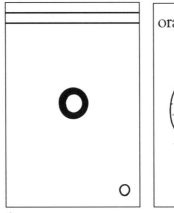

orange /ŏ/

face

reverse

Spelling Card

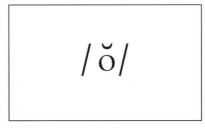

/ŏ/

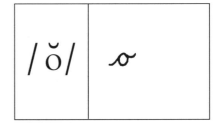

/ŏ/

face

reverse

Capital

printed
lower case

print to
writing

written
lower case

Introduce the reading and spelling cards. You might prefer to introduce only the short vowel sound at this stage. Only give the short vowel card for spelling. The letter can be tricky to write – it leaves from the top. Gently dip the leaving stroke down so that the next letter is approached in the same sort of inward curve as all the others.

Word lists at at 'o'					
regular words	irregular words	blends	vc/cv	affixes	'wild old words'*
cod nod	do	spot	hobnob	contend	most
dot pod	don't	snob		consist	post
hot top	doesn't	stock	see also	connect	host
not pop	done	stop	words	content	ghost
pot hop	one	cost	with	contact	
hod sock	once	pond	affixes	constant	
dock	son			continent	
hock	ton				
cock					

*These are words, mostly Anglo-Saxon in origin, that have a long vowel spelling and a short vowel sound. Others end in -ind, -ild, -olt, -old, -oll, -oth.

Sentences at 'o'
1. That pot is hot.
2. The lost sock is in the cot.
3. Stop! Don't hop on the ant!
4. I can contact Don.

Example worksheet at 'o': Making contractions. Write the two words without a gap. Cross out the 'o', and replace it with an apostrophe. Write the contraction.

does not	doesnot	doesn't
did not		
had not		
is not		
has not		
*do not		
*can not	(also take out an 'n')	

*Notice modified pronunciation of vowel sound.

Reading Card

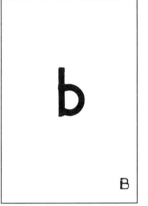

face   reverse

Spelling Card

   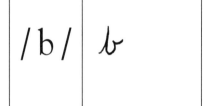

face   reverse

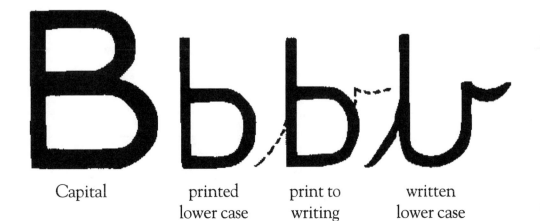

Capital   printed   print to   written
               lower case   writing   lower case

Introduce the reading and spelling cards. The cursive letter shape can be open or closed (𝒃 or 𝒃). Make sure the learner has established a firm link between sound and symbol before you introduce the issue of b/d confusion. Tackle it the next time confusion is demonstrated in reading or writing. Encourage the learner to take active responsibility for choosing a way of remembering that will work.

1. Write the word 'bed' on a card for the learner to keep for reference. Illustrate it.
2. Identify a word containing 'b' or 'd' which the learner always remembers (e.g. a name, or 'and'). Notice the starting position of the mouth. With /b/, the mouth starts in a stick shape. With /d/, the mouth starts in an open ring shape.

Word lists at at 'b'				
regular words	irregular words	with blends	vc/cv words	with affixes
bad tab	be	band	bandit	absent
bin cab	been	bend	bitten	
ban dab		bent	basket	
bid nib		best	Batman	
bat back		bank		
bib beck				
bit				
ban				
bet				
Ben				

Sentences at 'b'

1. Ben is in bed.

2. Is this the best bank?

3. The cat bit Dad's hand.

Example worksheet at 'b': Syllable division (two closed syllables). Put a 'v' over each vowel. Put a 'c' over the consonants between the two vowels. Say each syllable in turn. Read the whole word. Divide between the consonants.

(You can use some of these words for spelling. Teacher SAY the word. Learner REPEAT the word, then say each syllable separately. Spell each syllable as separate units before writing.)

bandit   Batman   basket

content   contact   hobnob

Long vowel syllable division pattern v/cv at 'b'

Before you introduce this pattern, you will need to add the long vowel sound onto the a, e, i and 'o' cards. Do this at a rate appropriate for the learner. At this stage, only introduce for reading.

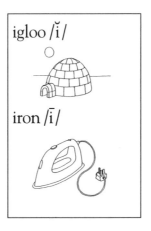

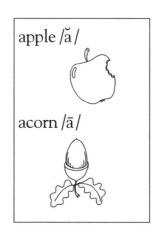

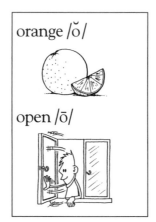

Example worksheet at 'b': Put a 'v' over each vowel. Put a 'c' over the consonant between the vowels. Divide after the first vowel. It will have the long sound.

$\overset{v}{b\bar{a}}\|\overset{cv}{sin}$	$\overset{v}{b\bar{a}}\|\overset{cv}{sis}$	$\overset{v}{p\bar{a}}\|\overset{cv}{tent}$
$\overset{v}{b\bar{a}}\|\overset{c\;v}{con}$	$\overset{v}{st\bar{a}}\|\overset{c\;v}{men}$	$\overset{v}{D\bar{a}}\|\overset{c\;v}{mon}$
$\overset{v}{t\bar{o}}\|\overset{c\;v}{ken}$	$\overset{v}{\bar{o}}\|\overset{c\;v}{pen}$	$\overset{v}{sp\bar{o}}\|\overset{c\;v}{ken}$

Reading Card

yoghurt /y/

Y

face   reverse

Spelling Card

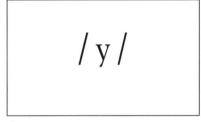

/ y /

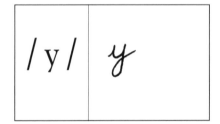

/ y /   *y*

face   reverse

Capital   printed   print to   written
               lower case   writing   lower case

Introduce the reading and spelling cards. The print form can be like a 'u' or a 'v' with a tail – we use the 'u' shape for the written form. The loop is necessary so that it can join on to the next letter. 'Y' is a consonant at the beginning of words and syllables.

Word lists at at 'y':	
regular words	irregular words
yes	they
yet	
yen	*my
yap	by
yam	say

*'my', 'by' and 'say' become regular when 'y' is introduced as a vowel, but are useful high frequency words and the learner might want to learn them quite quickly.

rR

Reading Card

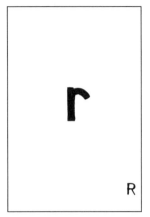

rat /r/

face   reverse

Spelling Card

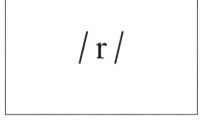

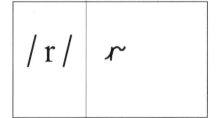

face   reverse

Capital   printed   print to   written
                 lower case   writing   lower case

Introduce the reading and spelling cards. This is the second letter that leaves from the top. Give practice in joining it to the vowels, and 't' and 'k'. Gently dip the leaving stroke down so that the next letter is approached in the same sort of inward curve as all the others.

You can add blend cards to the separate pack – 'tr', 'cr', 'pr', 'dr', 'br'.

Word lists at at 'r':					
regular words	irregular words	with blends		vc/cv words	with affixes (v/cv words)
ran	are	crab	brick	rabbit	prepack
rat	there	crib	brand	racket	pretend
rip	their	crack	print	bracket	repent
rid	trek	crop	prod	bracken	repack
rod		drab	prep	printed	
red		drip	prop	stranded	
rot		drop	prick		
rib		trip	sprint		
		trap	strict		
		trick	strap		
		track	strip		
		trend			

Sentences at 'r'
1. The rat ran in the pit.
2. The tap drips.
3. Ann has a red tin.
4. Ron can trap the crab in a crack.

Example worksheet at 'r': Put a 'v' over each vowel. Put a 'c' over the consonant between the vowels. Divide after the first vowel. It will have the long sound.

detest	detect	repent
depend	pretend	direct
noted	potent	coded

In these words, the 'de' and 're' are prefixes, and therefore unstressed. The long /ē/ sound is not really pure – it is pronounced a bit like an /ĭ/. But in practice it is very easy to modify from the unstressed sound to the stressed one, and a very useful clue for spelling.

Example worksheet at 'r': How many words can you make? Fill in the matrix, matching the onsets and rimes to make real words.

	ack	ick	ock	op
r				
tr				
pr				
dr				
cr				
br				

m M

Reading Card

m

M

face

man /m/

reverse

Spelling Card

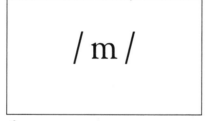

/ m /

face

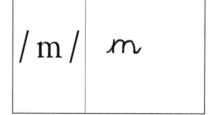

/ m /　　*m*

reverse

| Capital | printed lower case | print to writing | written lower case |

Introduce the reading and spelling cards. Say 'mmm' not 'mer'.
You can add 'sm' to the blend pack.

Word lists at 'm'				
regular words	irregular words	with blends	vc/cv words	v/cv words
man Pam	me	tram tramp	admit	omit
mat Sam	some	cram prim		demon
mad dam	someone	skim brim		item
met Kim	come	damp trim		stamen
map ram		camp smack		
men	*came	stamp		
dim	make	ramp		
hem		cramp		
him		scamp		
ham				

*Irregular until a–e is introduced.

Sentences at 'm'
1. The camp is damp.
2. The rats had the ham.
3. Some men came into the tent.
4. They hit the rats with sticks.

VC/V words

This syllable division pattern is not uncommon – there are about 40 common vc/v words (like 'planet', 'dragon'), and about the same number of vc/cv words (like 'magnet', 'rabbit'). The scales are tipped hugely by the words that have suffixes; when adding a suffix that starts with a vowel (like 'ing', 'ed' or 'er'), you double the final consonant of a word with a vc ending, and drop the e of a word with a vce ending. We end up with a spelling system where most vcv words have a long first vowel ('hoping') and most vccv words have a short first vowel ('hopping'). Thus vc/v words will be included in the column for irregular words. Don't try to give too much information at once; the information is here in case you need to answer questions from an older, observant learner. The stages will be gradually and logically covered by worksheets as the structure progresses.

Example worksheet at 'm': Some vcv words have a first short vowel. Put a 'v' over each vowel, a 'c' over the consonant between. Divide after the first consonant.		
p^văn^c|^vic	cabin	credit
atom	satin	habit

y Y
(vowel)

Reading Card

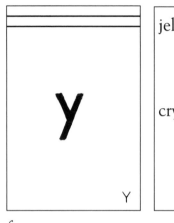

jelly /ĭ/

cry /ī/

face   reverse

Spelling Card

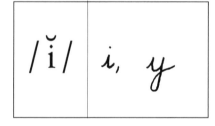

face   reverse

Introduce the reading and spelling cards. Use a vowel card. Explain that we hardly ever use the letter 'i' to say /ĭ/ at the end of a word – we 'borrow' the letter 'y', and use it as a vowel. There are a few exceptions: taxi, bikini, corgi, mini, and Italian pasta names such as spaghetti, ravioli. The Spelling Card response will now be: /ĭ/ 'i', /ĭ/ y.

The letter 'y' at the end of a word is sometimes a suffix. A suffix is an ending added to the end of a word which alters its grammatical use rather than the meaning. The suffix 'y' makes a noun into an adjective.

During alphabet work, ask the learner to make words like 'sandy', nasty' – first, secretly remove the letter 'i' and see what happens!

Word lists at 'y' (vowel)				
vc/cv words		v/cv words	with affixes	irregular
/ĭ/	/ī/	baby	risky	any
candy	my	tiny	trendy	many
handy	by	tidy	messy	pretty
brandy	cry		scanty	
sandy	try		skimpy	dye
penny	sky		tacky	rye
nappy	dry		handy	sty
Daddy	sty		rocky	
happy	pry			vc/v
nasty			deny	copy
pansy			retry	pity
berry				
Longer words: enemy, library				

Sentences at 'y' (vowel)
1. My hand is sandy.
2. Sit by me.
3. This pansy is so pretty.
4. Daddy is here, so try not to cry.

j J

Reading Card

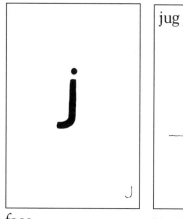

jug /j/

face   reverse

Spelling Card

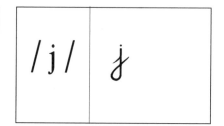

face   reverse

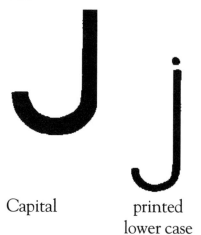

Capital

printed
lower case

print to
writing

written
lower case

Later you will be adding other spelling choices for the /j/ sound – leave space for them.

Suffixes and prefixes are often added to words which make sense alone. Here, prefixes are added to the base 'ject'. It derives from the Latin (past participle of *jacere*, to throw). Some older learners might find this a useful way to look at words.

Word lists at 'j'				
regular words	irregular words	with affixes	vc/cv words	v/cv
jab jam jet Jim Jack jot job	John	object reject subject inject project	jetty	Jason Jacob

Sentences at 'j'
1. Jim has a job.
2. John takes lots of jam.
3. The pet rat is sick so Jason can inject it.
4. The boss has rejected my project.

Reading Card

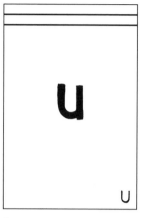

umbrella /ŭ/

uniform /ū/

face   reverse

Spelling Card

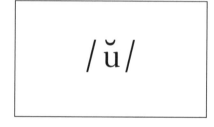

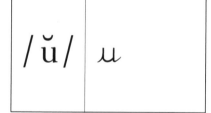

/ŭ/   /ŭ/   u

face   reverse

Capital   printed   print to   written
           lower case   writing   lower case

Word lists at 'u'					
regular	with blends	irregular	with affixes	vc/cv words	v/cv
but	just	us	submit	cactus	duty
cut	dust	plus	unrest	custom	jury
hut	must	bus	inhuman	mutton	stupid
jut	rust	four	unjust	button	cubic
nut	bust	pour	bumpy	possum	unit
cub	stuck	you	jumpy	puffin	union
hub	struck	your	mucky	muffin	crocus
rub	stun	January		rustic	music
dub	dump	out		summit	focus
bud	mumps			bonus	
mud	jump	*(oo)		human	
suck	bump	put		unit	
tuck	hump	push			
duck	stump	bush			
buck	pump				
muck	bunk				
bun	dunk				
nun	junk				
sun	hunk				
hum	bulk				
cup	sulk				
pup	hulk				

*Some Northern dialects rhyme 'put' and 'but'; there will be no need to put these words in the 'irregular' column.

Sentences at 'u'

1. Jim has lost his Cub cap.

2. Jack jumps in the mud. He is stuck.

3. This bun has nuts in it.

4. Put the junk in the skip.

Example worksheet at 'u': Look at the patterns of these word endings (rimes). Write them in the correct columns, then read them to your teacher.

put   dust   mud   jump   duck   cup   cut   stuck   just   nut

vc ending:	vcc ending:

Example worksheet at 'u': Look at the patterns of these two syllable words. Write them in the correct column. Mark where the syllables divide. Then read them to your teacher.

cactus   stupid   music   button   human   bonus   custom   submit

vc/cv	vc/v

Reading Card

G

face

gun /g/

reverse

Spelling Card

/ g /

face

/ g /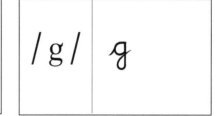

reverse

Capital

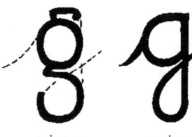

printed
lower case

print to
writing

written
lower case

Word lists at 'g'					
regular	with blends	irregular	with affixes	vc/cv words	v/cv
dig beg	stag	go	grassy	magnet	begin
big keg	drag	goes	groggy	maggot	grimy
rig hug	snag	gone	boggy	segment	pagan
pig mug	crag	gas			began
jig jug	drug	ghost			
gig bug	dregs	grit			
rag pug	grin				
bag dog	grub				
sag bog	grab				
tag cog	grid				
gag hog	gust				
hag jog	grand				
nag	grasp				
gun	gasp				
get	smog				
gut	smug				

Sentences at 'g'
1. Go and get a magnet. It can pick up the pins.
2. Empty the jug. It has bugs in it.
3. The gun is in the bog. We can not drag it out.
4. The big dog began to dig.

Example worksheet at 'g': How many words can you make? Fill in the matrix, matching the onsets and rimes to make real words.

	ig	ag	og	ug
r				
sn				
b				
dr				
d				
h				
j				
sm				
t				

ng NG

Reading Card

NG

face

ring /ng/

reverse

Spelling Card

/ ng /

face

/ ng / *ng*

reverse

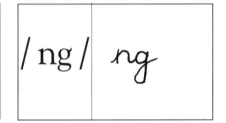

Word lists at 'ng'			
regular	with blends	irregular	with affixes
bang	sting	wrong	+ing
sang	bring	penguin	(e.g. singing)
hang	spring		bringing
gang	strong	ding-dong	+est
rang	prong	ping-pong	(e.g. strongest)
king	stung		
sing	strung		
ring			
gong			
song			
pong			
dung			
bung			
hung			
rung			

Sentences at 'ng'
1. "Ben, you can't sing," said Jason
2. "Yes, I can," said Ben.
3. "No," said Jason, "but you can bang the drum."
Draw attention to the punctuation. Use ordinary reading books or magazines to consolidate work on speech marks.

Example worksheet at 'ng': How many words can you make? Fill in the matrix, matching the onsets and rimes to make real words.

	ing	ang	ong	ung
r				
h				
s				
st				
b				

Example worksheet at 'ng': The suffix 'ing' forms present participles. It begins with a vowel. If your base word has a short vowel but ends in two consonants, JUST ADD the 'ing'.
Add 'ing'. Write the whole word. Use it in a sentence.

1. hand + ing   *handing*

Dad is handing me the bag.

2. rest + ing

3. stick + ing

4. grunt + ing

nk NK

Reading Card

nk

NK

face

tank /nk/

reverse

Spelling Card

/ nk /

face

/nk/ nk

reverse

Word lists at 'nk'		
regular	with blends	with affixes
bank ink	crank	cranky
tank kink	drank	kinky
sank mink	prank	
rank pink	stank	+ing (e.g. banking,
dank rink	brink	sinking)
bunk sink	stink	
punk honk	drunk	
sunk		
dunk		

Sentences at 'nk'

1. Pam has a pink hat.

2. Put the pots in the sink.

3. The tank is sinking in the sand.

f F

Reading Card

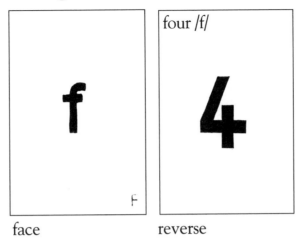

four /f/

face

reverse

Spelling Card

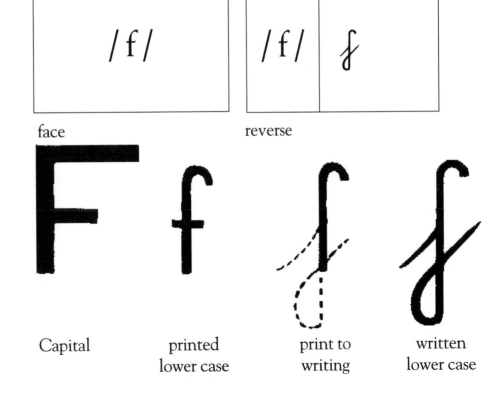

/ f /

face

/ f / ƒ

reverse

F   f   ƒ   ƒ

Capital   printed lower case   print to writing   written lower case

Word lists at 'f'				
regular	with blends		irregular	with affixes	vc/cv words
fit	fast	gift	friend	soften	often
fun	fist	rift	if	fasten	fifty
fin	frost	drift	of	defect	
fan	from	craft	for	prefect	
fat	font	croft	four	perfect	
	fond	raft		fitness	
	soft	daft			
	sift				
	deft				

Sentences at 'f'

1. Fred has a lot of fun.

2. Pam is his best friend.

3. They are fit, and can run fast.

4. The bed is big and soft.

Spelling rule at 'f'

At the end of a one syllable word with a short vowel, the sound /f/ is spelled 'ff'.

If you want, you can add the double 'f' to the Spelling Card, so that the response is:

/f/ 'f', /f/ 'ff'.

There aren't many common words; the rule only becomes interesting because of a group of letters that work in this way ('l', 'f' and 's'. 'k' doesn't double, but becomes 'ck').

off   cliff   sniff   stuff   puff

1 L

Reading Card

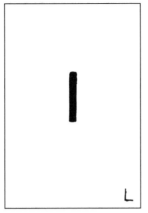

log /l/

face   reverse

Spelling Card

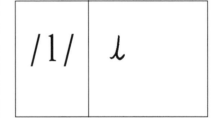

face   reverse

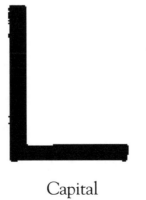

Capital   printed
lower case

print to
writing

written
lower case

Word lists at 'l'

regular	with blends			irregular	'wild old' words	longer words
lip	last	blank	plan	look	wild	vc/cv
lid	list	blink	plant		mild	splendid
let	lost	blend	plug	talk	child	hamlet
lad	land	black	plot	stalk		atlas
lot	lend	block	plum	chalk	bolt	blanket
	lent	clap	slam	island	colt	oblong
	lift	clip	slim	pal	jolt	mammal
	help	clock	slip	nil		dismal
	yelp	clasp	slick	palm	cold	
	elf	glad	slop	calm	bold	v/cv
	self	gland	slab	psalm	told	latent
	stilt	glint	sling		old	silent
	spilt	flip	slung	mild	scold	local
	gulp	flap	slant	child	hold	
	helm	flop	split	bold	gold	vc/v
	lilt	fling		cold	sold	planet
	silt			old		relic
	left			gold		salad
	milk			sold		limit
	silk			scold		camel
	felt			fold		Latin
	belt			told		label

Note that 'al' and 'el' endings are usually unstressed syllables, and their vowel sound is indeterminate. Encourage the learner to store the vowel as an accented syllable –
'loCAL', 'aniMAL', 'hospiTAL', 'camEL', 'labEL', so that it can be recalled for spelling.

Sentences at 'l'

1. Len cut his lip.

2. Here is a mug of milk. Drink it.

3. I left a lot of pens in my desk.

4. This is a splendid atlas.

The suffix 'ful' combines with nouns. It refers to amounts (cupful, armful) or qualities (joyful, painful). Unlike the word 'full', it has only one 'l'. It begins with a consonant, so you can JUST ADD it to all sorts of word endings.

Example worksheet at 'l': Add 'ful'. Write the whole word. Use it in a sentence.

1. play + ful   *playful*

The puppy is playful.

2. help + ful

3. sack + ful

4. cup + ful

The suffix 'ly' combined with adjectives to form verbs. It starts with a consonant, so JUST ADD it to base words.

Example worksheet at 'l': Add 'ly'. Write the whole word. Use it in a sentence.

1. rapid + ly   *rapidly*

They ran rapidly to get help.

2. bad + ly

3. final + ly

4. sad + ly

Spelling rule

At the end of a one syllable word with a short vowel, the sound /l/ is spelled 'll'.

If you want, you can add the double 'l' to the Spelling Card, so that the response is:

/l/ 'l', /l/ 'll'. Notice the oddities of pronunciation of '-all' and '-oll'

-all	-ell	-ill		-oll	-ull
all	bell	ill	frill	doll	bull
ball	dell	bill	grill	loll	cull
call	fell	dill	sill	moll	scull
fall	hell	fill	till		dull
hall	smell	gill	still	poll	full
small	spell	hill		roll	gull
mall	sell	kill		droll	hull
pall	tell	mill		scroll	skull
tall		pill		troll	lull
stall		spill		stroll	mull
		drill		toll	pull

> **Spelling rule**
> At the end of a one syllable word with a short vowel, the sound /s/ is spelled 'ss'. If you want, you can add the double 's' to the Spelling Card, so that the response is: /s/ 's', /s/ 'ss'. Notice pronunciation of '-ass'
>
> | -ass | -ess | -iss | -oss | -uss |
> |------|------|------|------|------|
> | pass | mess | miss | loss | fuss |
> | lass | Bess | kiss | toss | |
> | mass | less | hiss | boss | (bus thus) |
> | grass | press | bliss | moss | |
> | class | dress | | floss | |
> | glass | cress | (this) | | |
> | brass | stress | | | |
> | | bless | | | |
> | (gas) | | | | |

Now you have the 'floss' rule: at the end of a one syllable word, after one short vowel, double 'l', 'f' and 's'.

Syllable division – v/cv or vc/v

Two-syllable words follow strong patterns. These patterns are reinforced by the doubling of the final consonant when adding vowel suffixes to vc words (e.g. stopping, clapping).

- first vowel short sound: vc/cv
- first vowel long sound: v/cv

There are quite a number of common words that don't obey this rule – the pattern is vcv, but the first vowel is short. The learner needs to make a note of them as they come up in reading or writing.

Example worksheet at 'l': These two-syllable words have been printed twice. You have to decide how to pronounce the first vowel. Mark the vcv pattern, then decide which way it divides: V/CV (long vowel sound) or VC/V (short vowel sound). Tick the correct one, and read to your teacher.

v c |v plăn|et	limit	mason
v|c v plā|net	limit	mason
atom	robin	comic
atom	robin	comic
silent	Simon	Latin
silent	Simon	Latin

Reading Card

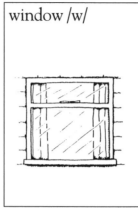

window /w/

face

reverse

Spelling Card

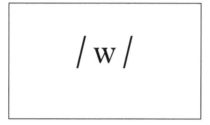

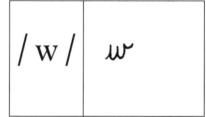

/ w /

/ w /

face

reverse

| Capital | printed lower case | print to writing | written lower case |

Some teachers and learners prefer to keep the points at the base of the 'w'.

Notice that 'wa' is usually pronounced /wŏ/. You can add 'wasp /ŏ/' to the 'a' card, or just treat it as a spelling rule.

Word lists at 'w'					
regular	with blends		irregular	vc/cv	wa = /wo/
wet	went	twist	two	witness	was
win	west	twig	walk	cobweb	want
web	wept	twin	woman		wasp
wed	wick	swing	women		wand
wig	wind	swill	water		swan
wag	wink	swell	were		swat
will	wing	swim	which		swap
well	weld	swam	who		
		swung	where		
		swift	what		
			when		
			why		

Sentences at 'w'
1. The man has a wig.
2. The twins went for a swim in the pond.
3. Wendy will win the cup. She can run the fastest.
4. The women can walk in the west wing.

Example worksheet at 'w': If you add a suffix that starts with a vowel, look at the rime of the base word. If it has one short vowel and one consonant DOUBLE THE FINAL CONSONANT.

run + ing *running*	stop + ing	fit + est	swim + ing
win + ing	put + ing	fun + y	wit + y

Now choose four of those words and put them into sentences.

Reading Card

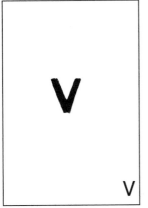

V

van /v/

face   reverse

Spelling Card

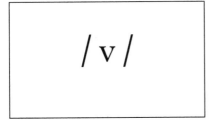

/ v /

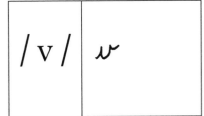

/ v /   *v*

face   reverse

Capital   printed   print to   written
               lower case   writing   lower case

Some teachers and learners prefer to keep the points at the base of the 'v'.

Notice the spelling rule: English words do not end in the letter 'v' Only one English word has 'vv': navvy.

Word lists at 'v'					
regular	with blend	irregular	vc/v	v/cv	vc/cv
vet	vest	have	oven	oval	invest
van	vent	give	seven	even	invent
vim		love	level	gravy	convent
		glove	devil	navy	velvet
		live	gravel	evil	victim
		dove	pivot	Venus	envy
		move	venom	vocal	vessel
			visit	rival	Vulcan
			Devon	raven	
			valid	David	+ing, ed
				naval	
				navel	
				vital	

Sentences at 'v'
1. The vet will give the cat a pill.
2. I love my Dad.
3. My Mum has invented a fantastic thing.

qu QU

Reading Card

question /kw/

face　　　　　　reverse

Spelling Card

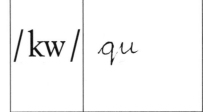

face　　　　　　reverse

Capital　　printed　　print to　　written
　　　　lower case　　writing　　lower case

Take care to establish that the learner can say the letter names correctly. In alphabet work, give lots of practice with sequential memory cards, presenting the letter names 'q' and 'u' at whatever level the learner is working. (e.g. Q T Z; M U X; or N Q S U; M Q T Y).

Notice that the sound /kw/ affects following vowels just like the letter 'w' does, so that 'qua' is /kwŏ/, 'squa' is /skwŏ/.

Word lists at 'qu'					
regular	with blend	vc/cv	v/cv	+ affixes	qua=/kwo/
quip	squid	squirrel	request	inquest	squash
quid	quest	quintet	equip	conquest	quad
quack	quilt		equal	equipment	squad
quick	squint			quickly	quadratic
quit			v/v	quacking	quantum
			quiet	quietly	

Sentences at 'qu'
1. The ducks are quacking on the pond.
2. Be quick, the bus is here.
3. There will have to be an inquest.
4. Here is a request for equipment.

Reading Card

face   reverse

Spelling Card

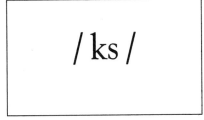 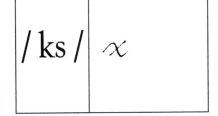

face   reverse

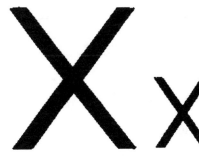  

Capital   printed lower case   print to writing   written lower case

The sound is hard to isolate and say – try saying /k/, then /s/, then running them together.

Explain that sometimes it can have a voiced sound, /gs/, as in 'exam'.

Spelling rules:
1. /ks/ is a sibilant (a hissing sound). Words ending in sibilants add 'es' instead of 's'. To make words ending in 'x' plural, add 'es' (boxes, taxes). To make the 3rd person singular of verbs ending in 'x', add 'es' (fixes, mixes).
2. When adding a vowel suffix, do not double (boxing, mixing, sexy).

Word lists at 'x'				
regular	blends	vc/cv	+ affixes	'x' = /gs/
fax box	flax	suffix	expand	exam
tax fox	flex	index	express	exact
wax pox	flux	expel	extend	exit
lax ox	crux	extinct	appendix	
pax cox	text	sextant		
six	jinx		(+ing, ed)	
mix	minx			
fix	next			

Sentences at 'x'
1. Ask Mum to fix the flex.
2. I expect him back at six.
3. If you stop mixing, it will go all lumpy.
4. You will find it in the index.

Example worksheet at 'x': Match a prefix with a Latin root. Write real words in a box.

	ex_ (out)	pro_ (forward)	re_ (back)
ject (throw)			
tract (pull)			
tend (stretch)			
pel (push)			
duct (lead)			

Do the 'translations' make any sense? How does 'project' link with 'throw forward'? How does 'expel' link with 'push out'? Discuss all the words you make.

zZ

Reading Card

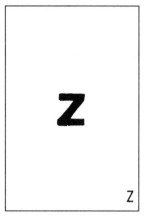

z

zebra /z/

face   reverse

Spelling Card

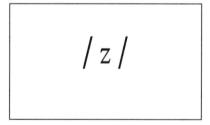

/z/

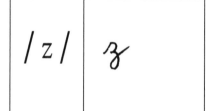

/z/

face   reverse

Capital   printed   print to   written
                 lower case   writing   lower case

The letter 'z' is used in very few high frequency words. You can almost treat each word as a 'one off', and deal with each one as it comes up in texts.

Many children are more familiar with its American *Sesame Street* name, 'zee'.

This is a good time to refer back to the voiced sound of the letter 's' (as in 'his', 'birds', etc.). Add the letter 's' to the Spelling Card.

Notice that at the end of a one syllable word, after one short vowel, use 'zz'.

Now that all the alphabet is covered for writing, alphabet work can take the form of writing out the whole alphabet. Homework can be copy-writing – make an illustrated book of favourite poems, or produce second drafts of free writing.

Word lists at 'z'			
regular	blends	vc/cv	v/cv
zip	zinc	zigzag	lazy
Zen	zest	zebra	hazy
buzz		frenzy	crazy
fizz		dizzy	topaz
jazz			zero
fuzz			Zulu

Sentences at 'z'
1. Help me, my zip is stuck!
2. I don't like fizzy drinks.
3. Listen to that buzzing. What is it?
4. I am not lazy, I am just resting a bit.

th TH

Reading Card

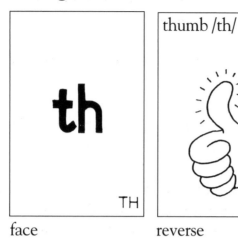

face   reverse

Spelling Card

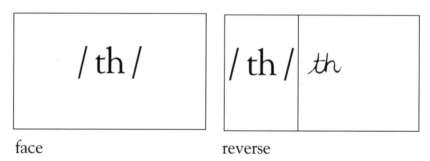

face   reverse

'th' is a consonant digraph – one sound, two letters.

    It has a voiced sound (this, that, breathe) and an unvoiced sound (thin, thick, thumb). Learners don't seem to find this much of a problem – a small oral modification is all that is required. A bigger hurdle is confusion with /f/ and /v/ – notice that the tongue parts the teeth when saying /th/, and the top teeth touch the bottom lip for /f/ and /v/. Use a mirror.

    Now that all the letters have been introduced for writing, guidance for the handwritten form is omitted. It is still very important for the learner to have a full multisensory introduction to the sound-symbol link, and to follow the handwriting routine – trace, copy, write from memory, write with eyes shut, saying sound and letter names.

Word lists at 'th'			
regular	with blends	irregular	compound words
this bath	thing thrust	their	blacksmith
then cloth	think width	there	withstand
with thick	fifth thrill	thus	withheld
the path	cloth thump	thumb	locksmith
them thin	froth length	both	themselves
that thud	throb strength	sloth	
than moth	plinth		
	thrift		

Sentences at 'th'
1. I think I will have a hot bath.
2. The man fell with a thud.
3. What did you do then?
4. There is the path!

Example worksheet at 'th': Give the strip of boxes, and five counters, to the learner. The teacher will say each word in turn. The
learner will listen to each word, repeat it slowly, stretching out the
sounds, and put a counter into a box for each sound. Next, look at
the word. Notice that the /th/ sound has two letters for one sound

th in (3) th is (3) th en (3) ba th (3) th rob (4) th rust (5) ten th (4)

sh SH

Reading Card

SH

face

sheep /sh/

reverse

Spelling Card

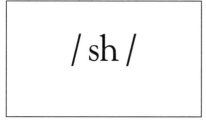

face

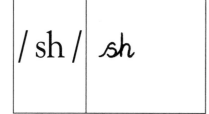

reverse

'sh' is a consonant digraph – one sound, two letters.
Present the Spelling Card carefully, with a full multisensory introduction to the handwritten form.

Word lists at 'sh'			
regular		with blends	irregular	with suffixes

regular		with blends	irregular	with suffixes
ash	shin	crash	wash	-ship
bash	shed	brash	sure	(e.g.kinship,
cash	ship	flash	surely	friendship)
dash	shop	slash	sugar	
gash	shack	splash	should	-ish
mash	shock	fresh		(e.g. selfish,
gush	fish	flesh		snobbish)
rush	dish	flush		
mush	wish	blush		
hush	shy	shrill		
		shrink		

The word 'should', like 'could' and 'would', is a difficult one to learn. Try the usual Simultaneous Oral Spelling method first; if it fails, a mnemonic might help. Try 'O! U Lucky Duck' as a mnemonic for the 'ould' ending.

Sentences at 'sh'
1. This fish is not fresh.
2. Rush to the shop, it shuts at ten.
3. There was a bad crash just by the bank.
4. Shall I mop up the splashes?

Children often mix up 'sh' and 'st' and 's' – usually, it's a problem rooted in poor auditory discrimination

Example worksheet at 'sh': First, read the word list. Notice the initial consonant sound: 'sh' makes one sound; 's' makes one sound; 'st' makes two sounds. Give the strip of boxes, and five counters, to the learner. The teacher will say each word in turn. The learner will listen to each word, repeat it slowly, stretching out the sounds, and put a counter into a box for each sound. Next, look again at the word.

step shop set stick shelf sock shell stink

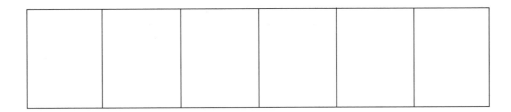

ch CH

Reading Card

ch

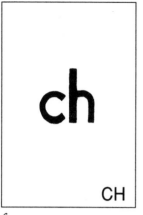

CH

face

cherry /ch/

reverse

tch

TCH

face

match /ch/

reverse

Spelling Card

/ ch /

face

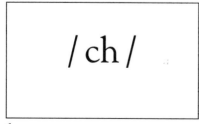

/ch/   ch tch

reverse

'ch' is a consonant digraph – one sound, two letters. 'tch' is a consonant trigraph – one sound, three letters.

Spelling choice: at the end of a word, after one short vowel, use 'tch'.

Word lists at 'ch'				
regular			irregular	longer words
chin	catch	notch	watch	kitchen
chat	batch	scotch	much	hatchet
chap	hatch	blotch	such	ratchet
chip	match	botch	rich	ketchup
chill	latch	crutch	which	
chimp	snatch	butch	sandwich	(also with suffixes,
check	scratch	hutch	ostrich	e.g. 'itching',
chest	itch			'chesty', 'chilly')
chick	stitch			
lunch	bitch			
munch	hitch			
crunch	ditch			
hunch	pitch			
	witch			

Sentences at 'ch'
1. Sit on the bench with me.
2. Stan will chop the logs for the fire.
3. Let's have fish and chips for lunch.
4. The witch has a tall black hat.

Example worksheet at 'ch': If your base word has a vcc or vccc ending, JUST ADD a vowel suffix. If your word has a vc ending DOUBLE the final consonant.

shop + ing	chop + ing	shut+ ing	rest + ed
shopping			
chill +y	crunch + y	thin + est	thud + ed

Notice that the suffix 'ed' behaves like the other suffixes, and obeys the same rules. It is special because it can be pronounced in three ways, even in quite common high frequency usages. Sometimes it makes another syllable, but not always.

Spelling Card

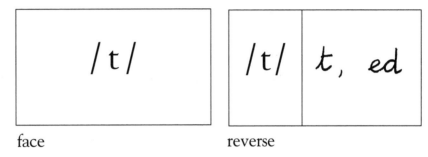

face   reverse

Spelling Card

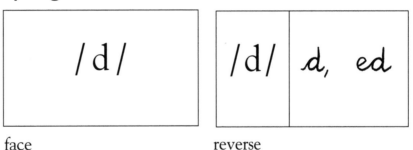

face   reverse

Look back at your spelling cards for the sounds /d/ and /t/. When the letters 'ed' are being used as a suffix, they do not always have the simple /ed/ sound (as in 'red' or 'bed'). Add these alternative sounds to your spelling pack.

Example worksheet at 'ed': Look at the words in the box; they all end in the suffix 'ed'. Say each word aloud. Think carefully about the 'ed' ending. How do you pronounce it? Is it /ed/, /d/ or /t/?

banged   kicked   rested   chopped   filled   messed
handed   mended   pushed   killed   fitted   pulled

'ed' = /d/	'ed' = /t/	'ed' = /ed/
banged	*kicked*	*rested*

Reading Card

hook /ŏŏ/

spoon /ōō/

face   reverse

Spelling Card

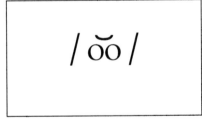

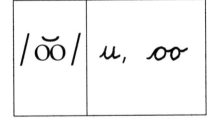

face   reverse

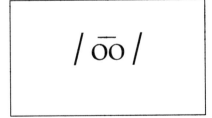

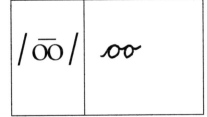

face   reverse

Add the letter 'u' to the Spelling Cards for the short vowel sound (as in 'pull', 'push').

Double 'o' can be quite difficult to write – give lots of multisensory practice – trace, copy, write from memory, write with eyes shut. For children with special difficulties, use big arm movements and various media.

Word lists at 'oo'					
short sound /o͝o/		long sound /o͞o/		irregular words	longer words
cook	crook	room	broom	loose	balloon
book	brook	boon	droop	moose	tattoo
took	stood	coot	drool	noose	pontoon
look	shook	coop	gloom	school	monsoon
nook		cool	scoop	floor	festoon
rook		doom	stool	door	lampoon
hood		food	stoop	poor	dragoon
wood		fool	spoon	to	cocoon
foot		goon	roost	two	baboon
good		hoop	troop		maroon
soot		loop	spook		racoon
		loom			lagoon
		moon			platoon
		noon			saloon
		pool			shampoo
		root			bathroom
		soon			
		toot			(also add
		tool			suffixes)
		too			

Sentences at 'oo'

1. This is a good cook book.

2. This room looks gloomy when the door is shut.

3. There will be a full moon, so we can walk in the woods.

4. We must get some more shampoo. There is none in the bathroom.

Example worksheet at 'oo': The letters 'oo' can be pronounced with a short sound ('hook') or a long sound ('spoon'). Look at the words in the box. Write each one in the correct column. This may vary according to your dialect.

soon moon look crook hoot foot wood food shoot shook

short /ŏŏ/ (hook)	long /ōō/ (spoon)

ar AR

Reading Card

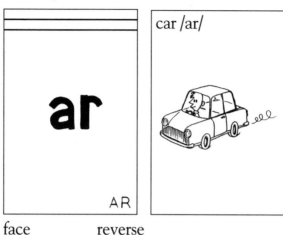

face　　　　　　reverse

Spelling Card

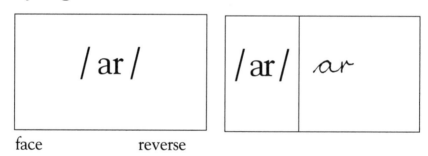

face　　　　　　　reverse

'ar' is a vowel-r combination. It is accented in one syllable words. Children often confuse the sound /ar/ with the letter name 'r'. Pay careful attention to writing – 'ar' and 'or' are easy to confuse in auditory discrimination, and impossible to distinguish unless the vowels are written correctly and carefully. Stress the need to push the downstroke of the 'a' down to the base line.

Word lists at 'ar'

regular		irregular	longer words
art	card	are	carpet
ark	farm	arc	garden
arm	hard	war	garnish
bar	harm	warpath	spartan
car	harsh	ward	carport
far	marsh	warp	bombard
tar	scarf	swarm	darling
jar	sharp	warden	garland
star	smart	bazaar	garment
bark	snarl	armada	harvest
darn	spark	guitar	embargo
dark	start		argument
dart	starve		armadillo
mark	garb		artifact
part	scar		(also + suffixes – e.g.
park	spar		harden, partly,
lark	carp		starting)
March	hart		

Sentences at 'ar'

1. I can't start the car.

2. The room was dark and gloomy.

3. That scarf looks very smart.

4. I think I am starting a cold.

Example worksheet at 'ar': Match a base word and a suffix to real words. Write the words in the box.

	-ing	-ly	-ness	-ful	-ed
dark					
harm					
harsh					
start					

Now choose one word with a suffix from each column, and use it in a sentence.

er ER

Reading Card

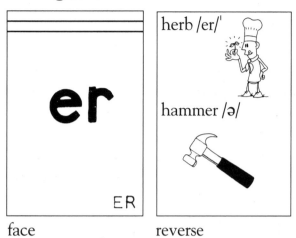

face   reverse

Spelling Card

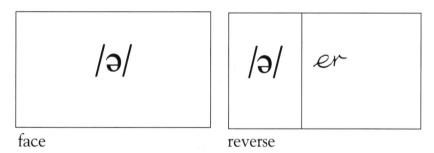

face   reverse

'er' is a vowel-r combination. It is stressed in one syllable words. It is most often found in its unstressed form, at the end of two syllable words. The suffix 'er' is an intensive (e.g. hard – harder) or an agent (e.g. teach – teacher).

Word lists at 'er'				
vc/cv		v/cv	irregular	longer words
anger	dagger	over	answer	cucumber
bitter	mutter	sober	other	September
bluster	pamper	trader	another	October
banner	scatter	safer	brother	November
copper	summer	later	mother	eternal
hammer	sister	glider	father	maternal
number	slumber	rider	smother	
plunder	winter	diver		also + prefixes
rudder	under	maker		over-, under-,
timber	dinner	baker		inter-
suffer	kipper			(e.g. under-
tender	tinder			hand, under-
trigger	letter			stand, overact,
thunder	rubber			overcome,
batter	flutter			interact)
butler	butter			

Words at 'er' (stressed)
her herd fern herb kerb Universe University diverse reverse

Sentences at 'er'
1. My socks are under the bed.
2. Jim can run faster than Oliver.
3. Tell her to bring her brother to the party.
4. It will be cold in winter.

Example worksheet at 'er': Add the suffix 'er'. Double the final consonant if the word has a vc ending. Just add to any other base. Did you double, or just add?

		Double or Just Add?
run + er	runner	double
hoot + er		
fast + er		
win + er		
shop + er		
cold + er		
fat + er		

Now choose four of these words, and write each one in a sentence.

i-e I-E

Reading Card

pipe /ī/

face　　　　　　reverse

Spelling Card

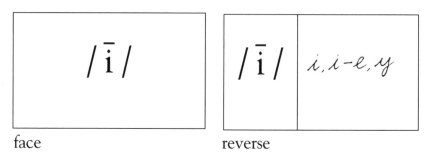

/ ī /　　　　　/ ī / *i, i-e, y*

face　　　　　　reverse

'i-e' is a split digraph. The 'e' has no sound. The 'i' has the long vowel sound. Notice that the long vowel sound is the same as its name. Children may be familiar with 'magic e', 'lazy e' or 'lengthening e'. When making the Spelling Card, refer back to page 208 – the 'i' can have the long vowel sound without the 'e' in words like 'Simon', 'pilot', etc. Look also at the 'vowel y' card – at the end of a word, use the letter 'y' for the /ī/ sound. If long explanations are too challenging for a weak working memory, just build in the simple response for the card, and work on words at the onset and rime level (see worksheet at 'i-e').

Word lists at 'i-e'				
		with blends	irregular	longer words
bike	fine	spike	while	inside
hike	mine	strike	white	confide
like	nine	stile	knife	respite
pike	pine	smile	rhyme	reside
bite	dine	stripe		beside
kite	wine	shine		
rite	vine	swine	dire	+ suffixes:
site	life	spine	fire	spiteful
mite	strife	bride	hire	likely
file	wife	stride	mire	wisely
bile	dive	tribe	shire	
mile	live	bribe	spire	
tile	five	drive	sire	
Nile	hive	quite	tire	
ripe	jive		tyre	
pipe	ride		wire	
wipe	side			
time	wide			
lime	tide			
mime	rise			
	wise			

Sentences at 'i-e'
1. The children can swim and dive.
2. Five men stood in a line.
3. This black bike is mine.
4. Shall we go inside?

Example worksheet at 'i-e': Match onset and rime. Write real words in the boxes.

	-ine	-ike	-ile	-ime
m				
n				
l				
sp				

Now choose one word from each column, and write it in a sentence.

Reading Card

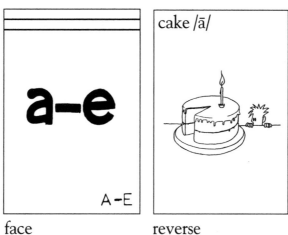

face　　　　　　　reverse

Spelling Card

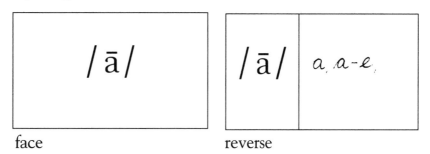

face　　　　　　　reverse

When making the Spelling Card, refer back to page 208 – the 'a' can have the long vowel sound without the 'e' in words like 'David', 'bacon', etc.

Word lists at 'a-e'		with blends	'are' words	longer words
cake	cane	blame	bare	cascade
bake	pane	flame	care	impale
rake	lane	frame	dare	inhale
fake	ape	brake	fare	mistake
lake	cape	stake	mare	escape
take	tape	flake	pare	encase
make	case	snake	rare	intake
ale	ate	plane	stare	rebate
pale	rate	crane	scare	prepare
male	fate	blade		insane
dale	late	spade		became
sale	date	crate		
fade	mate	slate		Drop 'e' when
made	rave			adding vowel
safe	wave			suffixes:
same	save			bake + ing =
fame	gave			baking
came	daze			scare + y =
tame	maze			scary

Sentences at 'a-e'
1. David is late.
2. Sandra gave me a present.
3. The snakes will escape from the zoo.
4. Cathy made a big mistake.

Example worksheet at 'a-e': When adding a suffix that begins with a vowel to a vce ending, drop the final 'e'.

dine + ing *dining*	mine + er	ripe + en	fine + est
late + est	like + ing	pile + ed	make + ing
hike + ing	blame + ed	bake + ing	bite + ing
line + ed	wide + est	dive + er	ride + ing

Now choose four of these words, and write each one in a sentence.

o-e O-E

Reading Card

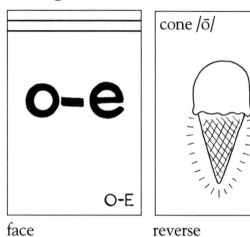

face   reverse

Spelling Card

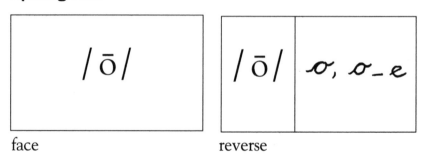

face   reverse

When making the Spelling Card, refer back to page 208 – the 'o' can have the long vowel sound without the 'e' in words like 'crocus', 'token', etc.

Word lists at 'o-e'		with blends	irregular	longer words
robe	cope	slope	come	global
rode	Pope	quote	some	lonesome
code	rope	smoke	one	expose
mode	dope	spoke	done	compose
poke	hope	stone	none	promote
coke	rose	stroke	gone	explode
woke	nose	strode	dove	trombone
pole	hose	globe	love	hotel
mole	doze	grope	ghost	
dole	rote		most	
hole	vote		host	
dome	tote		lose	
home	rove		move	
bone			wrote	
lone				
tone				

Sentences at 'o-e'
1. Jason rode his bike to the shop.
2. Simon left his book at home.
3. I fell over that stone and banged my nose.
4. Is it safe to stroke your dog?

Example worksheet at 'o-e': Mark the 'vce' endings of the base words. Just Add any consonant suffix. Drop 'e' when adding a vowel suffix.

		Just Add or Drop 'e'?
vce hope + ful	hopeful	just add
late + ly		
fine + est		
make + ing		
bone + y		
slope + ing		
wave + ing		
hope + ing		

Now choose four of these words, and write each one in a sentence.

Long vowel frame

There is a lot of regional variation on the pronunciation of sounds, and long vowel sounds are particularly hard to pin down. Before spelling was standardised, writers in different parts of the country would choose different ways of representing the sounds in print. David Crystal's (1995) *Encyclopaedia of the English Language* (p. 237) lists 20 long vowel sounds, and compares three different methods of representing them. Hickey stuck with the five alphabet vowels (a, e, i, o, u) and focused on their long and short vowel sound, adding only /oo/ as a long vowel sound – the vowel/r combinations were not included. This is complicated enough for most dyslexic learners, though it might help the teacher to be more familiar with the subtleties of linguistics.

It can help learners to sort the five key long vowel sounds into a frame, and add to the frame gradually. Make it part of the normal spelling pack routine. Give the learner a blank form, and when you reach a long vowel sound, give a reminder (if necessary) that the responses will be written in the frame. The frame here contains the vowels covered so far.

Long vowel frame			
sound	open syllable	middle	end
/ā/	*a*	*a-e*	
/ē/	*e*	*ee*	*ee*
/ī/	*i*	*i-e*	*y*
/ō/	*o*	*o-e*	
/ū/	*u*		

or OR

Reading Card

or

OR

face

fork /or/

reverse

Spelling Card

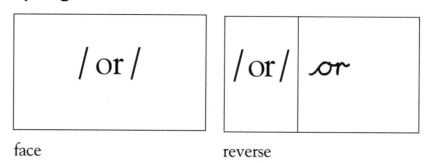

/ or /

/or/ *or*

face

reverse

Write carefully – 'ar' and 'or' can be easily confused.

Word lists at 'or'

	'ore'	with blends	irregular		longer words
or	more	scorn	Morse	bought	formal
for	snore	snort	horse	fought	important
cord	pore	storm	door	thought	morning
ford	gore	sport	floor	brought	normal
fork	sore	stork	oar	ought	record
pork	wore	sport	soar	sought	effort
cork	bore	thorn	roar		support
form	store	sworn	your		uniform
born	shore	short	four		transform
corn	core	North	pour		
horn	tore		sword		
sort	swore				
port					
fort					

Sentences at 'or'

1. Fill in the form.

2. Take a fork for your chips.

3. They had a holiday in the North of Scotland.

4. He thinks he's so important!

Example worksheet at 'or': A morpheme is the smallest unit of sound that contains meaning. Look at the long words, and divide them into morphemes. Put the bits of the words into the correct columns. Notice that the base is not always a complete word.

	prefix	base word	suffix
rejected			
unhopeful			
imported			
homeless			
smallest			
reprint			
conducting			

Example worksheet at 'or': Read the sentence. Put a ring round the base (the bit that isn't a prefix). Notice that prefixes are only stressed in nouns. Write the word in separate syllables, and mark the stressed syllable. Is the whole word a verb or a noun? Write the answer in the last box.

1. I object to men smoking in here.	ob ject'	verb
2. That is a fantastic object.		
3. I will not subject you to a long talk.		
4. The talk is on the subject of fishing.		
5. Our exports are up this quarter.		

Syllable division patterns: Final stable syllables

The two most common syllable division patterns are vc/cv (e.g. chan / nel) and v/cv (e.g. la / bel). A third pattern is vc/v (e.g. mod / el). Most words ending in 'l' behave differently, and although they are pronounced with an extra syllable, the vowel slips out of its central position. A useful way of handling these words is to put a ring round the 'final stable syllable', i.e. the last three letters. If the remaining syllable ends in a consonant, it will have the short vowel sound. If it ends in a vowel, it will have the long vowel sound.

Example worksheet at 'or': Put a ring round the final stable syllable (last three letters). Read the words to your teacher.			
sim ple	an kle	ta ble	no ble
can dle	bun dle	ri fle	cra dle
jun gle	bot tle	bi ble	ti tle
lit tle	puz zle	bu gle	ma ple
spar kle	ap ple	ca ble	tri fle
Now choose four of the words and write each one in a sentence.			

u-e U-E

Reading Card

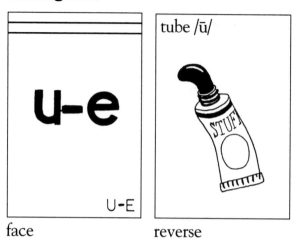

face   reverse

Spelling Card

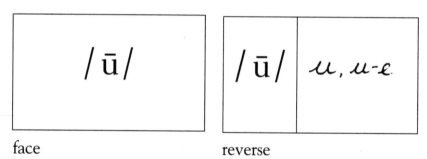

face   reverse

When making the Spelling Card, refer back to page 222 – the 'u' can have the long vowel sound in an open syllable in words like 'music', 'tulip', etc.

Word lists at 'u-e'

		with blends	irregular	longer words
cube	mule	flute	sure	duty
cute	muse	crude		useful
duke	nude			useless
dune	ruse	'ure' words		refuse
dupe	rude	cure		commute
fume	rune	pure		confuse
fuse	tube	lure		compute
June	tune	endure		computer
lute	use	impure		amuse
Luke				

Sentences at 'u-e'

1. The fuse has gone.

2. We can picnic on the sand dunes.

3. You will have to amuse yourselves, I am rather busy.

4. Billy is saving up for a computer.

Long vowel frame at u-e

sound	open syllable	middle	end
/ā/	a	a-e	
/ē/	e	ee	ee
/ī/	i	i-e	y
/ō/	o	o-e	
/ū/	u	u-e	

ee EE

Reading Card

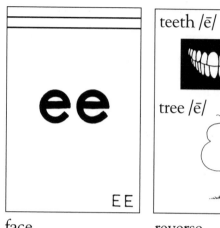

face

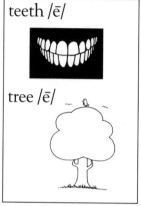

reverse

Spelling Card

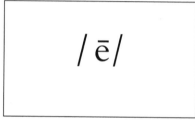

face

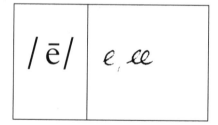

reverse

When making the Spelling Card, refer back to page 208 – the 'e' can have the long vowel sound without the 'e' in words like 'Steven', 'evil', etc.

Word lists at 'ee'

		blends	'eer'	'ee' end	longer words
feed	seem	bleed	beer	bee	canteen
deed	been	breed	deer	flee	fifteen
need	keen	freed	peer	glee	settee
reed	seen	greed	leer	see	coffee
seed	queen	speed	jeer	tee	indeed
meek	keep	Greek	cheer	tree	unseen
peek	jeep	steel	queer	free	asleep
seek	feet	green		three	
week	teeth	screen		(knee)	+ suffixes
leek		cheep			(e.g. sleepy,
feel		creep			greedy,
peel		fleet			creeping)
heel		greet			
		sleet			
		sweet			
		street			
		sneeze			
		breeze			
		freeze			

Sentences at 'ee'

1. Jane will feed the cat.

2. Steven is feeling a bit sick.

3. The greedy man ate three dishes of trifle.

4. My sister will be fifteen next week.

Long vowel frame at 'ee'			
sound	open syllable	middle	end
/ā/	a	a-e	
/ē/	e	ee	ee
/ī/	i	i-e	y
/ō/	o	o-e	
/ū/	u	u-e	

Reading Card

play /ā/

face   reverse

Spelling Card

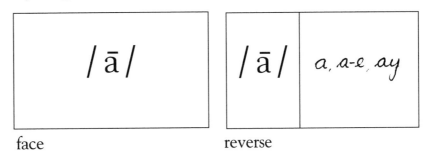

face   reverse

When making the Spelling Card, refer back to page 208 – the 'a' can have the long vowel sound without the 'a' in words like 'bacon', 'David', etc.

Long vowel frame at 'ay'			
sound	open syllable	middle	end
/ā/	*a*	*a-e*	*ay*
/ē/	*e*	*ee*	*ee*
/ī/	*i*	*i-e*	*y*
/ō/	*o*	*o-e*	
/ū/	*u*	*u-e*	

Word lists at 'ay'				
	blends	irregular	compound words	longer words
bay	stay	they	daytime	dismay
day	bray	grey	driveway	essay
gay	fray	obey	gangway	Sunday
hay	tray	Monday	pathway	yesterday
lay	pray	Tuesday	playmate	Friday
may	stray	Wednesday	haystack	runway
jay	spray	Thursday		decay
pay	slay	always		delay
say	play			display
ray	sway			
way	clay			

Sentences at 'ay'
1. Put the drink on a tray.
2. My grandson was born in May.
3. The plane is on the runway.
4. There was a beautiful art display in the hall.

Example worksheet at 'ay': Just Add consonant or vowel suffixes to a vv ending.			
see + ing	play + er	free + dom	glee + ful
decay + ed	display + ing	say + ing	stay + ed
Now choose three of the words, and write each one in a sentence.			

Reading Card

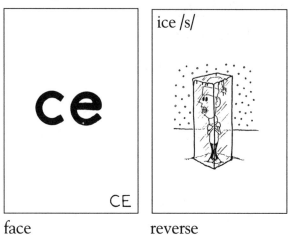

ice /s/

face   reverse

Spelling Card

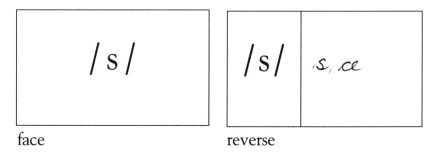

/ s /

/ s /   s, ce

face   reverse

Add 'ce' to the /s/ spelling card. Response is now /s/ 's', /s/ 'ce'. Notice that only in 'soccer' and 'sceptic' is the 'ce' pronounced /ke/. Americans write 'skeptic'.

    In many of the words the 'e' has two effects: the 'c' becomes 'soft' and the vowel sound lengthens. A rule with so many conditions is very challenging to children under nine years or so. Even with older learners explaining such complicated rules without overloading weak working memories is difficult. Give the routine reading and spelling cards, offer a simple initial explanation, but also give simple onset and rime exercises so that the ideas can gradually be absorbed at different levels.

Word lists at 'ce'					
	blends	'nce'	irregular	'ice' ending	longer words
ace	space	dance	soccer	/is/:	entrance
face	place	lance	sceptic	Alice	advice
lace	grace	glance	once	office	absence
mace	trace	prance	centre	bodice	instance
pace	brace	trance	police	crevice	sentence
race	spice	mince		malice	romance
ice	slice	prince		practice	device
dice	price	since		notice	pretence
lice	splice	pence			finance
mice	trice	fence		/us/:	licence
nice				menace	sequence
rice				necklace	advance
				terrace	
					+ affixes:
					produce
					reduce
					preface
					disgrace
					replace

Sentences at 'ce'

1. The mice ate rice.

2. Be careful of the ice on the steps.

3. The space ships took off and began the race to the moon.

4. Don't forget to put a full stop at the end of your sentence.

Example worksheet at 'ce': Match onset and rime. Write real words in the boxes.

	-ice	-ace	-ince	-ance
d				
m				
pr				
tr				
sp				

Now choose one word from each column, and write it in a sentence.

More words at 'ce': 'Soft c' is usually found at the ends of words. It can also be found at the beginning of some common word. 'ce' and 'ci' are more common than 'se' and 'si' in the middle of words. Read these words to your teacher. Learn to spell them gradually as you need them for free writing.

cell	cycle	except	accident	parcel
cent	cell	accept	recent	pencil
centre	civil	decide	recently	magnificent
circle	citizen	success	concern	incident
city	central	succeed	excite	concert
certain		necessary	medicine	decent
certainly		December	innocent	
century				

Example worksheet at 'ce': Read the sentences to your teacher. Copy each word that has a 'soft c' in it (you might want to photocopy and highlight or ring the words first).

1. He had an accident in December.

2. I am an innocent man. I did not even see the incident.

3. We live in the centre of the city.

4. Sharpen your pencil, then your writing will be magnificent.

Example worksheet at 'ce': Fill in the matrix to produce meaningful words. You will need to use the rules JUST ADD, DOUBLE, DROP

	-ing	-ed	-er	-ly	-ness
run					
race					
dark					
like					
jump					
deep					

ge GE

Reading Card

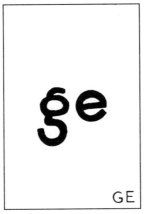

GE

face

cage /j/

reverse

Reading Card

ƆGE

face

bridge /j/

reverse

Spelling Card

/ j /

face

/ j / j ge, dge

reverse

Add 'ge' and 'dge' to the /j/ card. Spelling choice: at the end of a word, after one short vowel, use 'dge' . Always use 'soft g' instead of 'j' at the end of words.

'No English word can end in 'j'.
This is a rule you MUST obey!'

Word lists at 'ge'					
	blends	dge words	irregular	age = /ij/	longer words
age	stage	badge	sponge	cabbage	enrage
cage	stooge	hedge	gauge	rampage	engage
page	singe	edge	language	bandage	emerge
rage	fringe	ledge	massage	manage	upstage
sage	hinge	wedge	danger	ravage	infringe
wage	tinge	bridge	stranger	damage	indulge
huge	binge	ridge	suggest	savage	midget
merge	cringe	lodge	angel	plumage	lodger
verge	charge	dodge	imagine	dotage	budget
serge	large	stodge	magic	usage	badger
forge	bulge	fudge	intelligent		(+ ed, ing:
gorge	bilge	nudge	gym		drop final 'e'
	plunge	smudge	register		from base
		judge	engine		word)
					engaged
					rampaging

Sentences at 'ge'
1. This job pays a good wage.
2. Jane's fringe is very uneven. Did she cut it herself?
3. He always longed to go on the stage.
4. The car skidded onto the grass verge.

Sentences at 'dge'
1. Janet made a batch of fudge.
2. The bridge was swept away by the flood.
3. Here is a wedge to hold the door open.
4. You left your book on the ledge over there.

More words at 'ge': 'Soft g' is not so common at the beginning of words. Read these words to your teacher, and learn them for spelling as they come up in writing activities.

George	general	gem
German	giant	ginger
gentle	generous	gypsy
gently	genius	gin
gentleman	gesture	

Reading Card

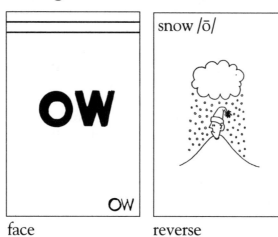

face   reverse

Spelling Card

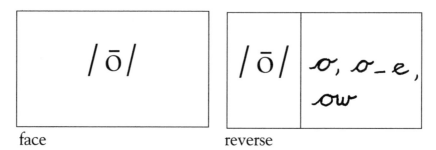

face   reverse

Long vowel frame at 'ow'			
sound	open syllable	middle	end
/ā/	*a*	*a-e*	*ay*
/ē/	*e*	*ee*	*ee*
/ī/	*i*	*i-e*	*y*
/ō/	*o*	*o-e*	*ow*
/ū/	*u*	*u-e*	

Word lists at 'ow'			
	irregular	longer words	compound words
blow	know	tomorrow	snowdrops
bow	bowl	arrow	snowman
crow	flown	barrow	snowflake
flow	grown	bellow	
grow	growth	burrow	
glow	own	billow	
low	shown	borrow	
mow	sown	elbow	
row	thrown	fellow	
show		bungalow	
slow	v/cv	undergrowth	
stow	shadow	(also with	
throw	widow	affixes)	
sow			
tow			
snow			

Sentences at 'ow'
1. Show me that book.
2. The weeds are growing in the garden.
3. Throw the ball to me.
4. A shadow fell across the window.

Example worksheet at 'ow': 'ow' counts as a vv ending (like 'ay'). Just add suffixes.

flow + ing	slow + ly	show + ed	mow + er
slow + ness	bellow + ing	borrow + ed	snow + y

Now choose three of the words, and write each one in a sentence.

Reading Card

face

rescue /ū/

glue /o͞o/

reverse

Spelling Card

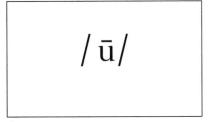

/ ū /

face

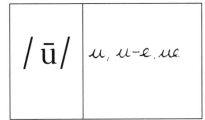

/ ū / *u, u-e, ue*

reverse

/ o͞o /

face

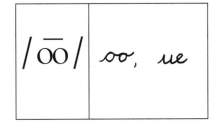

/ o͞o / *oo, ue*

reverse

Long vowel frame at 'ue': ('oo' addition optional)			
sound	open syllable	middle	end
/ā/	*a*	*a-e*	*ay*
/ē/	*e*	*ee*	*ee*
/ī/	*i*	*i-e*	*y*
/ō/	*o*	*o-e*	*ow*
/ū/	*u*	*u-e*	*ue*
/ōō/	*oo*	*oo, ue*	

Word lists at 'ue'			
	irregular	longer words	'que' ending
/ū/	queue	issue	antique
due	Tuesday	tissue	oblique
sue		rescue	unique
hue		argue	cheque
cue		subdue	grotesque
		continue	discotheque
/ōō/		barbecue	
blue		revue	
glue			
flue		vc/v	
true		statue	
		value	
		avenue	
		residue	

Sentences at 'ue'

1. Don't argue with me!

2. The dog is stuck in the pot-hole. Can they rescue it?

3. The last payment is due on Tuesday.

4. I will be very angry if you continue to be so rude.

Example worksheet at 'ue': Although 'ue' is a vv ending, drop 'e' when adding any suffix.

argue + ment	true + ly	value + able	rescue + ed
argument			

Now choose two of the words, and write each one in a sentence.

e-e E-E

Reading Card

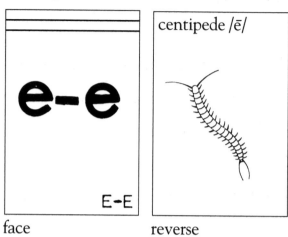

face   reverse

Spelling Card

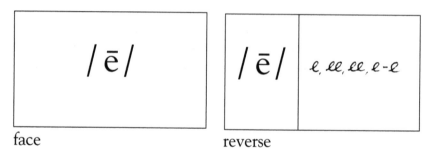

face   reverse

This spelling of the /ē/ sound is rare in one syllable words. It is the most common way of spelling the /ē/ in the last syllable of longer words.

Word lists at 'e-e'		
	irregular	longer words
eve	scene	adhere
eke	were	compete
theme	there	extreme
these	eye	stampede
mete	here	supreme
theme	mere	impede
	where	complete
	severe	delete
		serene
		concrete

Sentences at 'e-e'
1. These are my boots
2. Don't step in the concrete, it's not set yet.
3. Sometimes the thunder makes the cattle stampede.

y-e Y-E

Reading Card

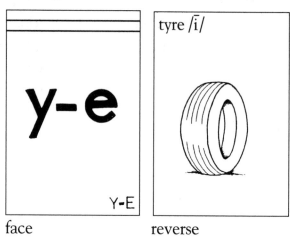

face   reverse

Spelling Card

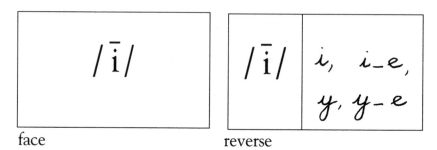

face   reverse

Another rare spelling. Many teachers don't bother to give the cards for e-e and y-e. They prefer to deal with them as irregular words as they come up in text. Biology students will find words ending in '-phyte', denoting plants, or '-cyte', denoting a cell.

Word lists at 'y-e'	
	longer words
tyre	analyse
style	acolyte
type	electrolyte
rhyme	paralyse
thyme	troglodyte

Reading Card

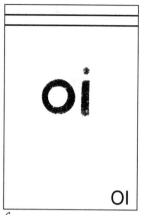

face

coin /oy/

reverse

Reading Card

face

toy /oy/

reverse

Spelling Card

/ oy /

face

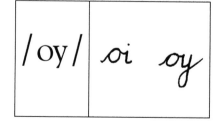

reverse

The /oy/ sound is usually spelled with 'oi' at the beginning or middle of a word or syllable, 'oy' at the end.

Word lists at 'oi', 'oy'			
'oi' words		'oy' words	irregular
oil	joist	boy	oyster
boil	hoist	toy	voyage
coil	foist	joy	boycott
foil	moist	coy	loyal
toil	joint	ploy	buoy
soil	point	Troy	
spoil	poise	enjoy	
coin	noise	employ	
join	voice	annoy	
loin	avoid	decoy	
groin	toilet		

Sentences at 'oi', 'oy'
1. It is rude to point.
2. Are you trying to avoid me?
3. We have been asked to make less noise.
4. Did you enjoy the concert?
5. There is so much unemployment in the North.

Reading Card

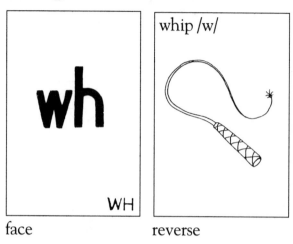

whip /w/

face   reverse

Spelling Card

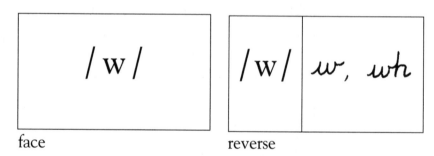

face   reverse

Very few English speakers aspirate this sound nowadays; it works better if it is treated as a second choice for the /w/ sound. Notice that many of the 'wh' words are high-frequency question words.

Word lists at /wh/		irregular	longer words	compound words
what wheel why white when whisk where whack whip wheeze whim whine whiff whale		which who whose whole whiz	whimper whiting whisper whisker whistle (+ with affixes)	whalebone whatever whoever wholesome

Sentences at 'wh'
1. What time is it?
2. The whale is a mammal, not a fish.
3. The dog is whining to be let out.
4. What long whiskers that cat has!

Example worksheet at 'wh': Read the question words in the box. Choose one to complete each sentence.

where   when   why   which   what   who

1. _____ can I visit the hospital?

2. _____ made that noise?

3. _____ bag shall I take?

4. _____ did you do it?

5. _____ can I do next?

6. I can't find my pen. _____ have you put it?

ou OU

Reading Card

face

house /ow/

reverse

Spelling Card

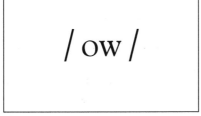

face

reverse

Word lists at 'ou'		irregular	'ou' = /oo/	'ou' = /u/
out	mount	doubt	you	country
bout	proud	flounce	wound	couple
clout	loud	pounce	youth	young
flout	cloud	our	soup	double
gout	bound	sour	routine	trouble
pout	sound	hour	coupon	touch
shout	found	your		cousin
stout	hound	could		southern
noun	mound	should		courage
house	pound	would		
mouse	round			
louse	sound			

Sentences at 'ou'

1. There are no mice in my house.

2. You must not shout! Don't make a sound!

3. I am in trouble. I lost a twenty pound note.

4. Let's gather round the fire.

Reading Card

face   reverse

Add 'cow, /ow/' to the back of the 'snow, /o/' card.

Spelling Card

/ ow /

/ ow /   *ou, ow*

face   reverse

Word lists at 'ow' /ow/

		longer words	compound words
now	crown	towel	township
cow	drown	tower	somehow
how	brown	bower	
wow	frown	vowel	
sow	gown	bowel	
row	prowl		
vow	owl	(also with	
brow	fowl	affixes, e.g.	
down	growl	crowded)	

Sentences at 'ow' /ow/

1. I would like a fresh towel.

2. Have you seen a little brown dog?

3. Rapunzel was locked in a tall tower.

4. The room was hot and crowded.

Example worksheet at 'ow' /ow/: Revise the rules covered so far. Mark the pattern of the base word ending (vc, vce, vcc). Is it a vowel or consonant suffix? Mark 'v' or 'c' above the first letter of the suffix. What rule will you use, just add, double or drop e?

word	suffix	rule	result
vc e hope	v ing	drop e	hoping
run	er		
like	ly		
home	less		
dark	ness		
big	est		
long	er		
weep	ing		
see	ing		

Example worksheet at 'ow'/ow/: When adding a suffix (except 'ing') to a word ending in consonant-y, change the 'y' to 'i'.

base	suffix	result
marry happy hurry worry duty pity mercy	ed ness ed ed ful ful less	married

Reading Card

au

AU

face

sauce /aw/

reverse

Reading Card

aw

AW

face

claw /aw/

reverse

Spelling Card

/ aw /

face

/ aw / *au, au~*

reverse

Word lists at 'au'			
'au' words	longer words	irregular words	augh = /aw/
Paul	bauble	laurel	taught
daub	saunter	gauge	daughter
cause	applaud	draught	naughty
clause	applause	laugh	caught
pause	audience		haughty
gauze	laundry		slaughter
haunt	automatic		manslaughter
launch	tarpaulin		
taunt	assault		
maul	somersault		
haul	Autumn		
fraud	August		
vault	saucer		
jaunt	because		
sauce	author		
	(also + affixes)		

Sentences at 'au'
1. The fraud squad is after him!
2. Paul has taken the blankets to the laundry.
3. Press that switch to use the automatic pilot.
4. I will not eat that because I am not hungry.

Word lists at 'aw'				
'aw' words			longer words	irregular words
jaw	brawl	lawn	crawfish	gnaw
law	drawl	dawn	hawthorn	dawdle
saw	crawl	fawn	outlaw	awkward
raw	sprawl	drawn	bylaw	
straw	scrawl	prawn	seesaw	
claw	trawl	brawn	trawler	
draw		sawn	drawer	
flaw			awful	
			lawyer	

Sentences at 'aw'
1. Raw carrots are good for you.
2. The socks are in the bottom drawer.
3. My little sister has drawn all over my text book.
4. Robin Hood was an outlaw.

ea EA

Reading Card

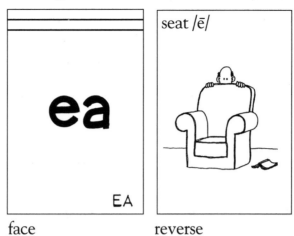

seat /ē/

face   reverse

Spelling Card

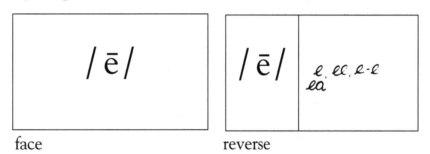

face   reverse

'ea' is the second choice for spelling the /ē/ sound. Like 'ee', it can be found in beginning, middle and end positions. Add to the long vowel frame.

Long vowel frame at 'ea'			
sound	open syllable	middle	end
/ā/	a	a-e	ay
/ē/	e	ee, ea	ee, ea
/ī/	i	i-e	y
/ō/	o	o-e	ow
/ū/	u	u-e	ue
/o͞o/	oo	oo, ue	

Word lists at 'ea'				
			irregular	longer words
bead	beast	clean	beauty	appeal
read	east	mean	beautiful	Easter
lead	sea	dear	seance	Eastern
leaf	tea	fear	idea	increase
beak	pea	gear	heart	beanstalk
bleak	flea	hear	hearth	underneath
freak	plea	ear		retreat
peak	beam	near	great	easy
weak	cream	please	steak	reason
speak	dream	meat	break	season
creak	scream	eat		easel
deal	gleam	beat		
peal	team	cheat		(also + affixes)
heal	lean	feat		
meal	bean			
seal				
feast				

Sentences at 'ea'

1. She fell into a dreamless sleep.

2. My Dad has eaten all the cream buns.

3. The branches were creaking in the wind.

4. We will have a quick and easy meal.

Example worksheet at 'ea': Copy the word. Do a quick drawing to illustrate its meaning.

heel	cheep	week*	meet*
heal*	cheap*	weak	meat

Write each starred word in a sentence.

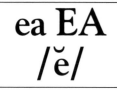

Reading Card

face

seat /ē/

treasure /ĕ/

reverse

Add 'treasure /ĕ/' to the reading card. Find the short vowel /ĕ/ card from the pack

Spelling Card

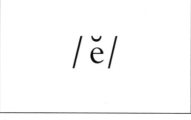

face

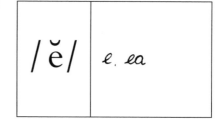

reverse

Word list at 'ea' /ĕ/			
		longer words	
head	wealth	feather	pleasant
read	health	heaven	steady
dead	stealth	heavy	weapon
bread	meant	ahead	weather
dread	leant	leather	ready
spread	sweat	meadow	
deaf	threat		(also + affixes)
realm			

Sentences at 'ea' /ĕ/
1. Are you ready?
2. This belt is made of leather.
3. What a heavenly sound!
4. It is important to eat lots of healthy food.

Reading Card

oa

OA

coat /ō/

face   reverse

Spelling Card

/ō/

/ō/ o, o_e, ow oa

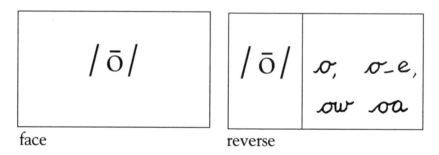

face   reverse

'oa' is the second choice for spelling the /o/ sound. It can be found in the beginning and middle of one syllable words. Longer words with this spelling are usually compound words, or made up of base words, suffixes and prefixes.

Long vowel frame at 'oa'			
sound	open syllable	middle	end
/ā/	*a*	*a-e*	*ay*
/ē/	*e*	*ee, ea*	*ee, ea*
/ī/	*i*	*i-e*	*y*
/ō/	*o*	*o-e, oa*	*ow*
/ū/	*u*	*u-e*	*ue*
/o͞o/	*oo*	*oo, ue*	

Word lists at 'oa'				
		irregular	compound words	longer words (also + affixes)
oat	oak	oasis	boatman	cocoa
boat	soak	boa	boathook	loafer
coat	cloak		oatmeal	unload
moat	croak		cloakroom	
gloat	road		carload	
float	load		oarsman	
stoat	foal		overcoat	
oaf	oath		topcoat	
loaf	boast			

Sentences at 'oa'

1. Kate and Mike were floating in the boat.

2. Soak the beans for six hours before cooking.

3. The man wore a long, black, shiny cloak.

4. It is so cold you will need an overcoat.

Example worksheet at 'oa': Read the story out loud. With a highlighter, mark every word where you can hear the long /ō/ sound. Write each word in the correct column below.

Robot showed Joan the small boat. They got in, and undid the rope. It began to float down the stream. 'I am so cold,' said Joan. 'Here is a cloak,' the Robot said. 'Do not moan. The stream flows past your home.' 'I hope so!' said Joan.

o	o-e	oa	ow

Reading Card

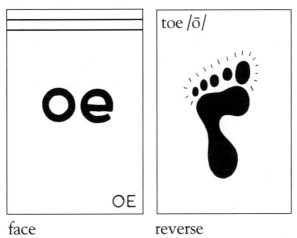

face   reverse

Spelling Card

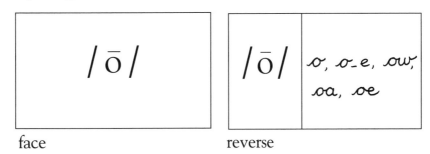

face   reverse

Not many words have this spelling. You can omit this card, and just deal with the 'oe' words as they come up in reading or writing. If you do include it, add it to the long vowel frame as a second choice for the /ō/ sound at the end of words.

'oe' words: toe, hoe, doe, woe, sloe, roe, oboe, mistletoe, foe

Spelling rule: Words ending in 'oe' just add 's' for the plural (toe, toes). The most common words ending in 'o' add 'es' for the plural (tomato, tomatoes; potato, potatoes; but stiletto, stilettos; embryo, embryos).

Sentences at 'oe'

1. Can you walk on tiptoe?

2. Put the potatoes on to boil at one o'clock.

3. Slice a large tomato into the salad.

igh
IGH

Reading Card

IGH

face

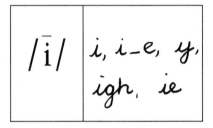

fight /ī/

reverse

Spelling Card

/ ī /

face

/ ī / i, i-e, y, igh, ie

reverse

'igh' is the second choice for spelling the /ī/ sound. It can be found in the middle of one syllable words, always before 't', and at the end of words. Longer words with this spelling are usually compound words, or words with affixes.

Long vowel frame at 'igh'			
sound	open syllable	middle	end
/ā/	a	a-e	ay
/ē/	e	ee, ea	ee, ea
/ī/	i	i-e, igh	y, igh
/ō/	o	o-e, oa	ow, oe
/ū/	u	u-e	ue
/o͞o/		oo	oo, ue

Word lists at 'igh'					
		irregular	'ite' words	compound words	longer words (also + affixes)
fight	blight	height	bite	moonlight	delight
light	plight	knight	kite	sunlight	twilight
might	flight		white	lamplight	alright
night	slight	pie	write	skylight	upright
right	high	tie	mite*	copyright	foresight
sight	sigh	die	site*		fortnight
tight	nigh	lie	rite*		tonight
bright	thigh				forthright
fright					

*Look up and discuss meanings.

Sentences at 'igh'

1. The plane is high in the sky.

2. We were delighted to get your letter.

3. Tonight, the moonlight is almost as bright as the sun.

4. Don't frighten the baby.

Example worksheet at 'igh': Match onset and rime to make real words. Write them in the matrix.

	ight	ite	igh
l			
k			
br			
s			
b			
th			
m			
r			
fl			

Example worksheet at 'igh': Read the story out loud. With a high-lighter, mark every word where you can hear the long $/\bar{\imath}/$ sound. Write each word in the correct column below.

It was a dark night. Simon, the brave knight, began to ride into the forest. A strange cry filled the sky, and his horse shook with fright. Still Simon rode on. He came to the gorge. The lovely Princess Diana was tied to a pine tree. The Dragon was hiding in the cave. 'Your time has come! You will die!' shouted Simon. There was a mighty battle, but Simon's knife plunged into the Dragon's neck. 'Will you be my bride?' asked Simon. 'I will,' said Diana with delight.

i	i-e	igh	y	ie

ai AI

Reading Card

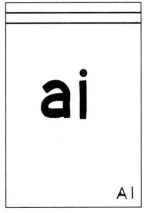

A I

face

rain /ā/

reverse

Spelling Card

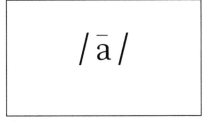

face

reverse

'ai' is the second choice for spelling the /ā/ sound. It can be found in the middle of one syllable words, usually before l, n and r.

Long vowel frame at 'ai'			
sound	open syllable	middle	end
/ā/	a	a-e, ai	ay
/ē/	e	ee, ea	ee, ea
/ī/	i	i-e, igh	y, igh
/ō/	o	o-e, oa	ow, oe
/ū/	u	u-e	ue
/ōō/	oo	oo, ue	

Word lists at 'ai'					
			irregular words	compound	longer words (also + affixes)
ail	chain	laid	straight	pigtail	complain
bail	plain	waif	praise	airman	complaint
mail	slain	brain	raise	airsick	detain
fail	sprain	drain		airship	explain
rail	saint	grain	in unstressed	overpaid	maintain
sail	taint	maim	syllable	underpaid	maintenance
nail	faint	vain			regain
pail	air	maid	bargain		ingrain
tail	fair	rain	mountain		obtain
wail	hair	paid	fountain		
jail	pair				
gain	chair				
main	stair				
pain	flair				

Sentences at 'ai'
1. The paint on the railings is still wet.
2. She fell down the stairs and sprained her ankle.
3. I am waiting to make a complaint.

Example worksheet at 'ai': Homophones sound the same, but have different meanings. Read these homophones. Draw a picture to illustrate each word.

fair	fare	pair	pare
hair	hare	mail	male
pail	pale	sail	sale
pain	pane	maid	made

Reading Card

face   reverse

The /er/ sound has been introduced for reading (see page 271, herb /er/, hammer /ə/). Take out the reading card, and show how 'herb' and 'bird' have the same vowel sound – sometimes known as a 'half-long' vowel, or 'vowel-r combinations'. Crystal (1994) classes these as long vowel sounds. For most English speakers, the sound is identical, but it is easy to detect the different vowels in Scottish speakers.

Spelling Card

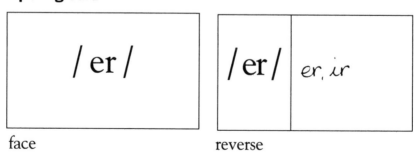

face   reverse

Word lists at 'ir'		irregular	longer words (also + affixes)
bird	flirt	souvenir	birthday
chirp	skirt	elixir	thirsty
dirt	shirt		dirty
firm	thirst		skirmish
first	swirl		swirling
mirth	twirl		thirteen
birch	squirm		thirty
fir	stir		girdle
sir	third		confirm
birth			infirm
			circumference
			circle
			circumstance
			circus

Sentences at 'ir'
1. Your shirt is dirty.
2. The thirsty birds gathered round the pond.
3. Thirteen is supposed to be an unlucky number.
4. What is the circumference of that circle?

ur UR

Reading Card

face

fur /er/

reverse

Spelling Card

/ er /

face

/er/ *er, ir, ur*

reverse

Word lists at 'ur'				
		irregular	longer words (also + affixes)	
hurl	burn	purr	turban	return
hurt	burst	burr	curdle	cursor
purl	curl		gurgle	turban
spur	fur		hurdle	murder
spurn	curt		purple	urban
spurt			urgent	

Sentences at 'ur'

1. The boy was badly hurt in the car crash.

2. She was asleep, curled up by the fire.

3. He ignored me except for a curt nod.

4. The murderer wore a turban and a silk shirt.

ew EW

Reading Card

new /ū/

screw /o͞o/

face   reverse

Even BBC journalists who speak for a living have trouble with this sound (as in 'nookiller bomb'). Many regional accents say 'noo' rather than 'nyoo' – you might be tempted to give the card just as 'screw /oo/', and add it only to the /oo/ spelling card.

Spelling Card

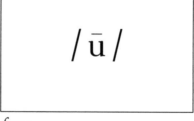

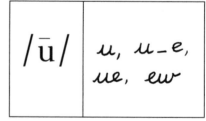

/ū/

/ū/ u, u–e, ue, ew

face   reverse

Spelling Card

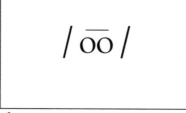

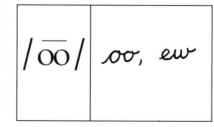

/o͞o/

/o͞o/ oo, ew

face   reverse

Word lists at 'ew'			
/ū/	/o͞o/	irregular	longer words
new	blew	view	jewel
dew	grew	knew	sinew
few	crew	sew	
mew	brew		
pew	threw		
stew	shrewd		
	chew		
	flew		

Sentences at 'ew'

1. Steven wore his new shirt.

2. We have sold quite a few automatic cars this year.

3. The wind blew harder, and the crew grew colder.

4. There is a lovely view from the upstairs window

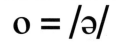

Reading Card

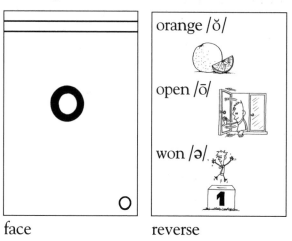

face   reverse

Find the 'orange, /ŏ/' card. Some of the words with 'o' saying /ə/ are high frequency, and have been introduced earlier as irregular words.

Spelling Card

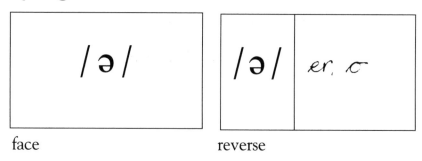

face   reverse

Word lists at o = /ə/			
regular	irregular	longer words (also + affixes)	
monk	come	nothing	comfort
ton	some	Monday	government
son	done	money	wonder
month	dove	shovel	wonderful
	glove	cover	another
	love	dozen	discover
	none	mother	above
	one	brother	London
	once		

Sentences at o = /ə/
1. I love Saturdays, but hate Mondays.
2. The cake had a dozen eggs and a pound of butter.
3. My brother Oliver had a wonderful birthday party.

ie IE

Reading Card

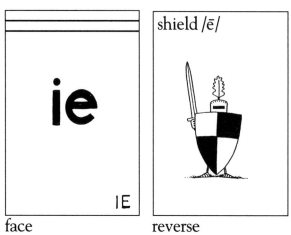

shield /ē/

ie

IE

face   reverse

Spelling Card

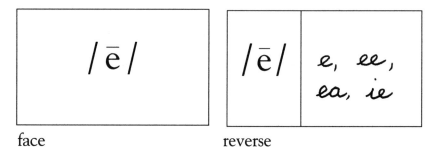

/ē/   /ē/   e, ee, ea, ie

face   reverse

Some of the words with 'ie' are important for reading. Add this third choice to the Spelling Card and to the long vowel frame if the learner confidently uses 'ee' and 'ea'.

Word lists at 'ie'			
regular words		irregular	longer words (also + affixes)
brief	priest	tier	mischief
chief	shield	pier	achieve
field	shriek	fierce	belief
fiend	siege	pierce	believe
grieve	wield	frieze	diesel
grief	yield	friend	relief
niece		tie pie	relieve
piece		die lie	reprieve
		retrieve	

Sentences at 'ie'
1. Have a piece of cake.
2. Sally's niece is coming to stay for a week.
3. A loud shriek pierced the silence.
4. I expect my son is getting up to some mischief.

Reading Card

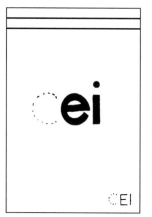

face

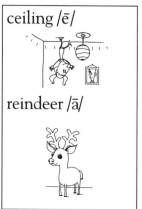

ceiling /ē/

reindeer /ā/

reverse

Most adults, when asked for a spelling rule, would probably say "'i' before 'e', except after 'c'". Yet it applies to very few words. Most of the words have prefixes combined with a Latin root derived from 'capere', meaning 'to take' or 'to contain'. You might want to add 'ei' as an extra spelling choice to the /ā/ card, though it is quite rare.

Word lists at 'ei'			
regular words – /ē/	regular words – /ā/	irregular	
ceiling	rein	forfeit	eight
deceit	veil	eiderdown	eighty
deceive	vein	counterfeit	eighteen
receive	skein	weigh	eighth
conceit		weight	
conceive		neighbour	
protein		sleigh	
perceive			

Sentences at 'ei'

1. There is a big crack in the ceiling.

2. I did not receive your letter.

3. Don't try to deceive me!

4. How much do you weigh?

ph PH

Reading Card

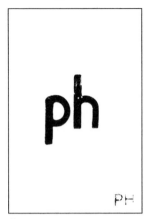

photo /f/

face   reverse

The consonant digraph 'ph' is used in words of Greek origin. English words with this spelling often have a scientific or technical connection.

Spelling Card

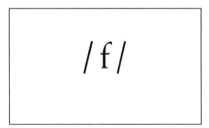

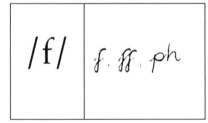

face   reverse

(Some teachers may have chosen to add 'ff' as a spelling choice.)

Word lists at 'ph'			
regular words	irregular words	longer words	
graph	cellophane	Philip	phantom
phrase	morphine	elephant	alphabet
sphere	sapphire	nephew	dolphin
lymph	semaphore	aphid	emphasis
phone	xylophone	trophy	orphan
phase	pheasant	physics	telephone
		pharmacy	telegraph
		triumph	photograph
		phosphate	paragraph
		phonics	graphic
		phoneme	microphone
		hemisphere	saxophone
		digraph	morpheme
		trigraph	

Sentences at 'ph'

1. A trigraph is three letters representing one sound.

2. The nurse will phone for an ambulance.

3. That paragraph is too long.

4. I would love to play the saxophone.

Example worksheet at 'ph': Look up these words in a dictionary. Each group share a morpheme. Discuss with your teacher the meaning of the morpheme.

-graph
graphic, photograph, grapheme

-phone
telephone, phonics, microphone

tri-
trigraph, tricycle, tripod

a = /ə/

Unstressed syllables

In unstressed syllables, the vowel sounds are often unclear. One way to deal with them is to store the sounds in 'spelling language'; the learner pronounces a word like 'hospital' in the usual way, but imagines the syllable with an accented pronunciation – 'hos – pit – AL', 'la – BEL', 'mag – NET'.

There are many words with the letter 'a' pronounced as the indeterminate /ə/. Many of the words that begin with an unstressed 'a' are derived from prefixes plus bases which are not used as whole words. For example, the base of 'agree' comes from a Latin root 'gratum', meaning 'pleasant'; the prefix 'a' is from an Old French 'a', meaning 'towards'. Some have more obvious derivations (e.g. 'ablaze', 'alike'). An etymological dictionary is a useful source of such information; Eric Partridge's *Origins*, first published in 1958, still provides endless enlightenment.

If you want, you can put 'canary /ə/' on the 'a' card. You might have to make a new card, making tiny sketches for the familiar words, thus leaving enough room for your new picture.

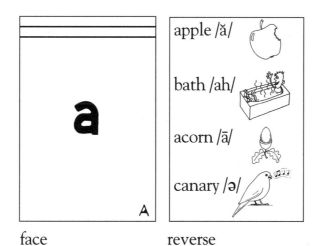

face   reverse

Spelling Card

/ə/	

face

/ə/	*er, o, a*

reverse

Word lists at 'a' = /ə/		
'a' as a prefix		'a' as an unstressed final syllable
aback	abolish	banana
abash	alike	Canada
about	alive	comma
abate	abound	cobra
abroad	alone	Cuba
abide	amid	fauna
abuse	acute	flora
ability	agog	Africa
ablaze	agree	quota
afar	ahead	tuba
abode	away	vista
abundant	abominable	camera
		zebra

Sentences at 'a' = /ə/

1. I was taken aback by his rudeness.

2. It was a pleasant afternoon; everyone was most agreeable.

3. He's gone away – a trip to Canada, I expect.

4. There is no evidence for the existence of the Abominable Snowman.

Reading Card

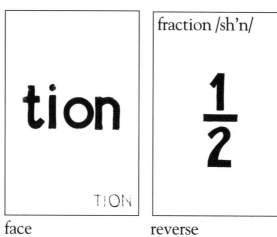

tion
TION

fraction /sh'n/

tion

TION

$\frac{1}{2}$

face   reverse

This is the most common way of spelling the sound /sh'n/ as a final syllable. There are no reliable syllable division patterns with words like this – cover the 'tion' and see if the rest of the word makes sense. By now, learners will be used to 'trial and error', and should be prepared to try both the long and the short vowel sounds in the first syllable of words like 'ration' and 'nation' in order to see which makes a real word.

Spelling Card

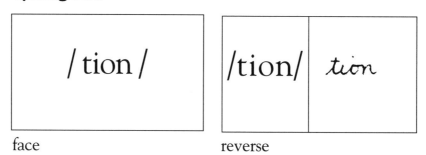

/ tion /

/tion/   tion

face   reverse

Word lists at 'tion'			
regular words	longer words	'-ation' words	'tion' says /ch'n/
action	addition	education	question
fraction	ambition	relation	suggestion
faction	expedition	vacation	digestion
option	subtraction	probation	exhaustion
auction	distraction	rotation	
caution	distinction	accommodation	
nation	indigestion	motivation	
station	induction	obligation	
notion	pollution	information	
friction	constitution	inflation	
section	institution	multiplication	
suction		carnation	
motion			
lotion			
potion			

Sentences at 'tion'
1. What action can we take?
2. Rub some of this lotion on the affected area.
3. My ambition is to have a career in education.

Example worksheet at 'tion': Put a ring round the 'tion'. Read the word to your teacher. How many syllables?

station (2)	inflation	relation	motion
adoption	information	motivation	indigestion
section	fraction	education	probation

ear
EAR

Reading Card

face

earth /er/

reverse

Spelling Card

/ er /

face

/ er /	er, ur, ur, ear

reverse

Word lists at 'ear'		
'ear' says /er/	'ear' = ea+r	'ear' says /ar/
earth	ear	heart
pearl	dear	hearth
earn	year	
learn	near	
search	rear	
earthquake	spear	
heard	fear	
yearn	gear	
rehearse		

Sentences at 'ear'
1. Father gave me some pearl ear-rings.
2. The search for the victims of the earthquake has begun.
3. Have you heard the news?
4. We have started rehearsals in the church hall.

Reading Card

ey EY

EY

donkey /ĭ/

face   reverse

Many southern speakers extend the final syllable, and prefer to represent it as a long /ē/ sound. However, true long vowel sounds are not found in unstressed syllables. When the 'ey' words are put into phrases (e.g. 'donkey-ride', 'parsley sauce'), the short vowel sound is more natural. When 'ey' is in a stressed syllable, it is more likely to be pronounced as /ā/ (e.g. they, obey).

Spelling Card

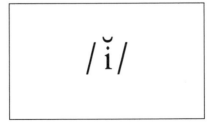

/ĭ/

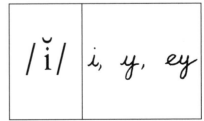

/ĭ/   i, y, ey

face   reverse

Word lists at 'ey'			
regular words		irregular words	'ey' says /a/
donkey	abbey	journey	grey
monkey	valley	key	they
honey	parsley	attorney	prey
money	kidney		obey
chimney	Jersey		disobey
turkey	abbey		survey
hockey	alley		
jockey	galley		
barley	chutney		

Sentences at 'ey'
1. Melinda asked for a slice of bread and honey.
2. The donkey can run freely in the meadow.
3. Telephone the chimney sweep and ask him when he can call.
4. Fish tastes good with parsley sauce.

our
OUR

Reading Card

OUR

colour /ə/

face   reverse

American spelling uses 'or' where we use 'our' (e.g. color, humor).

Spelling Card

/ə/

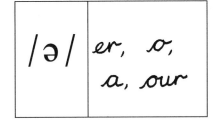

/ə/ er, o,
      a, our

face   reverse

Word lists at 'our'		
regular words		
labour	armour	vapour
harbour	arbour	favour
neighbour	fervour	flavour
odour	ardour	savour
vigour	humour	odour
colour	rumour	rigour
glamour	honour	splendour

Sentences at 'our'
1. Shall we buy Peter a colouring book?
2. Samantha attacked her work with vigour.
3. The wages will be delivered in an armoured car.
4. This soup has a very odd flavour.

ch = /k/

Reading Card

CH

face

cherry /ch/

chemist /k/

reverse

Add to the 'cherry, /ch/' card. The response will be 'cherry, /ch/, chemist, /k/'.

Many of the words with this spelling are connected with science or music, and are of Greek origin.

Spelling Card

/ k /

face

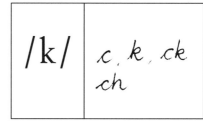

/k/   c, k, ck, ch

reverse

Add to /k/ spelling card. The response will be: /k/, 'c'; /k/, 'k'; /k/, 'ck', /k/, 'ch'.

$$\boxed{\text{ch} =/\text{sh}/}$$

Reading Card

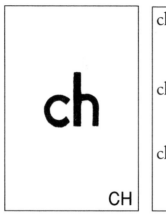

CH

face

cherry /ch/

chemist /k/

chef /sh/

reverse

Add to the 'cherry, /ch/' card. The response will be 'cherry, /ch/, chemist, /k/, chef /sh/'. Most of the words with this sound/spelling link are of French origin.

Spelling Card

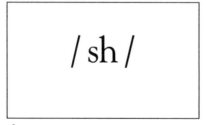

/ sh /

face

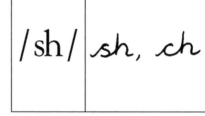

/sh/ | sh, ch

reverse

Add to /sh/ spelling card. The response will be: /sh/ 'sh', /sh/ 'ch'.

Word lists at 'ch', /k/ and /sh/			
regular words	longer words		ch says /sh/
ache	chorus	bronchitis	chef
chord	chronic	orchestra	parachute
Christ	echo	orchid	champagne
scheme	Christmas	christen	chivalry
school	character	Christopher	chiffon
chasm	chloride	chemist	chateau
	cholera	chemical	chauffeur
	chronicle	chemistry	chauvinist
	stomach	mechanic	chamois
	lichen	mechanical	chaise-longue
	monarch	mechanism	machine
	chrysalis	technical	
	chrysanthemum	characteristic	
		architect	

Sentences at 'ch', /k/ and /sh/
1. Take this prescription to the chemist.
2. Chris has chronic stomach ache.
3. My son sends me orchids on Mother's Day.
4. She is a first-class mechanic.
5. The college has a good catering course if you want to be a chef.

Silent letters

Explain that these letters were once part of normal pronunciation – we know that the monks transcribed speech as phonetically as they could, and some of these sounds still survive in dialect pronunciations. Use for reading practice, and notice as they come up in texts. Teach for spelling as they are needed in writing. They can be added to the Spelling Cards as indicated at the top of the columns. 'sc' is covered by the soft 'c' card.

Words at 'Silent letters'				
/r/ r, wr	/n/ n, kn	/n/ n, kn, gn	/m/ m, mb	sc
writ	knit	gnu	lamb	scissors
write	knight	gnome	jamb	scimitar
wrap	knob	gnarl	comb	scene
wrack	knee	gnash	tomb	scenery
wrench	know	gnaw	entomb	scenic
wreck	knew	gnat	womb	scent
wren	knife		bomb	science
wrist	knave	reign	limb	scientific
wring	kneel	deign	climb	scientist
wretch	knowledge	campaign	dumb	conscience
wrong	knuckle	sign	plumb	sceptre
wrangle	knoll	resign	numb	sciatica
wriggle	knobbly	ensign	crumb	scintillate
wrinkle	knot	assign	thumb	
wrestle		foreign	honeycomb	
wristwatch			aplomb	
writhing				
wrought				

Sentences at 'Silent letters'

1. Ray cannot write because he has hurt his wrist.

2. The knots were so tight that Janet had to cut the string with a knife.

3. The angry man gnashed his teeth in rage.

4. Emma's fingers and thumbs were numb with cold.

5. The forensic scientist was called to the scene of the crime.

<table>
<tr><td>

sion
cian

</td></tr>
</table>

Reading Card

face

mansion /sh'n/

television /zh'n/

reverse

'sion' has two sounds – you will need to make two spelling cards.

Reading Card

face

magician /sh'n/

reverse

'cian' is the third way of spelling the /sh'n/ sound. Add onto the /sh'n/ spelling card.

Spelling Card

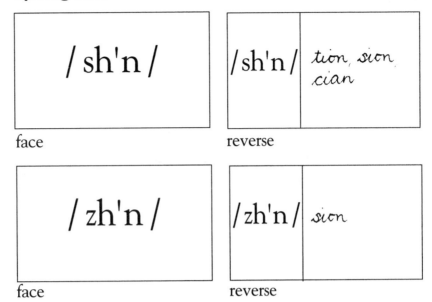

face   reverse

face   reverse

Sentences at 'sion', 'cian'
1. The optician will test your vision to see if you need glasses.
2. The class have covered addition, subtraction, multiplication and division.
3. I have done hours of revision for my examination.
4. The new house is small, but we could build an extension.
5. My children watch too much television.

Word lists at 'sion' and 'cian'			
sion = /zh'n/	sion = /sh'n/	cian (add to words ending in 'ic')	irregular
vision	tension	magician	Asian
incision	mansion	musician	Persian
decision	pension	logician	Russian
precision	extension	patrician	Venetian
evasion	compulsion	physician	Egyptian
fusion	revulsion	mathematician	Martian
erosion	repulsion	statistician	
occasion	convulsion	tactician	suspicion
dissuasion	passion	optician	
corrosion	mission		
explosion	expression		
intrusion	progression		
television	profession		
revision	procession		
supervision	possession		
division	compassion		
conversion			
version			
diversion			
immersion			

ar AR
(unstressed)

Add to the 'car, /ar/' reading card, and to the /ə/ spelling card.

Reading Card

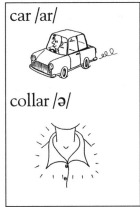

car /ar/

collar /ə/

face   reverse

Spelling Card

/ə/	/ə/	er, o, a, our, ar

face   reverse

Word lists at 'ar' (unstressed)			
pillar	dollar	regular	sugar
collar	beggar	calendar	
solar	polar	muscular	
vicar	cedar	circular	
burglar	vulgar	glandular	
popular	nectar		

Sentences at 'ar' (unstressed)

1. When the dog sees his collar, he expects a walk.

2. Parts of the UK saw a total solar eclipse on August 11th, 1999.

3. I wish I was as popular as my friend Pamela.

4. Janet has been quite poorly; she has glandular fever.

<table>
<tr><td>**or OR**
(unstressed)</td></tr>
</table>

Add to the 'fork, /or/' reading card, and to the /ə/ spelling card

Reading Card

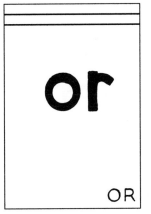

fork /or/

mirror /ə/

face   reverse

Spelling Card

|/ə/| |/ə/| er, o, a,
our, ar,
or |

face   reverse

Word lists at 'or' (unstressed)		
tutor	mirror	detector
anchor	terror	contributor
traitor	visitor	innovator
doctor	instructor	equator
factor	inventor	narrator
actor	solicitor	conjuror
horror	director	mayor
	contractor	professor

Sentences at 'or' (unstressed)

1. He was given help from a private tutor.

2. Miranda hopes for good A-level results; she wants to become a doctor.

3. The Earth Centre has not had as many visitors as we hoped.

4. The actor responded well to the new director.

Reading Card

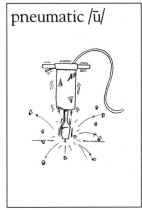

pneumatic /ū/

face   reverse

Notice the silent 'p' in the clue word – 'pneu' is from a Greek root, meaning 'pumping air through'. There are not many common words with this spelling for /u/ – you might not want to add it to the Spelling Card.

Spelling Card

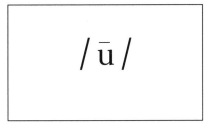

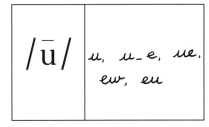

/ ū /

/ ū /   u, u_e, ue, ew, eu

face   reverse

Word lists at 'eu'	
Europe	neurosis
pneumonia	deuce
pneumatic	feud
neutral	eureka
feudal	neutralise
neurotic	neutron
neuter	euphemism
neutrality	

Sentences at 'eu'

1. Switzerland remained neutral in the Second World War.

2. The United Kingdom is part of Europe.

3. Modern life can make people quite neurotic.

ous
OUS
us
US

Reading Card

OUS

face

dangerous /us/

reverse

US

face

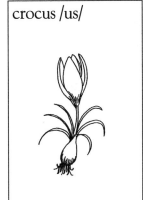

crocus /us/

reverse

Spelling Card

/ us /

face

/ us / ous, us

reverse

The /us/ sound at the end of words can be simply 'sounded out' for many words. However, it can also be a suffix, 'ous', added to non-word bases (e.g. 'frivolous') or to words (e.g. 'dangerous').

Word lists at 'ous', 'us'					
'ous' words			**'us' words**		
joyous	anxious	jealous	status	Venus	Pegasus
nervous	glamorous	serious	cactus	stylus	papyrus
grievous	perilous	generous	versus	bogus	platypus
virtuous	meticulous	obvious	census	genius	octopus
sumptuous	continuous	dangerous	mucus	surplus	tetanus
prosperous	deciduous	credulous	rumpus	radius	cumulus
tenuous	murderous	pompous	fungus	discus	stimulus
arduous	scrupulous	anonymous	sinus	impetus	nucleus
courteous	disastrous	frivolous	minus	omnibus	onus
fibrous	porous	marvellous	syllabus	focus	chorus
	ravenous	impetuous			

Sentences at 'ous', 'us'
1. An octopus has eight tentacles.
2. Bellerophon tamed Pegasus with a magic golden bridle.
3. That's a nasty cut, you will need a tetanus injection.
4. After the long hike, the children were ravenous.
5. Don't go so close to the edge, it's very dangerous.
6. Marcus felt very nervous as he went in for his interview.

ui UI

Reading Card

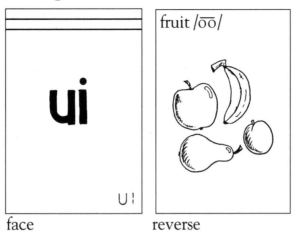

fruit /ōō/

face   reverse

There are only a handful of words with this spelling (fruit, juice, suit, cruise, nuisance, bruise all have the /oo/ sound; note also the irregular 'build' and 'biscuit'). You might prefer to ignore the cards, and just treat them as irregular words. 'ui' can be added to the /oo/ card.

Spelling Card

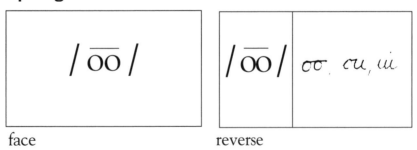

face   reverse

Sentences at 'ui'

1. Would you like some fruit juice?

2. When they retire, they will go on a world cruise.

3. That's a nasty bruise.

4. Roland wore his new suit at the wedding.

5. Can I have a biscuit?

Syllable division pattern v/v division

Two vowels together usually make one sound (e.g. rain, meat, soon, fruit, boat).

Sometimes two adjacent vowels belong to separate syllables. The vowel digraphs should already be familiar from the daily reading pack practice; notice that the v/v words usually reverse these familiar vowel combinations.

Example worksheet at v/v division: Put a 'v' over the vowels. Divide between the two vowels. The first vowel will have the long sound. Read to your teacher.

di et	poet	cruet
truant	friar	duet
dual	cruel	react
fluent	dial	quiet

Longer words with v/v division			
priory	aorta	priority	reality
pious	tuition	fruition	reactor
piety	vacuum	heroic	creative
annuity	creation	deity	diagram
diary	peony	diamond	poetry
radium	radius	onion	radio
tiara			

Sentences v/v division

1. Please be quiet while I listen to the duet.

2. I enjoy poetry much more when I read it aloud.

3. She needs a good, balanced diet with plenty of fruit and vegetables.

| e = /ə/ | Indeterminate vowel sounds (schwa) found in unstressed syllables cause persistent problems for dyslexic learners. Although they have been used at various points in the programme, it never hurts to revisit. You might want to add the schwa sound for 'e' to the reading and spelling cards. '-en', '-ence' and '-ent' are usually suffixes – look at the *Collins Cobuild English Guides, Word Formation* (1991) for a detailed study of words with these endings. Learners need to be aware of morphemes, and to develop an interest in the growth of our spelling system. |

Reading Card

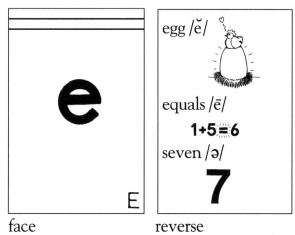

face   reverse

Spelling Card

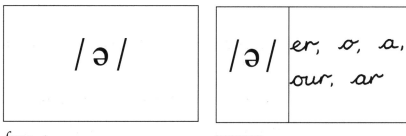

face   reverse

Word lists at 'e' = /ə/			
	'en'	'-ent'	'-ence'
label	blacken	absorbent	insistence
parcel	harden	dependent	dependence
rebel	darken	independent	existence
libel	flatten	persistent	emergence
cancel	lighten	student	preference
angel	sharpen	patent	subsistence
chisel	sicken	potent	reverence
funnel	widen	parent	absence
camel	ashen	moment	sentence
enamel	golden	accent	confidence
panel	leaden	silent	silence
channel	silken		resistence
tunnel	wooden		
kernel	waxen		
carpet	sudden		
basket	garden		
blanket			

Sentences at 'e' = /ə/
1. There was a sudden flash of lightening and a mighty crash of thunder.
2. The garden was flooded with a golden light from the rays of the setting sun.
3. Mop up the liquid with an absorbent cloth.
4. Sharpen your chisel before you begin carving the wooden box.

ure
URE

Regular final syllables

The 'ure' ending is usually found in an unstressed syllable, and affects the pronunciation of the preceding consonant. When it combines with a prefix (e.g. 'impure') its syllable is stressed, and has a different sound.

Words at 'ure'			
unaccented			accented
picture	puncture	pressure	impure
feature	structure	fissure	secure
creature	rapture	pleasure	insecure
signature	capture	measure	manicure
literature	scripture	exposure	procure
fracture	sculpture	composure	endure
temperature	torture	injure	manure
adventure	vulture	conjure	tenure
furniture	gesture	failure	
fixture	moisture	figure	
stature	future		
departure	texture		
culture	mixture		
lecture			

Sentences at 'ure'
1. Manure improves the texture of the soil.
2. It gives me great pleasure to present you with this picture.
3. The class had to endure a long lecture about literature.
4. If her temperature rises, give her some of this mixture.

More regular final syllables

Many of these will have been already encountered and discussed during reading sessions. It is worth giving them some special attention for spelling. There are regional variations in pronunciation.

'-ine' = /ēēn/	'-ain' = /un/	'-ive' = /ĭv/	'-ogue' = /ŏg/	'-ice' = /ĭs/
vaccine	mountain	adhesive	catalogue	service
plasticine	fountain	defensive	synagogue	novice
iodine	Britain	abrasive	dialogue	justice
sardine	bargain	evasive	epilogue	notice
machine	curtain	offensive	monologue	practice
	captain	expensive	prologue	office
	villain	explosive		
	comprehensive			

'-ine' = /ĭn/	'-ite' = /ut/	'-ate' = /ŭt/	'-ique' = /ēēk/	'-ace' = /ŭs/
crinoline	granite	syndicate	unique	preface
genuine	hypocrite	certificate	oblique	surface
doctrine	favourite	delicate	antique	palace
engine	requisite	duplicate	technique	grimace
masculine	exquisite	desolate	physique	necklace
feminine		triplicate	clique	menace
				furnace

Sentences with final stable syllables

1. Look in this catalogue for genuine antique furniture.

2. These curtains are too expensive. Have you any better bargains?

3. The palace has a unique granite fountain in the grounds.

4. She wore a necklace of exquisite workmanship.

Wordlist for Ref. nos 40 and 41

Irregular words

1. Introduce and teach the irregular words gradually. Use the spelling routine.
2. The irregular words need to be practised fequently until the pupil can spell them. To spell the words correctly in written work is the most difficult stage to reach. The pupil needs to be encouraged to reach this level. He should be given a lot of praise when he achieves this with any irregular word or tricky word.

References

Adams MJ (1990) *Beginning to Read: Thinking and Learning About Print*. Cambridge, MA: MIT Press.

Broomfield H, Combley M (1997) *Overcoming Dyslexia: A Practical Handbook for the Classroom*. London: Whurr Publishers.

Burtis P, Bereiter C, Scardamalia M, Tetroe J (1983) *The Development of Planning in Writing*, in Knoll B and Wells G (eds) *Explorations in the Development of Writing*. Chichester: John Wiley and Sons.

Cane B, Smithers J (1971) *The Roots of Reading*. Windsor: NFER.

Chall JS (1967) *Learning to Read: the Great Debate*. New York: McGraw Hill.

Clay MM (1972) *Reading: The Patterning of Complex Behaviour*. Aukland, NZ: Heinemann.

Clay MM (1993) *Reading Recovery: A Guidebook for Teachers in Training*. Heinemann.

Collins Cobuild English Guides (1991) *Word Formation*. London: Harper Collins Publishers.

Cox AR (1975) *Structures and Techniques. Remedial Language Training*. Cambridge, MA: Educators Publishing Service.

Crosby RMN with Liston RA (1968) *Reading and the Dyslexic Child*. London: Souvenir Press.

Crystal D (1994) *The Cambridge Encyclopedia of the English Language*. Cambridge: Cambridge University Press.

DfE (1994) *Code of Practice for the Identification and Assessment of Special Educational Needs*. London: HMSO.

DfEE (1998) *The National Literacy Framework for Teaching*. Crown Copyright: available from the Department for Education and Employment, Sanctuary Buildings, Great Smith Street, London SW1P 3BT.

DfEE (1999) *The National Literacy Strategy: Additional Literacy Support Modules 1 to 4*. Crown Copyright: available from the Department for Education and Employment, Sanctuary Buildings, Great Smith Street, London SW1P 3BT.

Frith U (1985) Beneath the surface of developmental dyslexia, in Patterson KE, Marshall JC and Coltheart M (eds) *Surface Dyslexia*. Routledge and Kegan Paul.

Gillingham A, Stillman BW (1956) *Remedial Training for Children with Specific Disability in Reading, Spelling and Penmanship*. Cambridge, MA: Educators Publishing Service.

Goodman K, Burke CL (1972) *Reading Miscue Inventory Manual*. London: Collier Macmillian.

Hatcher PJ (1994) *Sound Linkage: An Integrated programme for Overcoming Reading Difficulties*. London: Whurr Publishers.

Holdaway D (1979) *The Foundations of Literacy*. Gosford NSW: Ashton Scholastic.

Hulme C, Snowling M (eds) (1997) *Dyslexic: Biology, Cognition and Intervention*. London: Whurr Publishers.

Naidoo S (1972) *Specific Dyslexia*. London: Pitman.

Ott P (1997) *How to Detect and Manage Dyslexia*. Oxford: Heinemann.

Partridge E (1979, first published in 1958) *Origins, a Short Etymological Dictionary of Modern English*. London: Routledge and Kegan Paul.

Quillam S (1980) *Bright Ideas: Language Development*. Scholastic Publications.

Reason R, Boote R (1994) *Helping Children with Reading and Spelling: A Special Needs Manual*. London and New York: Routledge.

Snowling M, Stackhouse J (1996) *Dyslexia Speech and Language: A Practitioner's Handbook*. London: Whurr Publishers.

Stackhouse J (1990) Phonological Deficits in Developmental Reading and Spelling Disorders, in Grunwell P (ed.) *Developmental Speech Disorders*. Edinburgh: Churchill Livingstone.

Waites L, Cox AR (1969) *Developmental Language Disability; Basic Training; Remedial Language Training*. Dallas, Texas: Texas Scottish Rite Hospital for Crippled Children.

Wilson J (1995) *Phonological Awareness Training* (Parts 1, 2, 3) available from Jo Barnard, County Psychological Service, 25 Buckingham Road, Aylesbury, Bucks HP19 3PT.

Index

The Hickey Multisensory Language Course
Third Edition

Edited by

Margaret Combley BA(Hons),

Learning Support Teacher, Sheffield

W

WHURR PUBLISHERS

I A

© 2001 Tyrrell Burgess
First published 1977 by Kathleen Hickey Publications
Second edition published in 1992 and
third edition in 2001 by
Whurr Publishers Ltd
19B Compton Terrace, London N1 2UN, UK and
325 Chestnut Street, Philadelphia PA 19106, USA

Reprinted 2002

British Library Cataloguing in Publication Data
A catalogue record for this book is available from
the British Library.

ISBN: 1 86156 178 4

Printed and bound in the UK by Athenaeum Press Ltd,
Gateshead, Tyne & Wear